YORKSHIRE:
A Walk Around My County

Tony Whittaker

Published by Sigma Leisure – an imprint of
Sigma Press, 1 South Oak Lane, Wilmslow, Cheshire SK9 6AR, England.

British Library Cataloguing in Publication Data
A CIP record for this book is available from the British Library.

ISBN: 1-85058-457-5

Typesetting and Design by: Sigma Press, Wilmslow, Cheshire.

Text Photographs: A. Whittaker

Cover photograph: Hebden Bridge (photographed by Simon Warner)

Maps: Jeremy Semmens

Printed by: MFP Design & Print

Disclaimer: the information in this book is given in good faith and is believed to be correct at the time of publication. No responsibility is accepted by either the author or publisher for errors or omissions, or for any loss or injury howsoever caused. Only you can judge your own fitness, competence and experience.

Foreword

– by His Honour Judge James Pickles

As a born-and-bred Yorkshireman, I am delighted to write this Foreword to Tony Whittaker's book.

I was born in a small terraced house in the village of Warley on the outskirts of Halifax, West Yorkshire, in 1925. In the following 70 years I have always lived in or near Halifax – except for the time away at school and university and the year (1948) I spent in the Temple, London as a pupil-barrister. I practised at the Bar in Bradford from 1949 to 1976, when I became a circuit judge in Yorkshire.

My parents and grandparents, on both sides, lived in Halifax, as did my wife Sheila's forebears. Sadly four of my six grandchildren live in the south of England: a fate worse than life?

Until 14 February 1986 I was unknown outside Yorkshire. On that date the Guardian newspaper published my article on the so-called Kilmuir Rules by which Lord Chancellor Hailsham was trying to shut judges' mouths outside court. The media then took an interest in me and the rest is known to the public.

When asked why I am outspoken, I say I am a Yorkshireman. This irritates some who come from elsewhere. But we who do come from the biggest and best county pride ourselves on saying what we think. Others, including (dare I whisper it?) some soft Southerners, don't always do that.

I have worked in or visited many parts of Yorkshire. My wife and I have a motor-caravan and in recent years we have been more than once to North Yorkshire. We visited Whitby; once so prosperous from shipbuilding and (I regret) whaling. In writing this book, Tony Whittaker has passed through Whitby, going a little further north to describe beautiful Runswick Bay. He also writes about Beverley, that delightful mini-York where I used to preside at the Crown Court. I stayed at the Beverley Arms Hotel, formerly a coaching house. This is where, as I was paying my bill, the police rang to say my life had been threatened. A distressed woman had rung during the night, saying she intended to kill me and then herself. The police discovered that her son had been sent to Borstal: not by me, but by the recorder in the adjoining court. I said that if I was going to be knocked off, I hoped it would be for something *I* had done!

Tony Whittaker also includes Huddersfield in this book but not Halifax. Halifax and Huddersfield have always been rivals and it used to be said that the latter had more Bentleys per head of population than any other town. This book by-passes Halifax, but I do hope that it will feature in the second edition of Tony Whittaker's book. Meanwhile I must press our claims to fame. Halifax has a building that is unique in Europe: the Piece Hall, opened in 1798 for the cottage weavers to sell their cloth pieces.

Another famous Halifax institution was Crossleys at Dean Clough, which employed 3000 at the end. When that came, Sir Ernest Hall, as he now deservedly is, bought Dean Clough. He lets off units to small firms, and also has three artists in residence as well as a theatre. Regeneration indeed. Finally, Halifax still has the gibbet on which, until Cromwell stopped it in 1652, we dealt summarily with cloth-thieves. Some think we should bring the gibbet back, but on balance I am against it!

Forgive me for being so proud of my town, but we Tykes are like that. We speak our minds and are proud of our heritage. Those who want to go further into that should read this book. It is of great interest to Yorkshire folk, of course, but also to others who wish to know what has made us and our county so formidable.

His Honour James Pickles

Contents

Yorkshire: my county   **1**

Barnsley   **7**
"Walks like this? They'll nivver believe thi."

Sheffield & Dore   **17**
First King of All England, Champion County and Twenty-first Century Trams

Holmfirth   **25**
A pub trail and a failed attempt to avoid the Summer Wine.

Huddersfield   **34**
Fame and fortune and the search for an identity

Bradford   **44**
. . . and the escape to Ilkley

Hebden Bridge   **53**
The canal, the Pike and a hill village

Leeds   **60**
A city walk, and that famous Brewery Wharf

Harewood   **68**
Along the edge of the Dales – and a walk on the Royal side

Gargrave   **74**
The Leeds to Liverpool goes through here – night and day

Horton in Ribblesdale   80

Between the Three Peaks, plus a limestone pavement and a village from Norman times.

Hawes   86

Not quite the market town it was, but the tourists still like it.

Reeth   92

*Lead mining and sheep,
and the village is still going strong*

Middleham   97

Castles, Kings and other thoroughbreds

Middlesmoor   103

"Upstairs" via Little Switzerland

Ripon   111

Between Pennines and Vale

Coxwold   118

History and literature in another beautiful Yorkshire village

Masham   125

Here's health unto the family – and its black sheep

Runswick Bay   130

The place Neapolitans would choose to come and see before they die

Flamborough   135

A walk around the headland, the bays, the village and that famous light-house

Burton Agnes   143

A Hall that proves biggest isn't always best

Thornton le Dale   149

That village with the stream, on the road to Scarborough where you always meant to stop

Lastingham **153**
Challenger for the "most beautiful village" title

Castle Howard **158**
The big, big house

York **163**
No ghosts, just beauty from another angle

Huggate **170**
Still feels like the old farming village, with the best collection of Wold walks

Great Driffield **175**
Self-proclaimed capital of the Wolds, with cake shops that overcome your good intentions

Beverley **181**
Sir John Betjeman had it right when he said: "A place made for walking and living in"

Hull **189**
. . . or Kingston upon Hull to give it the name it has had since 1293, when created a port by Edward I

Brough **198**
Roman fording point and home of the Buccaneer

Pontefract **203**
Pomfret cakes, the hermit's cell and one hell of a finish

An Outline of Yorkshire History **209**

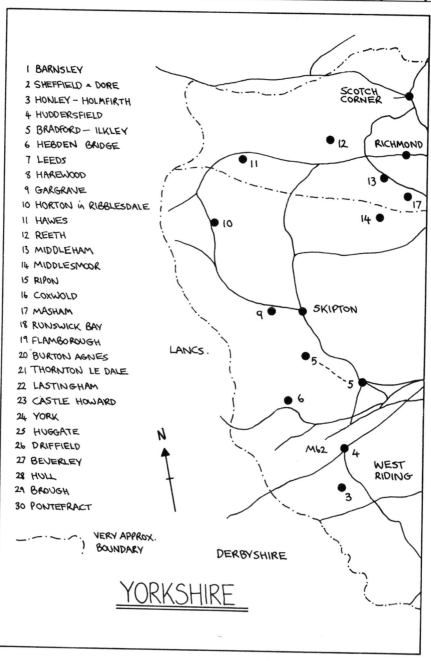

1 BARNSLEY
2 SHEFFIELD & DORE
3 HONLEY – HOLMFIRTH
4 HUDDERSFIELD
5 BRADFORD – ILKLEY
6 HEBDEN BRIDGE
7 LEEDS
8 HAREWOOD
9 GARGRAVE
10 HORTON in RIBBLESDALE
11 HAWES
12 REETH
13 MIDDLEHAM
14 MIDDLESMOOR
15 RIPON
16 COXWOLD
17 MASHAM
18 RUNSWICK BAY
19 FLAMBOROUGH
20 BURTON AGNES
21 THORNTON LE DALE
22 LASTINGHAM
23 CASTLE HOWARD
24 YORK
25 HUGGATE
26 DRIFFIELD
27 BEVERLEY
28 HULL
29 BROUGH
30 PONTEFRACT

VERY APPROX.
BOUNDARY

SCOTCH CORNER
RICHMOND
LANCS.
SKIPTON
M62
WEST RIDING
DERBYSHIRE

N

YORKSHIRE

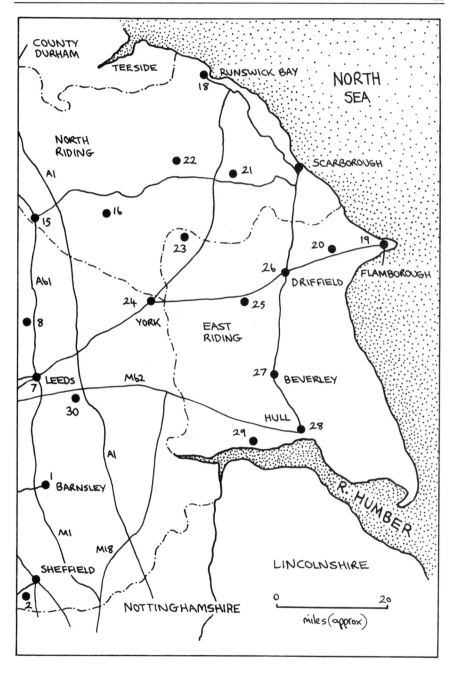

Yorkshire: my county

"My county," he says.

"Must be a Yorkshireman," says another.

"Aye, you're right," I interrupt. "Who else would be as proud of their roots? In England, anyway. I have known a few Scots who got a bit nationalistic now and again and, come to think of it, umpteen thousand Cornishmen have seemed that way these last few years."

But never mind them saying "you can't miss those Yorkshiremen," you shouldn't miss us. Our borders are equidistant from the Scottish border and the South coast of England with about 100 miles to travel to get across the county, so why not stop a while?

Not that this is written just for those who (we think) were unlucky not to be born here in Yorkshire, but also for those of us who wish to confirm that we live in the best county in England and are inquisitive enough to wonder if there are any good bits that we have missed. There are certainly some good walks in unexpected areas among those that accompany each chapter, none of them arduous, some of them unusual, all of them pleasant.

It is a while since the stage coaches struggled through Derbyshire on their approach to the county and the passengers saw the pit heads and the quarries, followed by the slag heaps and furnaces as they passed Rotherham and Sheffield. Further on came those dark satanic mills and some of the passengers felt sorry for the people who had to live up here. Now, even when they whizz up the M1, they cannot help noticing there have been a few changes. But will they see the beauty behind it all?

Northerners shudder at the thought of the vast sprawl of concentrated living areas "down South," and shrug off the occasional spell of weather that is not quite as good as it is in Surrey, by reminding themselves of the glorious landscape that surrounds us and the warmth of the people up here. Of course we are nosey too, but you must have noticed that any close and caring community has that characteristic. At worst it improves your chances of getting to know the natives.

We are, of course, ready to admit that the county has beauty and ugliness, is agricultural, industrial, frenetic, dreamlike, pragmatic and imaginative and if you think you don't like the people, it might mean that you haven't met more than a handful or you have heard that we boast a bit and are somewhat blunt in our manner of speech. Well, some of us do overdo the pride bit, and we like to think we are straightforward too. But judged as a whole I suppose we are only a little less varied than our countryside, cautious but welcoming, inclined to "ham it up" and with a tendency to be desperately loyal. So much so that I fear only Divine intervention could help, if I ever had to choose between friend and country. So come and meet a few more of us.

In all the Ridings we try to cultivate that type of democracy that has most of us believing that any one of us is equally entitled to earn the best in life. By practising that other Yorkshire saying, "courtesy costs nowt," we can get along with beggars or kings. I say "most of" because I find that the industrial area of the West Riding that gave many the opportunity to make a lot of money on the fringes of the woollen industry, also saw many of the next generation lose it almost as quickly. The result is that we have a few that are judged as over pretentious and a bit of a pain to the others. This is no doubt due to the fact that in the industrial areas particularly, we can be demanding of our neighbours because we have grown used to mutual reliance. More than half the county's villages are communities, one barely separated from the next, that owe their geographical position to the place of work, that is, along the valley, by the canal or near the pit. It may mean that there is a "herd instinct" despite our claims to being so very independent. What else ignites the passions that still flame for cricket, football, brass bands and choral societies?

Thankfully there were many successful Victorians. The conditions of employment they imposed would not be tolerated today, but they became very rich, ensured future security until long after the initial flood of Far Eastern goods and left their mark in most towns with fine buildings, subscription hospitals and the encouragement of learning and music. Sir Titus Salt went a bit further and built a village of sound houses for his employees (with a fine church and chapel, but no pub) as you will see in chapter 5. The thought did, of course, occur to him that they would be off work less often if he got them out of their insanitary hovels. Now it is obvious that his houses are proving to be better than a lot of those put up a hundred years later.

This strong mixture of people in the most industrial part of the county were the ones who had, over the last 200 years at least, a tougher time than those living in the rest of the county. Perhaps as a consequence, they are the warmest people you could meet; people who can hold their heads high in any company.

Yes, we are proud of our miners, our industrialists, our steelworkers and fishermen and we tend to take textile workers and farmers for granted. Perhaps the North and East Ridings, being largely agricultural, have not had such big swings from good to bad and back again. It has left longer established families and encouraged examples of mutual benefit such as the enthusiasm of Sir Christopher Sykes for better farming methods at the end of the 18th century. He convinced fellow agriculturalists that his ideas would bring enormous improvements and so changed the Wolds from barren wastes into one of the most productive and best cultivated districts in the county of Yorkshire.

It is a county of millstone grit, chalk hills, plains of rich loam, peat bogs and dales. Different: that's my county. We like to say "charity begins at home" and then are surprised when the Daily Telegraph reports that we give more to charity than any other county. It is a county that is always ready to find proof that anyone who is great, successful or famous, either comes from Yorkshire or that at least one of his or her forebears did. I am certainly convinced that William Blake had Yorkshire in mind when he wrote "Jerusalem" and no Yorkshireman is going to be surprised if he is told that it was probably a member of the Huddersfield Choral Society that set it to music. And it is a fact that it was on the Southern boundary of Yorkshire that a King became the first King of all England. But more of that later. For now, let me tell you I'm proud to ask anyone to come here and enjoy all that we have to offer. To paraphrase an advertisement, "the county to visit when only the best will do."

And what else can you expect as well as all these towns and cities, awash with history; walks through some wonderful countryside; first class sports facilities and so many fine buildings and monuments? Why, food and drink of course. Town pubs and country pubs, cafes and restaurants serving so many kinds of food. It would be unfair to list them for fear of upsetting the good ones I might miss out, although I will point out a few in the relevant areas ahead.

There are so many places where the food, drink and company are good, and with such a cross section of customers, you would be hard pressed to pick out the ordinary man.

The ordinary man? Figment of the politician's mind, grey, faceless figure who represents the average in all lists of population statistics, or what? He certainly isn't a Yorkshireman. We have history to uplift us in every field, to make us different, if not special. And that's when we are being modest. So we can at least understand what an ordinary Yorkshireman is not. Full of pride he may be, but only because he wants to share with you the glories of Britain's largest county. (Did you know, that at 3,923,359 acres within the proper boundaries, the acreage exceeds the words that are in the Bible?). We have no time for those, hopefully few, born in the county who use our reputation for being outspoken as an excuse to be gratuitously rude. Nor can we understand how, after winning the County Cricket Championship thirty times since 1893 (and there were no matches in 1915, 1916 or 1917 or from 1940 to 1945) we can do nothing for so many seasons, but allow the committee to fight among themselves and thereby contribute to the near-destruction of the team. (That is until we asked a Lincolnshire man, ex Chief Constable at that, to take over the Presidency.)

So we are not shrinking violets or grey, faceless shapes. Yes, we do have accents that you can sometimes fail to understand. But take a small group of us and supply us with a sufficiency of Tetley's - no missus, not the tea bags - and we can clearly and succinctly explain to you how to solve any problem.

But I am not sure that I could explain our emblem problem, the Yorkshire Rose. Which rose is it? We have one on the caps of our County cricket team which is not immediately recognisable as a rose, then the white replica of England's rose, the most frequently printed, and also the dog rose plucked from the hedgerows and worn in the caps of men of the East Yorkshire Regiment as they marched back from another victory. That became the more uniform shape when made a part of the regimental badge, in the centre of the Star of Brunswick. Maybe it is all intentional and represents the various types that go together to make a Yorkshireman. If you think this is male chauvinism creeping in, let me remind you that we have many fine examples of the Yorkshire Rose in people like that lovely lady, the Duchess of Kent, a right Yorkshire lass, daughter of Sir William Worsley, born and married at her family home in Hovingham (which just happens to have one of the loveliest cricket grounds) and who is constantly working to help any worthy cause. Or the present Madam Speaker, the Hon. Betty Boothroyd; now there's a no nonsense person who can sort out "that House" with firmness, good humour and charm.

I hope that you will meet lots of people and find out what Yorkshire is all about. I have avoided a lot of the better known places, taking you instead to where you will be pleasantly surprised; by the surroundings, buildings old and new perhaps, showing how centuries of hard work and good fortune have left their mark. How even the most industrial areas are surrounded by beautiful scenery and countryside. Challenge me with Turner if you must, but I believe that there is no better view across an inland waterway than that from the Yorkshire end of the footpath that crosses the Humber Bridge, looking westwards on a fine evening in autumn. Don't forget that Turner came up here to paint; unfortunately for him and us, the Humber Bridge wasn't built then.

No individual could take an intense personal interest in everything for which the county is famous. It was the death by overwork of an old David Brown tractor that intensified one of my interests, for example. A near-perfect crown wheel and pinion, a work of art, was exposed by the scrap merchant, when I had just heard that Huddersfield man David Brown junior had bought the Aston Martin factory for £20,000. Obviously such a combination could only amount to perfection, and my admiration for engineering excellence started the dream of owning one of the David Brown Astons, The companies have separated now, but they are still both leaders in their fields - and I am still dreaming.

I am tempted to start with a walk in the East Riding, which is where I belong, in an area I enjoy, that is linked to famous names. For example, Hornsea with Kay Kendall and Brian Rix, or Hull with Ian Carmichael, Tom Boyd and Amy Johnson. Instead, I want to start with a walk that begins in a town that is not only controversial, but also represents what the innocent, non-Yorkies, imagine that we are, fostering an exaggerated picture of cloth caps and clogs. At the same time, for some reason, it produces people who are undoubtedly famous, skilled and occasionally controversial, like Charley Williams, Arthur Scargill, Michael Parkinson and Brian Glover. Without stretching boundaries too much, I could include one of cricket's finest batsmen, Geoff Boycott, but the village of Fitzwilliam where he was born would be more than upset if I did. It's almost like in the days of Len Hutton, when, if you asked "where's Leeds?" you would be told "near Pudsey" (Hutton's birthplace!).

The town and the walk will be likely to turn out a pleasant surprise to you and will start off a series of pleasant surprises that will take you through the widely different parts of the county that are all gems in their own way.

From the Pennines to the coast, there is so much. The Vale of York, down through which all those dales rivers finally flow, the high chalk cliffs at Flamborough, the broad expanse of well kept farmland, the valleys that have a small representative collection of the mills that made Yorkshire textiles famous around the world; dockland and bustling cities, moorland gallops and market towns. It's all here, to see and enjoy, to tempt you to stay a while.

I know that I am not the first Yorkshireman to want to tell people what a grand place it is, but I still feel a little apprehensive. After all, look what happened to Captain Cook after he left Whitby to pass around a few brochures in the Antipodes.

Chapter One

Barnsley

"Walks like this? They'll nivver believe thi."

While all the other villages, towns and cities in this book are known for their history, architectural interest or industrial fame, Barnsley is pictured as the place at the centre of the pit strikes. A place of cloth caps, whippets and pigeon racing. Oh aye, an' don't forget tin bath in front a t'fire. The trouble is that the town isn't as big physically as its reputation suggests, so that visitors find all the industrial museums, open farms and other sites of interest are around the outskirts.

What makes Barnsley a worthy subject is the mixture of its people and its surroundings. So a stroll around part of the town is essential before experiencing the delights of a walk through the countryside around the town. This way you will soon see how different it all is to the place you might have imagined.

So few years after that last disastrous strike, the hard-won history of 500 years of coal mining in this area has ended. The desperation of men and their families trying to keep their jobs is almost forgotten. They were not a minority group being an irritant to some ministry by trying to change an esoteric minor law; they were part of a major national industry fighting for the future of their community. Many were Barnsley men who did not deserve to have the truth withheld from them, and certainly did not deserve to be ridden over by mounted policemen. Despite his 'Munich' style of oratory, it seems Arthur Scargill was right.

So if you are going to get any real pleasure from your visit to this town, you must meet the people and for that you should go first to the Market Hall, open every day except Thursday and Sunday. To get there, walk up Eldon Street from the bus or train station or the adjacent car park to the junction with Kendray Street and then turn right up May Day Green; the market is then a little way ahead on your left. First established in 1249, it has earned a reputation for

Barnsley Town Hall

variety and value for money and is also a great place for the atmosphere. From there, take the road straight ahead as you come out of the front of the market hall and turn right along New Street. At the end you go up Market Hill passing a fine Town Hall on your left, then opposite the second road on the left after the Town Hall is the Cooper Gallery with a good permanent collection as well as a changing contemporary exhibition.

After that, retrace your steps until you are again opposite the Town Hall and turn left down Regent Street and walk down to the bus station to catch a number 343 or 344 bus, asking the driver to stop at Locke Park, 46 acres of parkland, with bowling greens, tennis courts, and a glass house of rare plants. Have a stroll around. There is a cafe there, but be wary of the fitness course laid out there – it is tough.

On your return, you will probably agree that the town is still alive and well. The shops look good – it is hard to find one for sale, which other towns might envy – there is a theatre, a leisure centre, cinemas and many other forms of entertainment, including the famous cricket and football clubs. Now, once again from the bus station walk

The bandstand at Locke Park

along Eldon Street, on the trail of a truly local beer. When I attempted to track down Barnsley Bitter I found that it did, in fact, disappear altogether for a while. Then, about four years ago, two or three men got together to try and recreate it. Initial success was followed by disappointment and it took another two years of hard work to achieve that special flavour that was there every time. But where is it now? I found out that quite a few village pubs serve it, but I could only find two in the town. One is here in Eldon Street, The Beer Engine, which should be in sight by now. The place is run by a young Australian who serves Barnsley Bitter and other strong ales; it is worth the break to try the magic brew. Having decided to run an English Pub and chosen Barnsley as the place to do it, you will find you cannot stop him extolling the virtues of the place as well as the beer, with plenty of comment on the places to eat. His favourites included Armstrongs (stylish), Restaurant Peano (110, Dodworth Road, elegant and just out of town), and one of my favourites, Brooklands, home of the Barnsley chop.

Stranger still, it was my wife, possibly the future patron saint of dress shops, who told me that there is, in Barnsley, a boutique and a couple of men's shops that have a tremendous reputation for the latest fashions. When it got to quoting names and prices I was astonished. Looking a little surreptitiously into one of the rather posh-looking men's outfitters, I wondered if I could justify selling the remaining piece of family silver to buy one of those suits made from a worsted so beautiful to touch that it could only have come from Huddersfield. Speaking of the esoteric, there is also the Metrodome, Monk Bretton Priory (founded in 1153), and an industrial history that starts with iron mining in the 13th century, linen weaving and glass blowing, all well-recorded in the industrial museums outside the town, particularly Worsborough Mill Museum, Elsecar Industrial Museum and Wortley Top Forge.

Some locals go to great lengths to persuade you that they still breed 'em tough around here, especially their sportsmen and women, even influencing the "comers in". It's a place where fast bowlers have run-ups that start outside the ground and soccer players, especially defenders, don't take prisoners. I have believed it since training alongside Barnsley lads during National Service, and reading a lot of the stories of Michael Parkinson which often dwell upon the highly colourful career of one Skinner Normanton. Tales from the days when Association Football matches were worth watching, especially at Barnsley; the centre forward had a proper number on his back and was told that it was his job was to get the ball into the opponent's net which he usually did with style whilst, the aforementioned "Skinner" laid waste over-ambitious opponents. Martin Moxon and Darren Gough are from here too. Both important ingredients in Yorkshire's recipe for success.

If Barnsley people are soft at all, it's in the heart. The nicest thing I have seen written about a man's father is this: "He has been dead for a couple of cricket seasons now, but I still think about him because he was a special man and I was lucky to know him. He was a Yorkshireman, a miner, a humorist and a fast bowler. Not a bad combination. I only hope they play cricket in heaven. If they don't, he'll ask for a transfer." And the chap that wrote that is no softee. The same Barnsley man who would modestly deny that he was completely unruffled when Cassius Clay lost his temper with him and later survived an attack by that B . . . stupid emu.

Funnily enough, some of the best comedians have come from the Barnsley area, even if you might think that Charlie Williams has just come off a shift at the pit and consider Brian Glover to be Shake-spearean or the fella that sells bread in TV commercials. As for leading newspaper men and writers, besides "Parkie," there is Don Booker, editor, retired after 47 years with the Barnsley Chronicle, scout leader, churchwarden, magistrate, and sponsor of charities. He is also the writer of editorials to bring back corporal punishment and reminders of the fact that Barnsley cemeteries are full of men and women under 40. And Andrew Bark, film director. At the time Kenneth Branagh was hyping up reaction to his "Frankenstein" along came this Barnsley lad who, without any particular thought in mind had his talents awakened by the Barnsley College of Art and received world acclaim for his exceptional film, "Dark Waters".

Engineers too, like Josef Locke who was an apprentice of Stephen-son and then went on to be a successful railway engineer himself. He gave the town the 46 acre park which bears his name and contains the "double" memorial that started as a memorial to Josef Locke and then later attained a wooden "penthouse" dedicated to his wife which raised it to just over seventy feet. It also happens to be a place where there is confirmation that Barnsley is different, that it isn't enveloped in the wretched ugliness that the former mine owners imposed upon Mexborough and so much of the area. From Locke Park you begin to see the Yorkshire landscape and find out how much Barnsley people love the countryside. It was also in the park that I met a man exercising working labradors and I wasn't at all surprised to be told that each dog had won Champion Field Dog trials.

From the gate behind the Locke memorial you can get a view along and across the valley with three country mansions and a number of pleasant rural villages in sight. Enough to wonder why Anne Robinson, popular BBC presenter has to say "I live in Barnsley, the Gloucester one of course" If one of the houses of comparable size in Cawthorne was for sale, I bet she would be glad to swop.

So you see, to write about Barnsley you must write about the people. They make the town the sort of place it is and the places of interest that you do find are a bonus.

Now you have met the strong men and sampled the strong beer, it's time to try this walk in its beautiful setting and find out along the way how the Charge of the Light Brigade became part of Barnsley's history.

The Walk

The Route: Barugh Green – Cawthorne – Cannon Hill – Cawthorne Park – Barugh Green

Map: O.S. map Landranger series 110.

The start and how to find it: Take the A635 to Denby Dale for just under three miles, coming first to Barugh Green and then going under the M1 motorway. After four hundred yards you will come to a grass lane on the left with space to park on the verges. The starting point is at map reference 301081.

What the walk is like: Mostly green lanes, footpaths, fieldpaths and parkland with a little walking on quiet roads.

Distance: 6 miles.

From the starting point, on the left you will find that two paths join just off the road – take the right-hand one and then the next path on the left which takes you through a narrow woodland section with a wide variety of trees. Six hundred yards brings you out into the open with, at the bottom of the field on the left, a substantial modern house. Opposite this, a path heads across the middle of a field on your right that brings you to what looks like a restored farmhouse above Lower Norton.

As you step through the hedge, go to the left towards the road. At the road, turn right and walk into Cawthorne, a little over half a mile away. An unusual village of arty shops, museum, wonderful variety of houses, an unusual monument near the church and the Spencer Arms. The latter is a welcome oasis with good beer and reasonable food although the edge is taken off for me by the designer interior and the muzak, losing a lot of the village pub appeal that it had. When you think you can carry on, go right through the village, turning left with the road, ignoring the first two public footpath signs on the right, passing allotments and the Social Club until you come to Tivvy Dale Close and a road into a small housing estate on your right. Go right along the estate road, bearing right and then straight on to the end and a five bar gate, with a smaller gate at the side.

The path here will take you to the parkland surrounding Cannon Hall, so once through the second gate, go to the left and then down towards the lake to cross a footbridge below the weir at the end of the top lake. Keep going to the left after crossing so that you come to the car park, from where you can take a path up to the Hall.

Inside (admission free) you can follow a route through pewter and fine old furniture until you come to the stairs and the area that is the museum of the 13th/18th Royal Hussars. This will explain the connection with the Charge of the Light Brigade. It is a fact that from the early days of the 13th Lancers, Barnsley was an important recruiting area for them and as a consequence shared the glory in defeat of that ill-conceived and poorly-commanded charge.

Honour was upheld with more rewarding consequences when the Hussars went in with supporting tanks on D-Day.

Continue the walk by going across the front of the house. After the formal gardens on your right and the walled garden on your left, take the path that winds down to the right and go through the ruined arch, over a wooden footbridge that crosses the ditch dug below the wall of the "ha ha". You are now in the park following the direction of the hedge on the left.

It was here that I met an ex-miner who lived nearby who put forward the view that the Government would have saved money by setting up training centres before the pit closure programme was made public thereby attracting businesses to the area instead of paying all the redundancy money. His father had got out of the pit

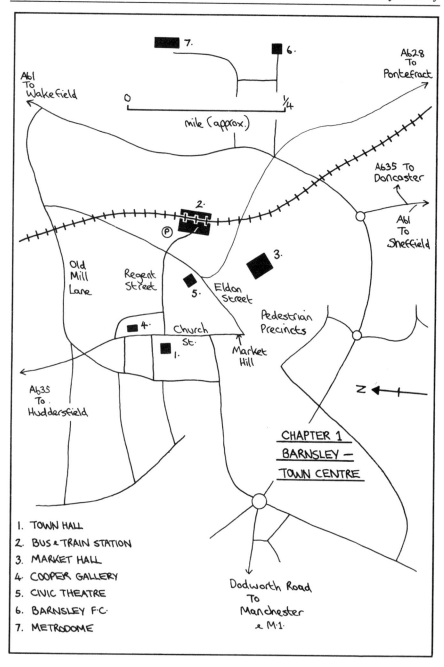

7.

6.

A628
To
Pontefract

A61
To
Wakefield

0   ¼

mile (approx.)

A635 To
Doncaster

A61
To
Sheffield

2.

Ⓟ

3.

Old
Mill
Lane

Regent
Street

5.

Eldon
Street

Pedestrian
Precincts

4.

Church
St.

1.

Market
Hill

A635
To
Huddersfield

Z ←

CHAPTER 1

BARNSLEY —

TOWN CENTRE

1. TOWN HALL
2. BUS & TRAIN STATION
3. MARKET HALL
4. COOPER GALLERY
5. CIVIC THEATRE
6. BARNSLEY F.C.
7. METRODOME

Dodworth Road
To
Manchester
& M.1.

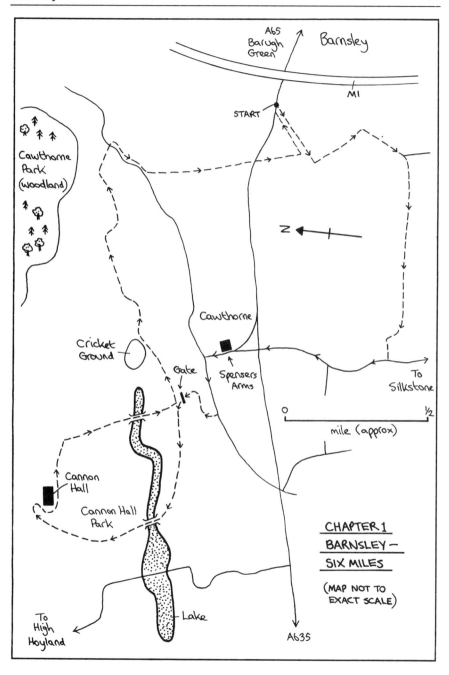

A65
Barugh
Green

Barnsley

M1

START

Cawthorne
Park
(woodland)

N

Cawthorne

Cricket
Ground

Gate

Spensers
Arms

To
Silkstone

0   ½

mile (approx)

Cannon
Hall

Cannon Hall
Park

CHAPTER 1
BARNSLEY —
SIX MILES

(MAP NOT TO
EXACT SCALE)

To
High
Hoyland

Lake

A635

by joining the Hussars and had been in the Normandy landings with them and survived, but he was just as sad as his son to see the end of a 500 year old industry whose dangers below ground had created such close communities. "People who don't live up here, they don't understand you know". With that, he swept his arm round to cover the whole park and beyond and said "And y'know, if you told 'em there were walks like this round Barnsley, they'd nivver believe thi'."

At the lake, go over the bridge and walk straight up the path opposite. Do not go through the gate at the top, but turn left before it and continue along the hedgeside. Keep going and pass the cricket ground on the left which has a cared for look with its well-kept field and plenty of seats around the boundary. Ignore the iron gate on the right and go through the hunting gate further on. Go on to the bridge and ford and then turn left, following the stream that is now on your left. Go through the next gap on your right and go to the left along the bottom of that field. At the end of the field there is a double plank bridge, through the gap, turn left when you are through it, over a bridge across the stream again and turn right.

Climb over the next stile you come to and cross the next grass field and then the next passing a farmhouse. Cross the farm road and keep on, straight ahead, crossing a large stone stile to go along the bank of the river. At the stonework of the weir, take the stile that is to the left. The stream now goes off to the right but the path is straight ahead. There is now a hedge along on your left and you will see you are heading in the direction of the bottom corner of the large wood that runs up on the left and is part of Cawthorne Park. Before reaching it, you will come to a stile and gate, both of which let you out onto a cinder track. Turn right to go along this track and come out on the road. Turn right along it, go over the bridge and keep walking along the road until you spot the path or bridleway going off from the road to the left. You can see the M1 from here and on the far side of it, the houses on the outskirts of Barnsley. When the path brings you to a road, cross it and continue along the path on the other side. A short distance ahead and there is a junction of paths. Take the first on the left and it will bring you to the road that goes under the motorway and is the one on which you have parked your car.

Chapter Two

Sheffield & Dore

First King of All England, Champion County and Twenty-first Century Trams

To anyone over 35, Sheffield means steel, then stainless steel, and they will believe, as I do, that the best cutlery in most houses anywhere in the world will have been made in Sheffield. Those who are younger will be more impressed by the stadiums, the pop venues, the two football clubs and the University; while all ages must grit their teeth and suffer the totally chaotic traffic situation caused by the continuing installation of the city's Supertram. With luck, things will be more peaceful by the end of 1996, so that by then you will

Supertram – super problem?

be able to see the sights of "Steel City" and still start a walk in one of the villages on the city boundary.

And this is still a steel city; October 1994 saw the installation of the new Master Cutler in a 358 year old ceremony. It has education programmes and charity functions but best of all it ensures that Sheffield Steel means just that. No two bit foreign company is going to set up a two room head office here so that they can put that mark on their Korean-produced product. And it is not too late, because Sheffield is producing more steel now than was produced at the time of greatest need in the 1939-45 war.

But at that time the area of Hallamshire, basically the steel producing area of Rotherham and all of Sheffield, had 176 furnaces. Now there are seven. That has meant a loss of 25,000 jobs, leaving an eighth of the original workforce to produce today's remarkable tonnage, 60% of which is exported. Stainless steel, steel for the aerospace industry, to build oil rigs, to make hand tools and to make "Gripples." A Gripple is a thingummy for joining wire. Australian sheep farmers think it's dinkum and Californian vineyard owners couldn't do without its support. In fact so many reasons for getting your ends together arose, that last year, five years after start up, the company avoided any puns and sold seven million Gripples.

Now here's a funny thing. An Arab from the Yemen came here in the fifties to work in the steel works and saved enough to buy two shopsto support his family which included nine children. One son, born here in Sheffield, went to his brothers to learn to box and defend themselves from bullies. If you meet him, you will find a pleasant young man who is engaging and often funny – unless you meet him in the ring. Then you would get some idea why I can tell you he is going to be the world bantam weight champion and maybe champion at other weights too.

His name is Naseem Hamed. Should you see him in action, I'll bet the phrase "fly like a butterfly and sting like a bee" springs to mind, for here is a Yorkshireman who measures people up like an undertaker and then if they are opponents, chooses his way to annihilate then#m just like his hero, Mohammed Ali.

So from the fortunate discovery of ironstone and charcoal, by the 14th century it was already famous for knives, as witnessed in Chaucer's Tales in which we are told "the Miller has a Sheffield dagger in his hose,". The industry was already established before the forests were denuded. Fortunately coal was also at hand and. Bessemer and Siemens went on to patent the methods that were to be used in the production of higher grade materials and armour plate. So Sheffield remains "Steel City" to this day. And more than likely the home of a world champion boxer too.

In Yorkshire, at least, it will also be known as the place where the County Cricket Club was formed and had its headquarters, even if usurped by Leeds in later years. Just as well as it turned out, when the football club that leased the cricket ground decided that their future plans were for football only. It was generally believed to be a good pitch and a sad loss, but a pleasant enough day can be spent at Abbeydale, which now hosts a county match each year. The city has some good Art Galleries and at least ten Museums. The museums include The Bishop's house, which is the oldest timber framed house in Sheffield and has displays to show life for those in this city in Tudor and Stuart times, a Fire Museum, one for glass, and another for buses. The Town Hall and the Cutler's Hall are both open to parties who pre-book, seven Theatres (you might have noticed that most of the televised snooker comes from the Crucible) and what would appear to be the most outstanding range of sports facilities anywhere outside London – without as far to travel – plus concert halls, cinemas and nightclubs.

Shopping isn't ignored. If you have driven north along the M1 to Leeds, you cannot possibly have missed the Meadowhall Shopping Centre, the biggest retail centre in Europe. Nearer the city centre, a framework of Victorian buildings at the Orchard Square shopping precinct or the old Barracks at Hillsborough, converted into a centre with supermarkets and speciality shops should please

"First King of All England" – Dore village green

you. Or perhaps Eccleshall Road, well-known for small, quality, individual shops that between them must have a specialist in everything.

And just when you thought you had heard everything about this city, it goes and rediscovers a canal dry dock, built in 1812. Found during restoration work on canals and warehouses in the City, it will now receive attention itself. It was originally built for the Keels, which were massive barges for an English inland waterway at 61 feet 6 inches in length with a beam of 15 feet 6 inches that used to bring coal to the steel works. And near to the city centre too; with the imagination shown by the city planners so far, I look forward to seeing what they make of it.

The Walk

The Route: From the Green—through village—Blacka Moor—towards Totley —Dore

Map: O.S. Landranger 110.

The start and how to find it: Leave the Ring Road at Bramall Lane and follow the A621. After two and three-quarter miles you will pass the Abbey-dale Industrial Hamlet, a museum of the old crafts of this area and then three or four hundred yards ahead on the right is the road to Dore. It is clearly marked, but if you see the Abbeydale RUFC and Cricket Club, you have just passed it.

With all those smart houses along the road, it is difficult to say where the village starts. There is a slight bend in the road, more a "kink" that goes to the right and it is the turning on the left after this, that goes into the village centre. If you see a row of shops on your left that has a Victoria Wine shop in the centre, turn around and take the first right. Go as far as the "Hare and Hounds" (making a note of this comfortable pub where pleasant staff serve excellent bar snacks and good beer, for future reference) and turn left between the chapel and the pub, which is then on your right, and go down to the left-hand side of the village green. There is usually space to park along this road providing no gateway is being obstructed. The start point is at map reference 308811.

What the walk is like: Easy walk through woodland, moorland and country lanes.

Distance: 5 miles — one sharp, but very short, climb.

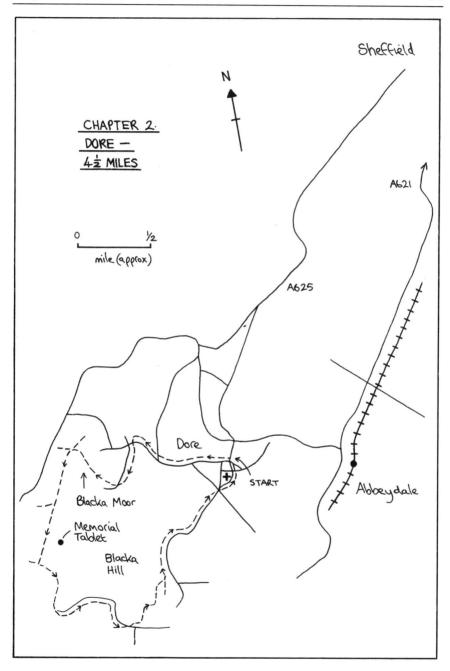

N

CHAPTER 2·
DORE —
4½ MILES

Sheffield

A621

A625

0 ½
mile (approx)

Dore

START

Blacka Moor

Memorial
Tablet

Blacka
Hill

Abbeydale

From the green, go towards the "Hare and Hounds" pausing for a moment at the stone at the end of the green. This was the deciding factor in choosing a typical Sheffield village that had style and good amenities but could also boast exceptional countryside on its doorstep. At least five qualify easily on those grounds but not one of them could boast having the very first King of All England gaining his title there. Indeed, this sandstone block in the shape of a Saxon shield, records the fact that Egbert, having gained wider power than his predecessors, had only Eanred the King of Northumbria remaining out side his control. So Egbert, with enough men to show the Northumbrians a thing or two, marched to Dore. But the Northumbrians weighed things up and decided they could do with some help against the Scandinavians who were still being a bit of a nuisance. Their leader then submitted to Egbert's rule and declared himself ready to assist in the consolidation of all England.

And so it was that King Egbert started his reign in the year 829 which lasted for ten years, leaving his grandson Alfred the Great to consolidate the position and show how little he knew about baking.

Now you can walk past the pub, cross the road and go along Town End Road, passing more shops, the fish & chip shop and Dore service station and garage. No lefts or rights, just go to the very end where it starts to go downhill and to the right. Do not take the lane on the right that is after the corner but go all the way down the hill, curving left at the bottom, over the bridge and start the slight rise in front. At the crossroads, turn left along the farm road ignoring the first and second footpath markers on the left, to go over the moor to see as much of this South Yorkshire countryside as we can in a short circular walk of just over four miles.

After the entrance to some farm buildings on your right, take the right-hand bridleway marked "To Blacka Moor" and then the right-hand one at the next fork. There is a map of the moors and plantations just after that which gives you some idea of the immediate area and a hint of the amount of open land there is near the cities and towns of the industrial north. There is a bridge over the stream on your left but continue straight ahead. Now you start to go up hill, a gradual slope through a good mixture of deciduous trees where any patch that gets some light on the ground has high ferns. Down to your left, a bridleway goes through the stream for a much shorter stroll that does not get onto the moor at all. The one you are on starts to make curves as it takes you to the edge of the moor and passes a sign that says "To Piper Gate". The climb starts to get steeper and you pass first an open patch and then a belt of pines and another path going off to the left, before you finally break out into the open. The moor in August and September is palette of colour with the heather in flower, and has some of the delight that woodlands offer in April and May when their floors have huge splashes of bluebells. Walk a few yards enjoying the rolling open land and then stop. Now turn around! South Yorkshire, nearly every bit you can see with perhaps just a touch of Derbyshire if you look half right. What a marvellous view isn't it? Go on, admit it. Go ahead again as you are nearly at the top and will see when you get there, at another junction of paths, notice boards without notices and one that forbids horses past this point. Ahead lies the Hathersage road and you can probably see the poles of the power line up that way. But turn left.

The path you are now on is going over Blacka Moor and ahead is the Derbyshire border. The hills to your right are often used for hang glider training and you might see the strange sight of a hang glider rising from the ground but being held at a certain height by people holding on to it with ropes. The next junction is where the main path goes to the right at a right angle bend and the path you want is the lesser one that goes ahead. You will soon know if you are on the right one as after about 20 yards or so you will find on the left a small low stone column supporting a plaque that tells you that the small area of woodland, mainly mountain ash, was planted in March 1975, by the Ramblers Association to commemorate the long service of one Noel Norton, who was for a long time their secretary.

Your route is still straight ahead and will continue until you meet a major path or bridle way that is running along the edge of the valley. Turn left and follow this path which starts going down hill and also has the occasional seat at the side. It also seems to have a devil of a lot of flies in late summer, providing the one other excuse for smoking a good cigar. Then take the right-hand path at the next junction under a power line through banks of ferns and back, for a short while, into woodland. Soon you find you are following a wall on your left down to a gate and parking area. Another copy of the map is there too to give you a check on where you are. This is also where you take to the road again and going to the left, walk along towards Totley Bents. Totley is another one of the many pleasant villages that form part of Sheffield's boundaries and which also has access to superb countryside. It was only the added interest of Dore's link with part of England's early history that made me choose the village from the three or four possibles as an example of how close is the richness of the land and the open country to those dark, black factories and pits.

As you go down the road, you can see one of the air-shafts for the railway tunnel over on the right and then you are in the village. At the end of Strawberry Lea Lane, join on to Lane Head Road and go to the left and take the next footpath sign pointing left at the entrance to the farm. At the gable end of the farmhouse, look right and you will see another familiar yellow arrow pointing to the right. Take a sharp right turn and cross the first paddock to the gate and then walk along the boundary of the next field, down the right-hand side, then along the bottom to the far left corner. Here is a house with a substantial stile built into the wall that also has steps down on the other side. Go down and through the entrance to the property, slightly left and along the lane to the house, Old Hay on the left. Just after it, go into the opening, over the bridge, up the steps among the beech trees and onto the road at the top. Pass the farm gate on the left and take the stile into the field which allows you to walk with the wall on your right, in the field instead of on the road. In the top corner, cross the stone stile and the short pathway onto the road again.

Now walk to the left along the road passing Old Hay Gardens, to the church. Go right here, going past the school on the right-hand side of Vicarage Green and an unusual but very nice old house also on the right, finally reaching the village cenotaph and the village green. You are back to your strting point.

Chapter Three

Holmfirth

A pub trail and a failed attempt to avoid the Summer Wine.

A lready introduced to millions through television, the beautiful Pennine scenery is now thronged with masses of "gawpers" looking for signs of the trio who have given the place a new kind of fame. It is not hard to understand why they do it, but there is something very strange about this common habit of standing outside an ordinary terraced house that is used as the background scenery for a fictional character to carry on her fictitious life for what, on the television screen, will be perhaps five to ten minutes a week. They then travel a few miles to "gawp" at what the film makers pretend is the "local" and are then surprised that the interior is nothing like the film set.

Whether this is of any benefit to the village and its residents must be hard to assess. Few shopkeepers are enthusiastic and locals, thinking of the parking problems, try to avoid the place at the weekend. But Holmfirth will survive. It has seen better – and worse, like the burst dam and floods sweeping down the river valley. The same valley that has also been relied upon as a source of power for the mills in this area, that produced the world's finest woollen yarns and cloth. The people of Holmfirth have an odd sense of humour anyway. Being the home of the original saucy postcard manufacturers, Bamforths, and having an "anthem" called Pratty Flowers proves that. And they profit from it too, with a picture postcard museum above the library on the route of our walk, £1.00 admission, and local brass bands that can play the "anthem". As locals join in, charity collection tins go round, possibly suggesting that more verses will be played unless enough is collected.

For some reason (which inhabitants might be able to explain to you) the immediate area has a much higher than average number of working artists of one kind or another. Ashley Jackson has many imitators, but few can get near the atmospheric effect he creates in his watercolour landscapes of the Pennines. Trevor Stubbley is a brilliant portrait painter in oils and, despite the impressive list of those who have sat for him, is probably at his happiest working in the brilliant colours he uses in his Mediterranean scenes. Potters and sculptors too. Less well-known, except perhaps to the regular customers of Harrods, is the miniaturist Jenny Shaw from Netherthong who produces exquisite pieces of porcelain. You will be very lucky if you manage to buy a piece or pieces, as demand exceeds supply. Glass blowers, sculptors, engravers, makers of jewellery and a person who makes scale replicas of local buildings to almost architectural standard are hereabouts. (Take note, the Annual Arts Week at the beginning of July offers the opportunity to buy examples of this local talent at less than usual prices and so help the Cancer Relief charities.)

But there is more to starting at Honley than the parking and the pubs. Walking from there gives you the chance to see the surrounding countryside before and after your introduction to this very individual Pennine village-cum-town.

The cricket ground between Honley and Holmfirth

The Walk

Route: Honley – Brockholes – Thongsbridge – Holmfirth – Netherthong – Deanhouse – Honley.

Map: O.S. map 110 (also on Pathfinder series SE 01/11 and SE00/10)

The start and how to find it: The walk starts at Honley. This is for ease of parking and because you might agree that The Jacobs Well is a pleasant enough starting and finishing place. Without trying to flatter, I can only say that the pints that are served there are about equal to the landlord's personality. The place is always full, so make your own judgement. Of course, behind every good (?) man, there is a good woman! The map reference for the start point is 137118.

What the walk is like: Easy.

Distance: 6 miles.

Having parked on the main road (the A6024) as near to The Jacobs Well as possible climb the steps at the right-hand side of the pub up to the Old Turnpike and turn left at the top. I suppose that if the bottom road looks a bit full, you could always park on this stretch. But for now, walk along this road and then along Far End Lane, which it joins. Quite a mixture of houses along here and not a few surprising modifications and extensions. Pass the first turn on the left and when you see a wide lane on your right, look to the left. There are steps down to the main road which, if missed, meet the bottom of the short lane that is the next turn on the left.

Either way, cross over and immediately after the entrance to the metal fabrications company, a path, marked by a sign, takes you into the field and along the edge that is just above the works' premises. Follow this path, first along the left-hand edge of the field, then straight on after the two houses (where the field boundary goes left), coming out at the far side, through a gap onto a lane. Turn left along an avenue of trees until you reach a hamlet and a road. Go to your right and after only a few yards go along a path off to the left which appears to go through the garden of the house by the road.

This leads into the wood via a line of silver birch and a path towards the river, taking you by the river but 25 or 30 feet above it. Keep to the well-worn path, taking the lower options at any junctions – except to avoid muddy patches – until you reach the bridge

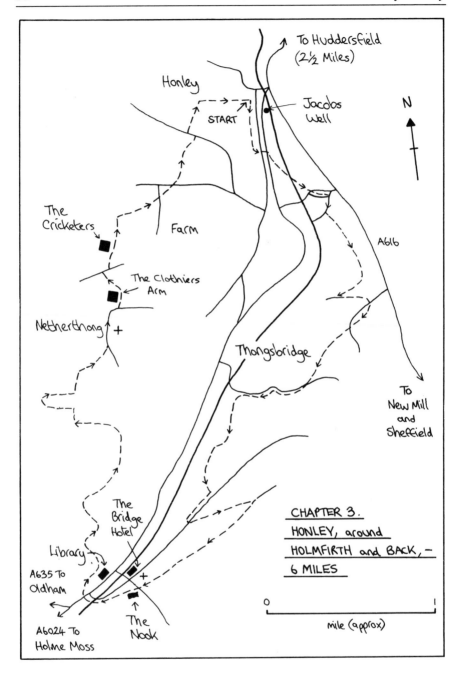

To Huddersfield
(2½ Miles)

Honley

START

Jacobs
Well

N

The
Cricketers

Farm

A616

The Clothiers
Arm

Netherthong   +

Thongsbridge

To
New Mill
and
Sheffield

The
Bridge
Hotel

Library

A635 To
Oldham

The
Nook

A6024 To
Holme Moss

CHAPTER 3.
HONLEY, around
HOLMFIRTH and BACK, —
6 MILES

0   1

mile (approx)

over this, the River Holme, and you are able to step out onto the track. Turn right for a short way, before turning right again to go through another gap in the wall with a footpath sign beside it and six steps to climb into the wood and then a few more as you climb upward swinging right and then left. The left turn brings you nearer to the edge of the wood, following the path in a line parallel to the stone wall.

At the point where the path comes out of the wood, turn left to follow the half metalled track, down the slope with walls and fields on either side. Immediately after passing the house on the right, turn right down a pathway beside the house which will lead you to a footbridge over the river, to the road, where you turn right and go around a left-hand bend. At that point you will find a path that goes up to the right along side the wall of a mill and rises so that you are again above the river.

By keeping along this path, you will pass behind a row of cottages followed by a good view of Thongsbridge cricket club and come to the end of Heys Road. Turn right here, going down the hill past a converted barn that is situated on a corner on your left. After that, on the same side is Berry Bank Lane, so cross over and walk up past the church to a vee junction ahead of you. Bear right here and past the blue painted shed, curving left with the road at the top of the hill. This is where you will find you are going alongside and above the old railway track. At the next junction go right so you are still above the railway line. A little further on, as the path drops down a bit, you will see a section of track with old goods vans, rotting away, in a line beside the track. Take the next bit of a path going upwards on the left (it avoids the scrapyard) to reach the main road and turn right. Take a few steps before leaning on the wall on your right – you will have a very good view of the other side of the Holme valley. Swing from left to right and you have a splendid panorama of views typical of this "off the tops" part of the Pennines, which that certain TV series has done well to use.

Now start to go down hill. You might see or hear a peacock on your right and surely notice the scrap yard sign. Then note the Kirklees sign to mark the Holmfirth boundary and the bus stop sign, for after this comes a road junction and the turn left into the other road. Approximately opposite the fourth house on the left, there is a turn to the right on a well-trodden footpath going uphill. From this path you will have good views of Pennine farms above mills large

and small that used the water power of the valley. In fact, not much
further on along this path is a well-placed seat at an excellent
viewpoint, with, at the right time of the year, a flowering rhododendron at your feet.

From here, the path takes you to a lane that is just after two or
three cottages. Once on the lane, walk to the right to a junction of
lanes. Take the one that is the next on the left after the cul-de-sac
and then, at the point where the road goes to the left, take the path
going down to the right. With a wall in front of you, you can go to
the left *or* right. Left for "Sid's Cafe" (I said we had failed to escape
them) or right, and the path goes down to the road near to the pillar
that records the height of floods. So now go along the road whichever
way you chose a moment ago. If you are thinking of something to
eat, or want to book Bed and Breakfast, look across to the right and
you will see across the river the Bridge Hotel, which should be able
to satisfy you – not that the place is short of good cafes and
restaurants. For a drink, turn left again and after the hardware store,
cross the road towards the newsagents and go down the left-hand
side of the shop to "The Nook". You will no doubt agree that there
are more impressive looking pubs, but take my word for it, the beer
is good and you will come out feeling happier and wiser.

Now, on your left along the river bank, is the house of the lady
that Charnos are probably pleased they did not have as a customer,
Norah Batty. At the next corner is the Toll House Bookshop where
second-hand books are better arranged than in most shops in the
same business, which means that you might find a bargain more
quickly or miss the pleasure of browsing through a jumble. So now
you can turn right along the main road, crossing over when you get
the chance and walk up to the library (that Bamforth collection is
upstairs). After the library, turn left, through the car park, up some
steps and through a small park. At the other side of that, you should
come out on Cooper Lane. Go left and to the top of the lane and then
turn right along Holt Lane. At the next junction, the path goes to the
right but a few minutes spent going to the left to see the small hamlet
there will not be wasted. Of course you have to return and go along
the lane to the right at the end of Holt Lane and the three houses on
the left-hand side which must feel well-pleased with their fine
views. The road now becomes a green lane and if you ignore two
paths that go away to the right you will follow the path as it turns
left, starts to go downhill, crosses a stream – there are stepping stones

– and then goes back up the other side of the valley, swinging left up a path that is more a watercourse in winter and spring.

A look back to pick out the backbone ridge of the Pennines over the top of Holmfirth and then on again to turn right at the next T-junction. You will pass a small housing estate, a path to the right and then come to the road. Turn right here, pass the church and at the next junction, go straight on along the minor road on which you will find (on School Street) The Clothiers Arms, a Free House. After this take the path downhill between the Netherthong Junior school and the Play Group premises. A housing development, where mills used to be, is over to your right and on the opposite side of the road a rising, twisting lane brings you to The Cricketers.

Some times open at lunchtime during the week in the summer, it is a reasonable pub if you can catch it when it's open.

The road ahead, passing the front of the pub takes you down to a gate where the owners have done a very good job of making a cattle-proof opening for walkers (who should ask themselves if they always remember to close gates). Into the field, up the hill along the edge to the end of the wall and then turn right to go through a gap in the wall ahead. After that, take a diagonal line to the left, aiming roughly for the left-hand side of a power line pole, before going through a gap and stile in the wall on your left. Now bear right to cross the field and also get a good view of Castle Hill ahead with the monument and the pub in clear view. The path leads you to a narrow, fenced path that goes to the right alongside an immaculate lawn, ending at a stile to cross. Head down to the road.

At the road turn right and then go across it to turn left at a small hunting gate. As it springs back behind you, walk down to the far end of the field. The next field has a very obvious, well-used path for you to follow diagonally. It ends by running along the wall for a few yards before a gap lets you out onto the road. Turn left here, cross the road, go to the bus stop sign and go through the next gap/stile on the right. Another diagonal line across the field, this time towards some modern houses on the left. The gap here opens on to a short grass lane between houses, then onto the road on the housing estate. Take the turn to the right as far as a block of garages. From here you can cross the playing field to get to the far left-hand corner, which you will find is the wall of the cricket field. Walk down the side of it to the road, passing what is now a smart little mews, a development of what was once a classic-car restorers

premises, and you will find Far End Lane. To the left, the Old
Turnpike, where I hope you will find the steps down to The Jacobs
Well and your car.

And that anthem. The story goes that it was written by a local
man, Joe Perkins, in the mid-18th century and dedicated to a friend
living at Sand House, Holmfirth. The local choir liked it and, when
asked to lead the audience at a concert in Huddersfield Town Hall
in the singing of the National Anthem, they came out with this:

"Pratty Flowers" outside a pub in the Summer Wine country

Pratty Flowers

Abroad for pleasure as I was walking
It was one summer's evening clear,
There I beheld a most beautiful damsel,
Lamenting for her shepherd dear.

Repeated by all

Dearest evening that e'er I beheld thee,
Ever, evermore with the lad I adore;
Wilt thou go fight yon French and Spaniards?
Wilt thou leave me thus, my dear?

Repeated by all

No more to yon green banks will I take thee,
With pleasure for to rest thyself and view the lands
But I will take thee to yon green gardens
Where the Pratty Flowers grow.

Repeated by all

. . . and from then on, it was known as the Holmfirth Anthem.

'Pratty' Flowers ? Not, I'm afraid, something to do with the gardener, merely an old word used in the area for "pretty".

Chapter Four

Huddersfield

Fame and fortune and the search for an identity

The local paper, The Examiner, has been running an exercise called "Pride in Huddersfield" If there is a need for that, it must say something about what the people hereabouts usually think about the biggest town in Britain. And it is nothing new. From the time when the mills first started to line the power source, the River Colne, Huddersfield has been a place for industry, and let the people find a place to live as best they can.

The lucky ones worked outside what is now the town and could walk to work from comparatively decent hillside cottages (though they say it was only when the mills closed for the holiday week that

Huddersfield narrow canal

they could see the other side of the valley). The town became a sprawling mess and it was only thanks to more organisation by the successful businessmen that any order came about. As it grew in the 18th century, plans were put into effect by the then Lord of the Manor, Sir John Ramsden, so that the town got a passable street layout from which to start. Substantial buildings followed; the Cloth Hall was not exactly a thing of beauty but it inspired others to do better. Fortunately, successful men were seldom modest, so the result was bigger and better buildings, like the railway station, the classic grandeur of which makes it one of the finest in the country.

Of course, these are the buildings – stations, hotels and blocks like Lion Buildings – that bring in a little profit as well. But nothing in the way of direct profit came out of the workers' dwellings. They would often be crammed in behind the place of work in the town, in yards. Only Wormald's Yard survives in a form easy to imagine as mid-19th century. To some the yard may be of architectural interest; to most, it remains to remind us of the domestic squalor from which it was difficult to escape. And this was the norm, when at the same time mansions were being built all along Halifax Road. No Titus Salt in Huddersfield.

Part of Huddersfield Railway Station

So if the Examiner does stir any feeling that Huddersfield is a place of which to be proud, it will probably be among those who lived here in the 40s, 50s and 60s, when housing started to improve and the 97% who were employed could say "it'll take more than a slump to put this town down" and point to the fact that all the mills were working, the gear works had full order books and the tractor works continued to grow. On top of that there was the manufacture of mill machinery, electric motors and the many successful dye-works. And the famous names – who usually took pains to live out of town – like the owners of Brook Motors, Major Holliday (as famous for his racehorses as for his dye-works), the David Browns, Hopkin-sons and the mill owners, all felt confident and made few changes to the benefit of employees, although Browns took the lead later, when it was almost too late. A pity, perhaps, that they didn't take note of some of those dramatic scripts of that other Huddersfield man. No, I meant James Mason not a certain Prime Minister and leader of the Labour party.

Yet many of the people who live here were born here, have never been obsequious or servile, always been friendly, supported the Union, held a firm grip on the rights of man and the Methodist Church and do, in fact, harbour some civic pride. So maybe The Examiner isn't so daft. It's just that they will need to do a bit of mouth to mouth resuscitation.

The pubs along Leeds Road will be sure to have customers who can tell you about the great days of football here when "Town" were in the First Division. They will be men who are probably in their 60s and start off with: "Do you remember Peter Doherty then?" and go on to forecast the great things that are going to happen in the new stadium. You need optimism in this town, but I hope he is right.

Then you must stand in the main street and be quiet for a minute and most likely you can hear the ghosts saying "there's nowt we're not good at". Now the West Indian bus driver says to me as he stops at the sixth set of traffic lights in half a mile – and half of that was ring road – "this town sure knows how to mess up the traffic. With all these lights, Blackpool must be getting real worried". But the main trouble is, where can you find employment? But beware, maybe like the Test team, never strong unless Yorkshire CCC is strong, so it might be with industry in England. When Huddersfield flourishes, etc.

As in most West Riding towns, the atmosphere of a town pub changes with the hour of the day. In Huddersfield, few pubs rise above the mediocre, but an exception is The County opposite the Town Hall; a steady regular trade, augmented by members of most visiting orchestras during their concert interval, ensures that it is different. The fact that it seems to appeal to most age groups without any unpleasant commotion merits a recommendation as an oasis.

I suppose that Huddersfield isn't a bad place to live near to, so who can blame those who prefer to live in the surrounding villages? They make up more than the workforce, they also make up the Colne Valley Choir and the world renowned Huddersfield Choral Society. They also see to it that the town gets a good name for sport with League cricket being the nursery of many a county cricketer and a small collection of Olympic Gold Medallists. Incidentally, Rugby League started here and held its first meeting in the George Hotel a hundred years ago. That's the hotel you see in that square in front of the railway station. But the villages are also full of people who go to town to catch the train to shop in Leeds. And how many of them had their honeymoon in Huddersfield?

Just the same there is pride here and that makes it appropriate to start with an opportunity to see some of the buildings which make those who live here proud. Then a canal path walk that starts with empty mills or empty spaces that once had mills and on towards those villages that gave work and play, and finally Pennine scenery at its best. Then you can ride back to town.

Stop Press: when you have tried to be down-to-earth about a place you know well, and been forthright about the pubs in the town, it may be because you know that there are many good places to choose from in the villages that surround Huddersfield. All the more reason to praise the exceptional; this time in the shape of the old Court House, which, next to the old chapel resurrected as the Lawrence Batley Theatre, has been praised for the sympathetic manner in which the restoration has been completed. It was opened just in time for Christmas, 1994, as the Old Court Brew House, and a jolly good thing too. I have managed to squeeze in three visits before rushing this off to the publisher, so that you will get the chance to visit a really good town pub. A judgement based on the interior (warm, lots of good woodwork and cosy corners), the customers (all age groups seem to be there) and, most important, the beer. Lots to choose from and, if you decide to stick to their most potent brew, it could be a close thing as to which runs out first, your mind or your pocket. It ain't cheap, but what is there that is this good?

The Walk

The Route: 1½ miles through the town, followed by a walk along the Huddersfield Narrow Canal to Marsden and Tunnel End, 6.5 miles, to return by public transport.

Map: O.S map 110. Map reference 142165.

What the walk is like: Mostly flat and easy.

Distance: 6 miles

Start in front of the station after having a good look at it and reflecting that this is what you could get for £20,000 in 1850, the year it was completed. The George was completed at about the same time, not as impressive architecturally, but very convenient. In front of you is the Lion Building with the fibreglass lion on its roof that replaced the original stone one. A jumble of shop fronts at street level perhaps, but with well-balanced upper stories. Nevertheless it isn't a patch on the building on the other side of the square, the Britannia Building, almost Italianate in its fine proportions.

Turn right along the main street, John William Street, and then take the first left down a street that leads to Byram Street which, with the public gardens, crosses your front. Turn right and you will see the parish church of St. Peter where you turn right again. Now cross the road and walk up to the Market Place and its modest market cross which dates from 1671. This was the year when the first Sir John Ramsden was granted a Royal Charter to hold Greenhead Park, while the stalls went off to the covered market below the Town Hall or to the splendid "open" Victorian market hall that operates on Mondays and Thursdays.

Walk past the front of Barclays Bank and between an estate agents and the Royal Bank of Scotland there is a path to the left. This is Market Walk and as you turn the corner you will pass Fillans the jewellers who have one of the few Victorian shop fronts left in town, its curved glass, moulded wood and painted panels having so far escaped the destruction suffered by the others. At the end of the Walk, turn left down King Street, a street bordered by some of the "names", Boots, M&S, a Burger King and W.H. Smith's. After passing the latter, turn right to go along Queen Street, (unless of course you would like to see Wormald's Yard, which is just a few yards down

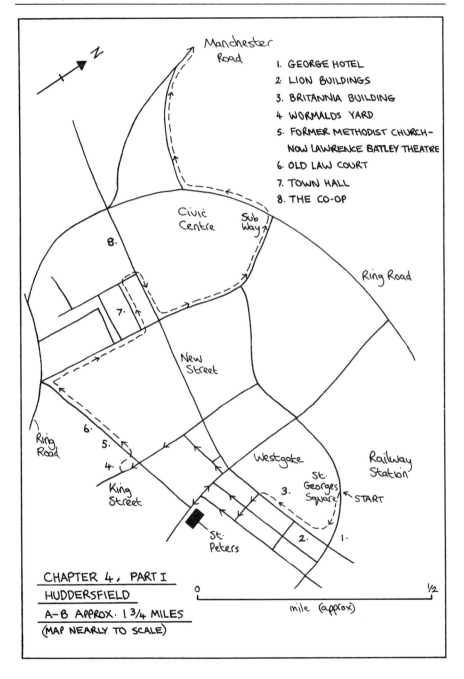

Manchester Road

1. GEORGE HOTEL
2. LION BUILDINGS
3. BRITANNIA BUILDING
4. WORMALDS YARD
5. FORMER METHODIST CHURCH-
   NOW LAWRENCE BATLEY THEATRE
6. OLD LAW COURT
7. TOWN HALL
8. THE CO-OP

Civic Centre

Sub Way

Ring Road

New Street

Ring Road

Westgate

St. Georges Square

Railway Station

START

King Street

St. Peters

CHAPTER 4, PART I
HUDDERSFIELD
A-B APPROX. 1 3/4 MILES
(MAP NEARLY TO SCALE)

0   1/2
mile (approx)

on the right of the street in front), and then come back to Queen Street.

Along here, on the left, you will pass what was the old Wesleyan Chapel of 1819 which could seat over 1700 people. The building was saved by the successful conversion to a squash club and now looks like having a longer future with its recent conversion to the Lawrence Batley Theatre, which has played to full houses since it opened in October 1994. How odd that 1994 was the 10th anniversary of the death of that great actor from Huddersfield, James Mason, and not a word was said. From a TV short he made, it seemed he loved Huddersfield rather more than the town loved him.

Then comes the old Court House building. with its classical facade. In contrast, at the end of the road before you go up the steps on your right, there is the modern Queensgate frontage to the covered market. At the top of the steps you will see the entrance to the market on your left and ahead and to the right the excellent, helpful and well-stocked Library. It started as a subscription library, founded in 1807, but the present building was not completed until 1940. To me, it is one of Huddersfield's two prize possessions. Keep walking and you come to the other, the Town Hall, which I admire because it contains a wonderful concert hall, of a standard that this very musical area deserves.

But now pass the front and turn left down the far side. At the far end, turn right, to the pedestrianised shopping area to turn right again, but not before looking to the left at the Co-op building, built in two parts, the second bit being seen as very daring when it was built. Not as modern as the Midland Bank building, further down New Street, at the far end of the pedestrian precinct, but impressive at the time for its use of new techniques.

Walk to where the road crosses your path with Ramsden Street on your right and High Street on your left and go left to pass the Civic Centre and the Law Courts. If I cannot persuade you to take the canal walk, this is the point where you take the street on your right. This way, if you are not dazzled by the forest of traffic lights, you will pass Sainsbury's (route check) and be able to go straight ahead, crossing only one more road to reach the station. Otherwise go down the pedestrian subway to your left and take the first left at the bottom. You are on the other side of the ring road now and should walk past the Fire Station going right, down Outcote Bank. Then just keep going until you get to Charlie Brown's.

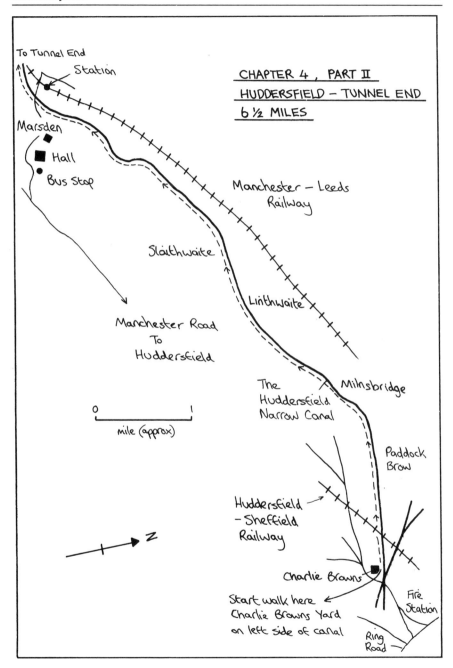

To Tunnel End

Station

Marsden

Hall

Bus Stop

CHAPTER 4 , PART II
HUDDERSFIELD – TUNNEL END
6 ½ MILES

Manchester – Leeds
Railway

Slaithwaite

Linthwaite

Manchester Road
To
Huddersfield

0 _____ 1
mile (approx)

The
Huddersfield
Narrow Canal

Milnsbridge

Paddock
Brow

Huddersfield
– Sheffield
Railway

Charlie Browns

N

Start walk here
Charlie Browns Yard
on left side of canal

Fire
Station

Ring
Road

Go into their car park, through the gap in the wall on your right and turn left along the canal path. You are now on the Huddersfield Narrow Canal. Signs of refurbishment are soon seen, particularly of lock gates. You will see the unusual site of cleaned up locks and gates on either side of a blockage like the one near F.M. Woods, where a road goes over at a low level.

At another restored lock the approach to Milnsbridge becomes obvious with turning areas for barges and a recently restored road-bridge for the road coming down from the Manchester Road. It is worthy of note that even in an urban environment canals look so calm, so laid back, so safe. And they are not. At locks particularly, children who have quickly got used to the placid atmosphere can be taken unaware by the dangers if they are not carefully supervised.

At the double bend in the canal there is a narrowed section which is the top of the bridge over the river and the weir. The next bridge is at a road into Trident Carpets, and would need to be raised or swung before a barge could get through. The rise in the canal "pounds" is becoming obvious and the lock gates at the lower end of locks are now two half gates for ease of operation. It is now easy to see how the system works. Also to be seen on this section approaching Linthwaite is an old mill pond, taking the overflow from the canal, used in the past as back-up for the water driven power from the river. There is also a bridge here dated 1826.

The view starts to open up from here and the canal is cleaner, or so you might believe as you start to meet fishermen sitting on the canal bank. Through Linthwaite and past their cricket ground (no village should be without one). There are domestic geese on the canal now and the scene is generally more rural, although the approach to Slaithwaite is dominated by large mills on both sides. In fact Slaithwaite council were probably the first to fill in their section of the canal, a fact that becomes obvious as you first walk along a raised bank before having to go down onto the road on the left. Turn to the right at the next road and then go left through a gap in the railings.

This is the path on top of the canal and the landscaped (?) site, also provides a notice board full of unexpected facts about Slaithwaite. Well, look around; would you expect it to be a Spa? Next comes a car park, then the streets. Go left along the first and cross the road, (straight across) at the cross roads. Another car park, grassy banks, a block of concrete that was a lock and then the canal again.

Another surprise. Here is the Moonraker, a floating cafe offering the usual fare as well as breakfast at any time of the day.

From the Moonraker to Marsden is just three miles and the countryside is getting better all the time, the houses taking on a more individual identity and mini- lakes and reservoirs appearing more frequently. You can opt out at Marsden where the road, canal and railway all come together. The extra half mile after Marsden – and half a mile back – is recommended, however, as this brings you to Tunnel End and the small canal side museum. It is planned to restore the roof of the tunnel and open it to traffic at some time in the future. You will see railway tunnels that are still in use go through alongside the canal tunnel, but to see the details of construction and the manner in which the barges were propelled through, you must go into the museum. There is, by the way, quite a good pub on the road just above.

When you return to Marsden, there are timetables on the boards next to the station car park. There are trains back to Huddersfield, but I recommend the bus, which may take a few minutes longer, but will give you views of the walk you have just done from another angle, together with views of the other side of the valley that were not always visible from the canal path.

In any case, the "Railway" is not open on weekday lunch times. But take heart, two minutes downhill into the village is the Swan, with a decent pint. So now is it train, bus or a drink before the next bus? They run every half hour from the Mechanics Institute, at 5 minutes past and 25 minutes to. Decisions, decisions.

Chapter Five

Bradford

. . . and the escape to Ilkley

Bradford has been associated with wool for so long that it's hard to understand why there aren't any mills around. There are a few in fact, but not on the grand scale of the almost feverish days of invention and expansion, when the giant mills along the valley employed thousands and before the Second World War when it was said that Bradford had more Bentleys and Rolls-Royces than any other city bar London.

The city had no option but to become what it was, the wool capital of the world. At first, the valleys that ran towards the saucer in which Bradford sits provided power for the mills and on the slopes, grazing for the sheep. Then the factories grew and the sheep lost out. But we had our Empire and merchant fleet so we could import raw materials from anywhere and sell the finished products everywhere.

Big names and big deeds, that was Bradford. Isaac Holding and the combing machine, James Noble and the Noble comb, still used today, Samuel Cunliffe Lister – later Lord Masham – and Sir Titus Salt, both of whom devised new cloths such as the lightweights with the right combination of wool and cotton, or others from alpaca, mohair, and waste silk. Sir Titus is also famous for his own model village, Saltaire, which he built (after making "a few bob" in Bradford) out of concern for his workers and no doubt to benefit from enhanced production from workers in decent homes who were off work less often. It took twenty years to build and most of it still exists today even if used for different purposes, like the enormous mill built in the style of an Italian palace. But more of that later. Bradford has always been more than just wool, even in the days of the multi-millionaire mill owners.

Four of the Brontës were born at Thornton, then a Bradford suburb. Charlotte, Emily, Anne and Bramwell. Delius was born here too, even if he did live most of the time in France. All his life he sang the praises of the Pennines, which I suppose is reasonable if you are snug and warm in France. John Wood and Richard Oastler led the long fight to get the ten hour bill passed mainly to safeguard the child workers who had been forced to work much longer hours. And there is J.B. Priestley too. His statue stands outside the National Museum of Photography, Film and Television and the Library. Now there's a place to go. So if you start at the Interchange, where the

railway station, bus station and a large car park are sited, first walk down Bridge Street past the Victoria Hotel and St. George's Hall, the concert hall, behind which are the new and old offices and machinery of the Telegraph and Argus, Bradford's respected evening paper, turn left and cross the front of the City Hall. Go to the far end of the police station, through the subway and out in front of that museum. Once there, make sure you have time to see the films that are on at the IMAX cinema. It's terrific.

J.B. Priestley

The Walk

The Route: Bradford City (1½ miles), Saltaire Railway Station and Dick Hudson's, above Bingley.

Map: O.S map 104. Detailed map in book for City walk.

The start and how to find it: Park in Interchange car park signposted from A641. Start by walking out through bus station shopping area, adjacent and below car park. Part 2. Bus from Bingley station to Lane End above Eldwick to start by walkingfrom there to Dick Hudsons.

What the walk is like: Easy.

Distance: 4½ miles.

Try to make an early start on this one as it includes more of the city, train and bus journeys, a diversion to a gallery, a walk across that moor which famously warns of the consequences of not wearing a hat (not that it would rate very highly today as the place to go for any serious courting), and then to an early spa town. Perhaps five or six hours, not counting any self-inflicted delays in any place of refreshment.

So go to the left as you come out of the photography museum and have a look at the Alhambra. Large amounts of money were spent on its restoration and all to good effect. Tours of the theatre are sometimes available and very interesting. Perhaps you just want to pop in to book some seats; the programme usually tries to please all tastes and is about 85% successful. From there, I recommend going through the subway again in the direction of National & Provincial House (easy to spot) as the road is approaching kamikaze status. Then when on the road facing that building, go to the right, passing the City Hall on the opposite side of the road with its fairly obvious hint that a Bradford merchant of earlier times had visited Florence. Bear left and walk down Hustlergate noting the old Cloth Hall on the left. At the bottom, you join Market Street at the entrance to the Wool Exchange, no longer used for its original purpose but, as you will see, with some impressive stone work.

It is in this area before the "developed" parts, that you can see the quality of the Victorian stone and more examples of the mason's skill and evidence of a confident stonecutter. A sharp left turn at the end of Market Street takes you into Cheapside to the left of which

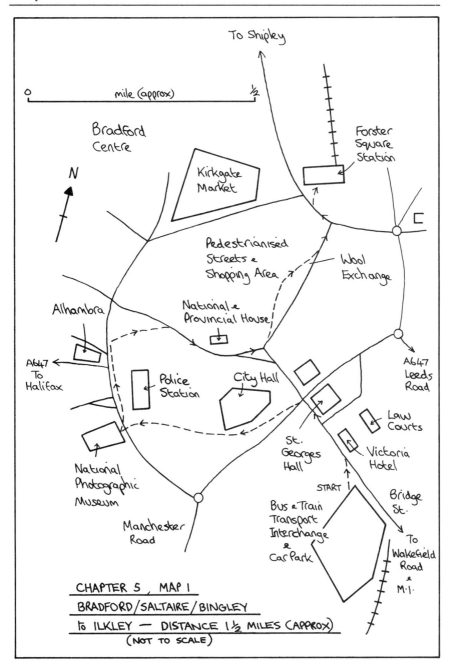

To Shipley

o   mile (approx)   ½

Bradford Centre

N

Kirkgate Market

Forster Square Station

Pedestrianised Streets & Shopping Area

Wool Exchange

Alhambra

National Provincial House

A647 To Halifax

Police Station

City Hall

A647 Leeds Road

Law Courts

St. Georges Hall

Victoria Hotel

National Photographic Museum

START

Bridge St.

Manchester Road

Bus & Train Transport Interchange & Car Park

To Wakefield Road & M.1.

CHAPTER 5, MAP 1
BRADFORD/SALTAIRE/BINGLEY
To ILKLEY — DISTANCE 1½ MILES (APPROX)
(NOT TO SCALE)

there is one of the ubiquitous shopping centres. Going further up the hill, you would need to cross two streets on your left before coming to the covered market. Without that excursion you will see that Forster Square station is on your right. There is lots more to see of this city such as the Cathedral, the other markets, some exceptional Indian restaurants, the colour museum and the Design Exchange. But for now, walk down into the station and take the train to Bingley. If you haven't already done so, it might prove to be a good, money saving idea to buy a bus/train Metro day rover ticket. You can use it on all public transport in the Metro area for as many trips as you like in the day and it really is a good saver. Trains to Bingley run from here every hour, on the hour and take 15 minutes.

Two thirds of the way to Bingley is Saltaire (first stop after Shipley) and that famous mill containing many business ventures. With all the publicity given to "the local lad made good", the main reason for breaking the journey here is the gallery which almost continuously has exhibitions of the work of David Hockney. Some people are less than enthusiastic about his work, as some of the comment greeted his commission to illustrate the cover of the Bradford telephone directory showed. But you only have 60 minutes to the next train, so why not have a go? At least you might judge for yourself if any of his wide range of skills and his originality please you. Almost opposite the steps up from the station is the mill and there's no shortage of signs to get you to the gallery.

The village of Saltaire was built by Titus Salt for his workers, dependants and local old people and was opened by him on his 50th birthday in 1853. It covers 25 acres and has 22 streets – all named after members of his family – for the 850 houses, schools, almshouses and the Congregational Church. A wealthy and generous man, Sir Titus also built a church at Castleford and a Sailors' Orphanage at Hull, both of which he continued to support during his lifetime. He died at the end of 1876 and it is recorded that 100,000 people lined the route that the funeral procession took from Bradford to Lightcliffe.

Once outside Bingley station you will see the bus stop opposite from where you can take the bus to Lane End up above Eldwick. From there, continue along the same road on foot until at the junction with the Otley Road you will come to "Dick Hudson's" The real name of the pub is The Fleece, but it has long been known by the name of an earlier landlord, so much so that when buses came

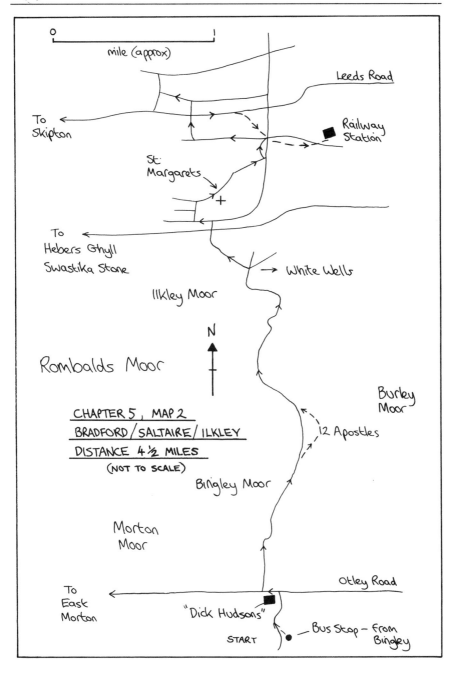

0 _____ 1
mile (approx)

Leeds Road

To
Skipton

Railway
Station

St.
Margarets

To
Hebers Ghyll
Swastika Stone

White Wells

Ilkley Moor

N

Rombalds Moor

CHAPTER 5, MAP 2
BRADFORD / SALTAIRE / ILKLEY
DISTANCE 4½ MILES
(NOT TO SCALE)

Burley
Moor

12 Apostles

Bingley Moor

Morton
Moor

To
East
Morton

Otley Road

"Dick Hudsons"

Bus Stop - from
Bingley

START

further up the lane, their destination boards read "Dick Hudson's". Though now a more designer-type pub, the food and beer is still good.

You will also see that the cricket club have managed to get the only piece of flat ground for miles. What a remarkable coincidence that it should be next to the pub.

Now it is only a matter of crossing the road from the pub to start the four and a half miles to Ilkley by taking a gap in the far wall onto Morton Moor. This, like Ilkley Moor, is a part of Rombalds Moor, the whole stretch of open country stretching from Airedale to Wharfedale and very nearly to Shipley. The open space that was an escape from the mills on high days and holidays. You can see now why they prayed to God to spare them from Hull, Elland & Halifax; they must have felt the same about Bradford, Shipley and Keighley. God spared them in the shape of the Bank Holiday Acts of 1871.

The first part, between two walls, is stepped and steep, but short. A stop at the top makes it worthwhile to turn round for the view in anticipation of the pleasures to come. These come immediately in the form of a good footpath, paved in places from packhorse days and boarded or bridged in others from the traffic it gets in the present day. There are also little detours around plots planted to start the restoration of the cover and grazing. Certainly, the path is clear enough to see in anything but the blackest night.

There are usually a few walkers coming the other way and most of them on arrival at the top of the moor will go over to your right to have a look at the circle of stones that are called the Twelve Apostles. I heard two fellows putting forward views on the circle's origin. One was sure it was only the boundary of a burial ground while the other was holding a piece of newspaper that apparently stated that they stones represented the signs of the Zodiac.

It is quite possible that about a hundred and twenty five years ago, a gang of youths after their share of carousing, decided to have a race up to the top, each carrying a large rock. Only twelve of them finished the course and they decided to drop them in a circle. No one noticed them for two or three years and then the trippers started to come, so the "racers" took turns to guide groups up to the magic circle for a penny each and, to achieve a little credibility, called them the Twelve Apostles. They also took great care to see that they appeared as such on all the maps. Well, they do, so it could be true.

Downhill now and a ravine to go down and up before the path

Part of the Twelve Apostle stones

curves to the left and opens up views of Wharfedale, so that very soon you can see the sports grounds on the other side of the River Wharfe and the town of Ilkley. A group of trees with a seat below them stand on a knoll to your right, and offer an alternative path straight down instead of following the path which goes a little further to the left before curving to the right. Both lead to the same place, the recently renovated White Wells bath house with a natural spring bath where Victorians once took the waters. There are still the mounting steps for the ladies to mount the donkeys that took them back into Ilkley. The town grew mainly on its reputation as a spa and became "a good address" for many a business man and woman, especially after the coming of the railways in 1865. More about this is displayed in the Countryside Service Information Centre housed in the bath house, with its displays on its history and details of former services.

Go around the left-hand side, following the path to a bridge. Instead of crossing the bridge go down the path on the right just before it and then at the road, walk to the left and take the next on the right. This, by keeping to the right, leads to St. Margaret's church and the Panorama Stone, the most accessible, here in the public gardens opposite the church, of the many "cup and ring" marked stones that are in this area. You are now on Queen's Road; had you not turned right off Westwood Road (the one at the edge of the moor) you would have passed the reservoir and arrived at Heber's Ghyll and the Swastika Stone, which is thought to be Yorkshire's oldest rock carving.

Back to Queen's road, turn left at the bottom along Wells Court, and up to the cross roads. Turn left again along what is The Grove and where a lot of the town's smart shops are; antiques, tea shops, bistros and fashion shops. After these, bear right with the Memorial Gardens on the left and into Bolton Bridge Road. Cross – with care – the main Skipton to Leeds road, go down the lane opposite and turn left at the Riverside Gardens. A little way along Bridge Lane, turn into the gardens. Here, beside the river, you can hire boats and get a view of the Old Bridge. There is also a pub, but although convenient and quite reasonable, it is like most town pubs, lacking any strong features. The food is O.K. but there is a wide choice of places to eat in Ilkley and most of them serve drinks. I always find them more relaxing and more in keeping with the atmosphere of the town. So don't expect to see fish and chip shops here. I saw some, but the chips looked white and the pigeons in the nearest park looked suspiciously fat.

Walk back either along the river to the New Bridge and turn right up into the town or back along the main road crossed earlier and turn right at the Box Tree restaurant and up through a shopping area of pleasant shops with Betty's Coffee Shop and Tea Rooms at the top.

A stop at one of Yorkshire's finest tea shops (the others are their branches in York and Harrogate) is essential. Not for just the wide choice of teas and almost sinfully delicious cakes but because a little time spent here restores the spirit enough to think that perhaps the world isn't so bad after all. For here the customer comes first – once you have got a seat – and you feel you could easily become friends.

A walk along the tree-lined streets wouldn't do you any harm as there is every amenity here, yet it remains peaceful. So, it is either up New Brook Street (from the river) and turn left at the second crossroads or, coming out of Betty's, go left to the crossroads then straight across. Both ways lead to the station for trains to both Bradford and Leeds.

Chapter Six

Hebden Bridge

The canal, the Pike and a hill village

The title says it all. Hebden Bridge is strung out along the river, canal and railway, between the Pennines rearing up to Stoodley Pike on the south side and the hills and valleys to the north. To say that you should find your way around the town and its attractions and then take to the hills for a wonderful but mildly strenuous walk would be sadistic. Instead, you have a choice of starting points. At the station of course, if you have just stepped off the train; or at the dock or the marina on the canal, if you have just parked your car or got off a bus. Directions start from the station and connect with the

Hell Hole Rocks, Hebden Bridge

other starting point after the dock. This way you will see the surrounding countryside, get panoramic views of the town and surroundings which will help you to understand why Hebden Bridge has been a place of importance from medieval times. Then, at the end of that occasionally strenuous walk, "nosing around" can be done with some feeling for the place with the additional pleasure of feeling that you have really earned a break when you finally sit down with a glass of something refreshing.

Of course, the pedantic will say we are cheating. The area covered – hills and valleys once entirely committed to the production of clothing, blankets cotton and the machine tools that go with such industries is really Hebden Royd. Nowadays I would bet you have to live here to know that in 1937 Hebden Bridge and Mythholmroyd were allegedly united. But the walk still starts in Hebden Bridge.

The Walk

Route: Hebden Bridge station – canal through town – Stoodley Pike – canal – Heptonstall – Hebden Bridge

Map: O.S. Map 103

Start at: The railway station; map reference 993268.

What the walk is like: Moderate, with occasional steep paths.

Distance: about 6 miles.

Coming out of the station, walk down the road, over the bridge across the River Calder until, just before the main road (Burnley Road), there is a left turn into a gateway and the park. Although it isn't obvious at first, this path runs alongside the Rochdale canal. Go to the other end of the park, past the first lock and then over an aqueduct where the canal crosses the river.

Anyone starting at the marina will have walked a little way along New Road then turned left to go along Holme Street to the bottom and crossed the bridge over the canal to join the route just before the aqueduct. Now we are all able to take the small footbridge on the left and up some steps on the other side to the Shelf road. Go to the left, through the traffic lights on the Z-bend and along the road until you see on your left, a house with a large wooden summer house in the garden and on your right a driveway that after a few

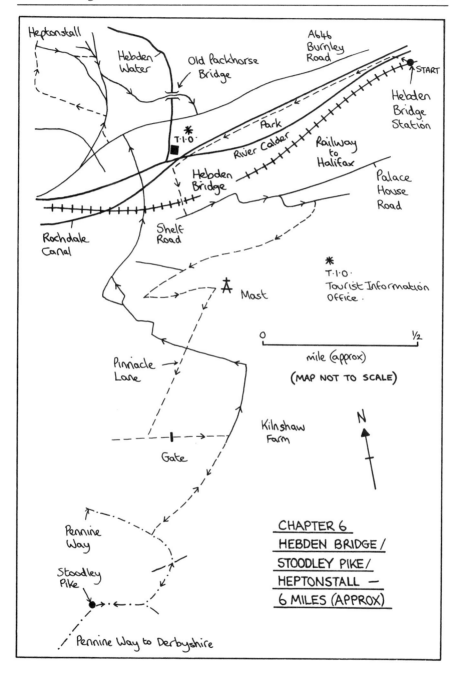

Heptonstall

Hebden Water

Old Packhorse Bridge

A646 Burnley Road

START

Hebden Bridge Station

Park

River Calder

T·I·O·

Railway to Halifax

Hebden Bridge

Palace House Road

Rochdale Canal

Shelf Road

Mast

* T·I·O·
Tourist Information Office.

0   ½
mile (approx)
(MAP NOT TO SCALE)

Pinnacle Lane

Kilnshaw Farm

Gate

N

Pennine Way

Stoodley Pike

CHAPTER 6
HEBDEN BRIDGE /
STOODLEY PIKE /
HEPTONSTALL —
6 MILES (APPROX)

Pennine Way to Derbyshire

yards, curves to the left. After about 25 yards, take the well-worn path that goes up on your right and is angled to the right and which will appear to go to the corner of the wood. Halfway up, a look to the right gives a wonderful view of nearly all of Hebden Bridge and many of the surrounding hills and valleys. Carry on through a small stile-cum-wicket gate, towards the house ahead and the adjacent metal gate with vertical bars. Through this, to walk along a short track as far as the meeting of four lanes, then take the left-hand one and keep to it, going around a hairpin bend.

Not long after this, a wireless mast will come into view, so look out for the path that crosses the one you are on before reaching the mast. To the left, it goes down through the wood, to the right it points towards Pinnacle Lane. That is the one to take. Over the stile and along the edge of the field going straight up to the brow of the hill and there, way in front of you, is Stoodley Pike. One field after this a narrow road is crossed, the path still straight ahead.

The lane continues through walls and stiles, pleasant walking all the way. Then after a gap between wall and copse, cross a grass field that has a farm house over to the right. You will come to a gate and stile which lets you into a lane with stone walls on either side. Turn left, go through the next gate and straight on to the next T-junction. Here is Kilnshaw Farm and a right turn.

You are now on Kilnshaw Lane and should continue along it, passing a house on the right and walking to the end of the stone wall after the house. Here, follow the pointer of the Pennine Way sign to the left. A short sharp climb, a wall to get over (with the aid of a ladder stile) and turn right. You can see the immediate objective quite plainly, a good place for that snack you brought, while taking in the stupendous views of the Pennines.

The building of Stoodley Pike started in 1814 as a peace monument, by public subscription, but with a break in construction from the time of Napoleon's escape from Elba until we gave him the final what for at Waterloo. Unfortunately it fell down in 1854, so the Anglo-Russian peace treaty was used as an excuse to rebuild it to 120 feet on a hill over 1300 feet above sea level.

The return trip starts with a retracing of steps back down to Kilnshaw Lane. Go back along this too but go straight ahead to pass the junction where you joined it on the way up. This becomes a gated road and has some improved old houses, coming to Erringden Grange on the left. Soon after this join the metalled road that goes to the left, over the crossroads, and along the narrow winding road to the hamlet of Horsehold. The T-junction there marks the point to turn left and follow the road with its steep side and good views of the valley, down to the A646 Todmorden and Burnley road. Cross the main road and go to the left. After a small restaurant, look out for a small opening on your right. This is Stoney Lane and is the start of steep steps which don't go on forever – just seem to. I'm sure there must be more than those up to Whitby Abbey. At the top you will find yourself on Heptonstall Road, so turn right.

When you reach a short terrace of houses on your right, you will see on the other side of the road a signpost pointing to the left which reads "Hell Hole Rocks" and "Heptonstall" Take this path which follows the curve of the hill as it climbs steadily upwards. Stopping for a breather will let you absorb the surrounding beauty and give you time to notice how the valley bends and narrows. Other valleys join it, many within sight and possible tracks over the tops are not difficult to pick out. The road, railway, river, and canal all have to run almost shoulder to shoulder on this important east-west commercial link, and thus created at the river crossing point on the Halifax to Burnley pack horse route the beginnings of an important textile centre.

After about a mile along this path the Rocks seem to block the way. In fact, looking at what seems to be a giant stage backdrop you do not immediately notice the flight of steps "in the wings" of the stage. Climbing them is not quite as hard as the earlier flight and there are not as many of them. At the top are the backs of a few modern houses and a path that goes between them. It turns out to be a very pleasant little development of attractive designs with decent sized gardens. At the other side, cross a road, then follow the one at the other side going round the church, keep going round and you come out into the village street near to the post office. Further up the street and on the left, are two pleasant looking pubs. The first one, The Cross Inn has Timothy Taylor's and the next one The White Lion, Whitbread's, a pleasant enough choice. A walk around this outstanding example of a Pennine hill village yields a few pleasant surprises including the old Grammar School, the two churches (the roof fell in on one) and the Octagonal Chapel, founded by John Wesley. Together with the chapel at Yarm on Yorkshire's Northern boundary this is one of the two oldest chapels in continuous use in England. A short way up a lane opposite the one to the Chapel (well

signposted for a small village) you will see a plaque on the wall that
tells you that Whitehall Farm was originally called "Bentleys" after
the original copy holders, many of whose offspring became famous
literary figures in their day. Most famous of them was Dr. Richard
Bentley (1662-1742), the brilliant classicist who became Master of
Trinity at Cambridge.

The thing that mystifies me is the Mummers' play held here at
Easter. The name "Pace Egg Play" is odd enough, but nowadays,
when each Good Friday sees St. George, a juggler, enemies galore
and a lot of ribald laughter, two hundred or more turn up in
Heptonstall for the morning and afternoon performances hoping, I
presume, to find out what it is all about.

Back at the Post Office, to continue the walk, take the road
downhill on the left to the footpath that starts on the left-hand side
of the road. Down steps this time and a turn to the right on the road
at the bottom. A little way along take the cobbled path on the left
that goes past the old cemetery which now seems to be part of the
garden of the bungalow also by the path. This easy down hill walk
called The Buttress is an old pack horse route and ends at the bottom
road appropriately enough, after the "Hole in the Wall" pub, near
the old pack horse bridge (explanatory plaque at the entrance tells
all). At the other side and facing you is the "White Swan" so that
there is a pub on either side providing good beer and food at very
reasonable prices.

The options now are:

1. Turn right up Bridge Gate and turn left and you can walk along
the main road to the left to reach your car or the railway station.

or

2. Go right at the top of Bridge Gate and then right again down Old
Gate, Hanging Royd Lane to the Hebden Crypt and the Turret
Gallery.

or

3. Turn left after the Pack Horse Bridge and go along to St. Georges
Square and explore the three or four streets on the right.

You will find lots of interesting shops as well as places to eat and
drink. The town is trying to shed its hippy centre image, but there
is still some colour around from people who feel they have to be

different. It is really why the walk came first without a complete run down on the town. It is a place you have to experience and it is a place that seems to make a different impression on each visitor, or inhabitant. Hebden Bridge has long been attractive to visitors, as you will see if you drive or walk up to Hardcastle Crags, where in 1902 Gibson Mill, no longer able to compete with the larger mills, was converted into a dining saloon. It was then very popular with the day trippers and so it extended its attraction with boating on the mill ponds, a roller skating rink and a dance hall. The Edwardian forerunner to the theme park – and they are going to restore it.

Should you want to go on exploring, the A6033 runs out of the middle of Hebden Bridge, past the Pack Horse Bridge, to Haworth, once the home of the Brontës, and Keighley. Haworth is about six miles. Less than two miles along the road is Pecket Well and a mill that still weaves fustian and corduroy. You can't miss it, it is just before the Robin Hood Inn, a place for a good pint and a bar snack.

Yet more bits of Yorkshire you will have to come and see.

Chapter Seven

Leeds

A city walk, and that famous Brewery Wharf

As the third largest city in the country, the thought of a walk in crowded streets and business areas may make you stop and wonder what kind of walk this is. Neither area is avoided and other areas are added, but remember, Leeds has been at the game of attracting people for a long time and in consequence has learnt how to make it a pleasant experience. If there is a snag, it is that Leeds is too big to show you all the interesting parts in one walk, so as much variety as possible has been packed into a walk that is mainly central. The cricket and rugby league Test Match grounds are reluctantly left out in the belief that those who are interested, know them well and anyone with the desire to get to know them will have them down as the object of a special trip. And for the others caught between masochism and membership of the county cricket club, who wonder why the individuals who are good cricketers cannot play together as a winning team, could go along to Headingley and suggest that players salaries are frozen and they are paid a bonus on the basis of a percentage of the gate money (including members). We might get more entertainment that way – and they like value for money in Leeds.

Even the monks had that in mind when they were led here by Abbot Alexander in 1152. They built their monastery in the Aire Valley, an area known to have had the resources for at least cottage industries, a place now known as Kirkstall Abbey (and now also "out of town"). But then the collection of villages began to grow and the one that had the church also happened to be the largest. So by 1207 it had been granted a charter to make it a borough, a place of special privileges. Then a new street was made called Briggate, with thirty building plots on each side. These were let out with cash rents, making an urgent need for crafts and industry to bring in that cash.

Success came and so did a second charter from Charles the First in 1626 and growth, if slow, was sure. Leeds was on its way.

By 1721, 17,000 people lived here and the town had a General Infirmary, (rebuilt in 1867 to become the finest medical school in the North) industry, the University and inventiveness. Although iron and coal mining were already a major source of wealth (and there was a railway from Middleton Colliery to Leeds before Stephenson had a Rocket), cloth began to take the lead. The first Jewish settlers arrived in 1800 and surprisingly stirred up a great deal of anti-semitism at the time, but went on to play a major part in the city's economic explosion into the Victorian era, as respected citizens.

At least we can be proud of the buildings of that period, left for us to enjoy. The City Hall certainly has classical grandeur and many a citizen must wish that Park Square still had private houses in at least part of it. But the city has acres and acres of parks, galleries and museums by the dozen, sporting centres, concert halls, theatres and lo and behold, for your sophisticated taste in the exuberance of nostalgic variety in entertainment, The City Varieties, home of that popular television programme, "Those Were The Days". Of course we have all heard of the Mother in Law that came north and could not be deterred from a visit to that lovely theatre, only to find that,

The Museum of The Pub, Leeds

when not on television, it had some of the finest strippers in the
business, twice nightly and two matinees.

But then Leeds was always sophisticated. Did they not have a
super football team that was the star turn of "Match of the Day",
stage managed by Don Revie, that were beaten in the Cup Final by
Second Division Sunderland? And haven't they now the most pala-
tial block of offices ever seen in a government department, set up to
see how they could avoid spending money in the National Health
Service? It's all possible. So let me explain the route to take to see
what could be typical of such a city.

The Walk

The Route: City Sqyare – River Aire – Brewery Wharf – Parish Church –
West Yorkshire Playhouse – Kirkgate Market – Briggate – The Headrow –
Town Hall – Metropole – City Square

Map: Leeds is on O.S Map 104, but the sketch map in this book shows the
route in greater detail.

The start and how to find it: You start right in the middle of City Square.

What the walk is like: Easy, all on city streets

Distance: 3 miles

In the city square, you are guaranteed the company of some
beautiful women. It would seem, however, that there is a shortage
of such delightful examples of the gentle sex, as all those here have
been placed on pedestals. Tearing yourself away from them, face the
station and move over to the left to cross the roads in front of you
and end up walking down the road at the side of the station and
through the road tunnel. Two thirds of the way through, an illumi-
nated sign points to the right and Granary Wharf. Follow the arrow
and after crossing the River Aire you will arrive at the old granary
and a canal quay side. Here are all the shops that you might expect
of such a place. Not tatty by any means, but full of the things that
look nice and you would love to buy but never intended to go out
and get. River trips start here if you fancy an hour on an old barge.
Return to the road the way you came in and turn right. After a
hundred yards or so, passing the Stakis Hilton and Casino, the road
goes over the River Aire at Victoria Bridge and a path at the other
side lets you go down to the left, to walk a little way along the

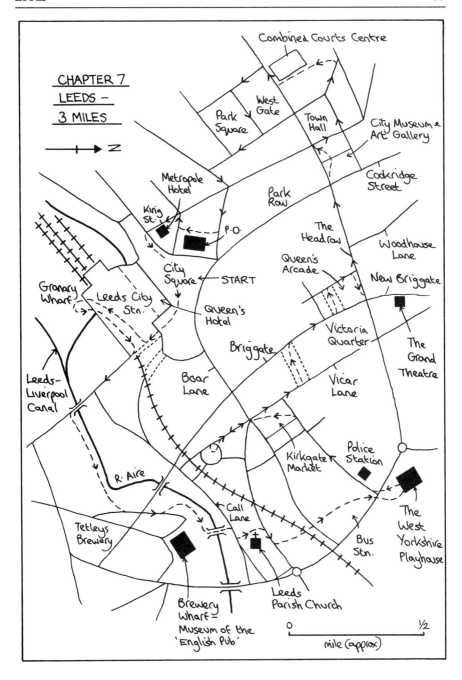

CHAPTER 7
LEEDS –
3 MILES

Combined Courts Centre
West Gate
Park Square
Town Hall
City Museum & Art Gallery
Cookridge Street
Metropole Hotel
Park Row
King St.
P.O.
The Headrow
Woodhouse Lane
Queen's Arcade
New Briggate
City Square
START
Granary Wharf
Leeds City Stn.
Queen's Hotel
Victoria Quarter
The Grand Theatre
Leeds-Liverpool Canal
Briggate
Boar Lane
Vicar Lane
R. Aire
Kirkgate Market
Police Station
The West Yorkshire Playhouse
Call Lane
Bus Stn.
Tetleys Brewery
Brewery Wharf =
Museum of the 'English Pub'
Leeds Parish Church

0   ½
mile (approx)

riverside. When you have to come up to the road you see that you have to cross the main road and go down Dock Street, which is opposite.

A little way along Dock Street, go left into Navigation Way, take the first right, walk along to the end of that block of buildings then left (the sign says, to Fly Boat House) and there you are, back by the river, chain guarded at the edge. Some of the traffic on the river, as you might see, is still commercial, but mostly leisure craft. What is good to see is the mixture of styles used in bringing life back here with restoration work. Modernised offices, flats and the rebuilding of warehouses using almost the same lines as when first built. I think if we followed Prince Charles's ideas to the letter we might still be living in caves as he doesn't appear to want to change anything. On the other hand we have too many planners who agree to modern designs as long as they all fit the same pattern, so that in two or three hundred years people will look back in horror at the end of the 20th century when everything looked the same. But not in Leeds.

At the place where there was a dock, turn right and go over the solid footbridge passing the pool where fountains usually play. Then left to continue along the riverside again to the place where river cruises start and see the futuristic building beside it. This is Brewery Wharf and the buildings you can see over to the right will give you a clue, if you need one, that this is the museum of the English Pub through the ages. You need to allow yourself a couple of hours if you are going to take a break here. Whether you do or not, the next step from Brewery Wharf is to go over the suspension bridge that spans the river.

When you are over the pedestrian bridge, turn right along The Calls until, opposite Langtons Wharf, you will see a gateway in the railings that is on the same side as and just after a parking ticket machine. Go up the steps and across the yard, finding yourself in what remains of a cemetery. It is also the site of Leeds parish church, a fact you cannot miss, no matter how long you stayed in the brewery's museum. After walking a little way along to the right to get a better view of the church, turn left and cross the road. When you have done that, you will notice two things; that there is also a "cut down" grave yard on this side, and that there are still a few shops in business in the railway arches. Well, the railway had to take the line it did and the road was widened, so goodbye graveyard. "Business is business", as they might say in Leeds, in any other part of Yorkshire that practices pragmatism (that should cover a fair part of the county). The shops under the railway, on the other hand, show a determined sort of optimism, as it is difficult to park and people do not seem to think of coming this way. A pity because there are some good shops there.

Now go under the arches and by going ahead in the same direction, go right through the bus station. When you reach the far end and look to the right, the West Yorkshire Playhouse appears. On the whole, a good theatre, or theatres as there are two in the building. They try hard to cater for everybody – always a dodgy way of business – so that musicals, high drama, comedies and thrillers all get their chance. So too do some of the more weird productions when you wonder whether to look at the stage or the audience for entertainment. They also have a really good bar and cafe that is light and airy, a great place to drop in if you need refreshment now and a pleasant spot to sit if you come early for a performance, when there is usually some live music. Kay Mellor the Leeds playwright had her premiere of "A Passionate Woman" here and in 1995 she has sold the foreign rights to 12 countries, had four offers for the film rights and all this while it is a "smash" in the West End.

So from the point where you stood thinking about visiting the Theatre, turn left, up the side of Millbank Police Station and carry on up the street towards the sign you can see on a building on the right, Harwin, pass the jewellers, fish shops, et cetera, then after the newsagents turn left into the doorway that lets you into the main part of Kirkgate market. First look up at the roof supports, a great bit of Victoriana. Then make your way diagonally across to the far right-hand side. That should be interesting enough but once out at the other side, walk to the left along the main road that is on your right when you come out of the market. (Vicar Lane) On the left, on the corner after the bus shelters is a large circular building, The Corn Exchange. It has been completely refurbished and now contains shops and a cafe or two, well worth a look.

Now go back up Vicar Lane so that you pass the market hall again and cross over to the left and walk up to the block diagonally opposite the end of the market block and you will see a glass door entrance into what is now called the Victoria Quarter, a move to put one of Leeds' many famous arcades upmarket. Looks good, especially the modern stained glass, but the work seems to have put the prices up too. You come out at the far end, on Briggate, the part of the shopping centre that has most of the well-known stores. It also has Arcades, some still as they were, others like the Queens Arcade, looking new and fresh but without a lot of the former stores and businesses who now say they cannot face the new rents. Then the alleyway pubs. Good places for a quick bite or even a quick drink or maybe a spell away from all that shopping. The other end of Queens Arcade comes out onto Lands Lane so go right and, at the top, turn right along the Headrow. This was Leeds' first step in modern city planning – "go straight through the City" – they said.

The City Varieties theatre is on the right-hand side and having seen it, cross over to the left and at the corner of Lewis's, look left up New Briggate. The Odeon on the corner and the Grand Theatre further up. That's alright then. So turn around and walk down the front of Lewis's, along the Headrow. You will pass an open area, Portland Square, with a jolly looking statue of a man with a cask and then start to go downhill. As you reach the flat, the art gallery is on your right. It has some excellent exhibitions but I remain in awe of the man who gave the gallery his entire collection of paintings which almost fill one room. Leeds industrialist Sam Wilson had a very wide range of interest when it came to painting and statuary, not without knowledge and/or taste; I fancy that there is at least one painting here that you will particularly like. It may not be the same one that has taken my fancy, or the one that my wife might exchange the house for.

Next is the north of England's finest Town Hall. Stand before it and you would be afraid to disagree. It is quite awesome, with huge stone lions, imposing clock tower and a concert hall of international fame. Majestic.

Now turn right before passing the front of that building. At the crossroads another beauty of another architectural age, the Civic Hall looking like a galleon in full sail coming towards you from slightly to the right and ahead. The Banqueting Hall in this building now hosts chamber music concerts. Part of the Lord Mayor's private accommodation, Sir Thomas Beecham is said to have declared it to be the finest music room in Europe. But your path is to the left. First the back of the Town Hall, then on the right a wonderful music shop, Forsyths, which can supply anything from "First steps on the Penny Whistle" to the full score of "Cavalleria Rusticana". Ahead of you now is the L.G.I. It has a more business-like name now but it remains Leeds General Infirmary in many minds and hearts. It has earned respect for being a top class teaching hospital. The nurses were always good looking too. I do not know about now, so you had better turn left at the Water Hole, a wine and food bar, into Oxford Row which has the High Court of Justice on the right with a facade familiar to those who watch 'Look North'. It also has a massive seal set in a high brick pillar outside. Ahead you will see the Town Hall

Tavern which is on the other side of the Headrow. Cross over towards it (for a lunch-time sandwich and a decent drink of Tetleys, it isn't bad for a town pub) and then go to the right, which, though an extension of the Headrow, is called Westgate. Take the next turn on the left which takes you into the western end of Park Square. Turn left again and admire not only the well-kept gardens on your right and the statue in the centre but also the nicely proportioned town houses around you. Alas, they are now all offices and this London square look-a-like is the only one in Leeds. At the other end of the square, a blue plaque on the wall notes: "The elegant square formed part of the Wilson family plan to create a high class residential estate on the site of the medieval park which was part of the manor of Leeds. Its residents were merchants, clergy, lawyers and surgeons. It was built during the period 1788 to 1810."

Now turn right and walk down to the bottom, St. Paul's Street and turn left opposite Levi & Co., solicitors, to head towards the Sun Alliance building and for the next few streets an area of amazingly varied office buildings, which can give rise to various emotions but are all interesting in some way. At the end of the street, cross over from the Bank of Ireland to the left-hand side of the Allied Irish Bank, with Pavorotti's on the left.

After about fifty yards you can turn right through the gates of Cloth Halls Court, past the back of the Yorkshire Bank Chambers, turning right at the bottom to look at the three blocks of buildings each built in a different style, material or colour of brick or stone. Not that the side you are on lacks variety of style. Makes you wonder which planet you are on, never mind in which era. A walk to the right brings you to the Cloth Hall Court building. Cross over to go left past the King Street side of the King's Court building which is different and yet "fits in" as do all the buildings in this exuberant city.

As you walk down King Street, the Bank of England is on the right but more interesting is the Hotel Metropole on your left. Once one of the smartest hotels of Leeds, you will see from the plaque on the wall that it was erected in the 1890s on the site of the old White Cloth Hall. It also claims to be the best example of terracotta work in Leeds, or one of them as we have just passed a few. When you come to the bottom of the road, the Tourist Information office is opposite so that you can pop in to collect more information about what is on offer in this city. From here, it is a left turn to head towards that large white hotel that you can see, "The Queens", and you will find yourself back at the square with those ladies you left at the beginning.

Chapter Eight

Harewood

Along the edge of the Dales – and a walk on the Royal side

A s you sweep down the hill on the A61 from Leeds to Harrogate, you may get a glimpse of solid looking stone houses on the right and you will be bound to see the signs for Harewood House. You may not realise that you have passed the centrepiece of the Harewood Estate, the house and park, comprising of nearly three square miles behind those stone walls, well before the village. What is more, a lot of it is freely accessible to walkers with access by admission fee, to the House, gardens, aviaries, etc. Unlike a lot of estates which have yet to fulfil their promise to give greater free access to the public in exchange for the waiving of inheritance tax, Harewood has always maintained a lot of pathways and bridleways and explored ways of giving greater freedom. Such an example is only to be expected from the family of the previous Princess Royal.

It wasn't always like that of course. The Estate came into being through shrewd use of privilege and power – in this case gained from inheritance – and it was Edwin Lascelles who benefited from his father's good business sense and good fortune.

That business sense had been exercised as founder and senior partner in a West Indies merchant company; the good fortune lay in being able to buy the adjoining estates of Gawthorpe and Harewood. When his son decided, in 1759, that he needed the sort of house that would add to his standing in politics as well as society, he started to devote much of his ability and energy to the task. Many of his peers had failed in their attempts to build in the grand manner, but Edwin possessed all the necessary abilities. Besides which his vast wealth must have made things easier, especially when his confidence continued to prove well-placed.

By the beginning of the 1900s, things were not looking so good. In fact, paying nearly £3000 for the installation of electricity in 1901 made the 5th Earl, Henry Lascelles' forget about any other improvements that he might have had in mind. Despite London houses, a house in Newmarket and a yacht, cash was very short. Then, with the luck that had frequently smiled on this family and just when the eldest son was living on £600 a year (in 1910) dear old great-uncle pops off and leaves him £2.5 million, a derelict castle in Ireland and a noteworthy collection of paintings.

In 1922, the same eldest son married the eldest daughter of King George V and Queen Mary and they started an enthusiastic restoration of Harewood House, which had to be restarted after the war, during which the house had been used as a convalescent hospital. In this same war, the then Viscount was wounded and taken prisoner. As the present Earl, he was able to open the house to the public in 1965, not long after the death of the Princess Royal, displaying its treasures, a study centre, bird garden,. and garden centre so that Edwin's house of the 18th century became a home and a commercial venture.

The house and the estate, dominate everything else in the area, in a setting that could not be bettered. It is a house of fine proportions with its very valuable paintings, carvings and any number of antiques in porcelain, precious metals and furnishings – and it leaves me thinking, what a nicely laid out museum. But I surrender totally in my admiration for the gardens. The formal gardens are a like a jewel laid upon a green cloth that is the undulating park designed by Lancelot "Capability" Brown. Even that has been improved upon, the open spaces created when many trees were lost in the storms of the 40s and 50s being filled with many varieties of rhododendron to add vivid splashes of colour to Brown's stage set. And even the briefest, most casual visit should include a lakeside walk, beautiful when the flowers and plants are in full bloom from spring to mid summer but exceptionally so in Autumn.

Continuous improvement seems to be the main principle of estate management here. A great deal has been made possible with grant aid from European Community funds, and to judge by the Parterre at the rear of the house, is a good investment. The Parterre, with its statue in the centre instead of the original fountain, has been modelled on Italian lines but to me, still looks essentially English. More schemes are in the planning stage and the only thing I find slightly out of keeping with the continuance of the image of an English country estate is the increasing use of modern machinery which has apparently reduced the numbers employed.

The road outside the estate is busy and there is little room for more houses. The few that live here probably wonder why they came if they don't work for the estate. In fact the main reason that most people come here is to look at the house, enjoy the park and learn more about this family that have made such an impression on this part of the county for hundreds of years. Even so, in doing so they miss the fine collection of alabaster memorials in the Church of All Saints and will probably never know that there are the remains of a castle, now in a ruinous and dangerous state that was rebuilt upon Norman foundations in the reign of Edward III. It was here that Edward Baliol, King of Scotland, took refuge after being driven out of his own country. And then there is the walking around here.

The Walk

The Route: Harewood Arms in village – path above Stockton Farm – Garewood Wike Road – Estate Lodge house on Leeds road – Circle estate to church – Harewood Arms

Map: O.S.Map 104

The start and how to find it: Start your walk at the Harewood Arms for the convenience of its good position, comfortable interior and good service – you will be coming back to here; map reference 321452.

What the walk is like: Easy – farmland and parkland plus a short stretch of country lane.

Distance: 6 miles

First go to the left-hand side of the Harewood Arms, the opposite side to the one with the telephone box, and walk up the lane away from the A61. This goes for some way passing a house on the left that appears to be a very stylish barn conversion. After that, a gas pipe valve station (or Martian refuelling point, they look quite similar) followed by a gate to go through before walking the length of the field. Along here you get your first view over the Wharfe valley, although soon after you are on the edge of the escarpment and can look down towards Stockton Farm. It is a little way ahead but is easily identifiable by the roadway that starts in the bottom of the valley with a couple of "wriggles" then a straight stretch, a curve and an uphill section before going out of sight. This is the Harewood

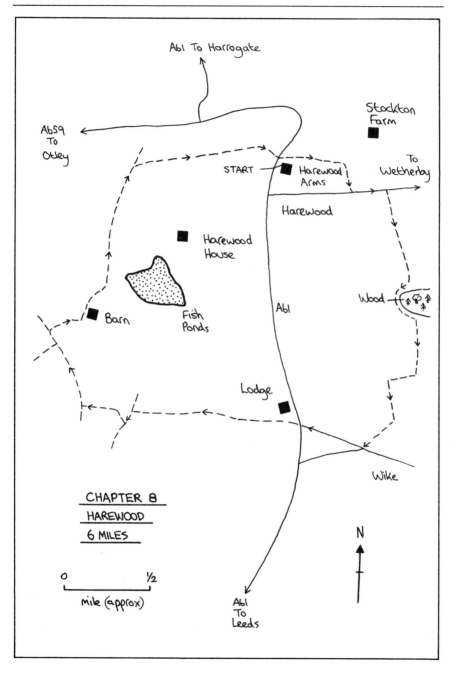

A61 To Harrogate

Stockton
Farm

A659
To
Otley

START

Harewood
Arms

To
Wetherby

Harewood

Harewood
House

Wood

Barn

Fish
Ponds

A61

Lodge

Wike

CHAPTER 8

HAREWOOD

6 MILES

0   ½

mile (approx)

N

A61
To
Leeds

Hillclimb course used for club hillclimbs as well as the British Automobile Racing Club Championships. Then, just as you are thinking you might be going to get a view of the last corner and finish, you go through another gate and immediately go to the right over a stile to walk down the edge of the field to the road. A little bit of a nuisance that you have to walk about 400 yards to the left along this road until you see on the other side a farm road to New Laithe Farm and livery stables. Walk straight down towards the farm veering slightly left as you near the house, passing its left-hand end before starting to go downhill to cross the valley. Approaching Hollin Hall you will find notices to say that the route has been officially changed asking you to follow the arrows. This is no problem at all and the markers are well-placed, sturdy and clearly painted with yellow tops. Near the bottom you pass a small fishing lake on your right after which you bear right to go through a gap in the woods so that you can then go left and walk along the other side of the wood.

Near the end of it, curve off to the right (another yellow topped pole in sight) and go uphill towards the gate. Way over to your right you can see the village of East Keswick, something of a gem to note for future visits to the area. The path soon meets another, crossing your front and is part of the Leeds Country Way which you follow to the right. At a metal six bar gate go left up to the road, on which you have about half a mile to walk to the right. The A61 has to be crossed then, but at the other side, the cheering sight of a lodge (modernised) and gates into the park. Go through the small one at the right-hand side, and a couple of other gates out of a sort of storage area and into the park proper on a good footpath. Here is a rare view of Harewood House in the distance, seemingly set on the hill side.

As the parkland appears to get more wooded with a good mixture of trees in well-managed plantations, the path starts to go downhill, through a gate then curving slowly to the right before going into the wood, crossing the stream by the bridge, with a pond and weir to the left. Take the left-hand track, which a few yards on goes to the right. Follow it with confidence and when you see fields opening out in front of you, turn right and go down and up to cross the stream by an overgrown bridge. Further along this path a gate appears. It has been opened up a bit on one side for cyclists. Go through it and from the two or three signposts pick the one with "Ebor Way" on it. There are two, but take the right-hand one that goes down hill. And at the bottom of that short stretch go right, negotiate a roughish surface and take the next path on the left. This goes downhill too and passes a disused farm building. Through a gate here and you are in open parkland again with the fish ponds in view in front and to the right. The path follows the left-hand boundary and then the track going left and through a gate. Next, on your right you pass the end wall of part of the walled gardens and the private entrance to Harewood Gardens. Keep to the tarmac road that goes to the left.

Next comes a crossroads, straight on here, over the bridge and up the short hill, still going straight on to a sign post at the side of the road and a letter box set in the corner of the building ahead on the right. This is Stank, one of the old villages within the estate that was engaged in spinning and weaving. The Palladian style of building on the right was formerly to do with a large aviary. Keep going straight ahead and up hill to the gap in the tree line ahead of you and over the cattle grid. Now you are on a concrete road to the next cattle grid where a right turn just after it, starts you on a steady climb. Some massive beech trees are at the roadside here but as the road starts to level off, the trees thicken and restrict the view, so you are pleased to arrive at signs of habitation, even the police house. It is a very short stretch along this road to the A61 now. When you get there, turn right and over the road, is the Harewood Arms.

Chapter Nine

Gargrave

The Leeds to Liverpool goes through here – night and day

Once a place where you could hear the river gurgling its way under the bridge, now bearing much more traffic on the road that runs through the middle, masking all other sounds from late March to October. Fortunately the areas on both sides of Gargrave offer pleasant walking country, and the Pennine way passes this way. Even though the Aire valley has its sprinkling of likeable villages along the river, this is the one that the valley seems to pivot upon, perhaps in the natural gap in the Pennines, the Aire Gap, where road, rail and canal take advantage of less-difficult gradients.

The church at Gargrave

Turmoil in the past has been conveniently spread out over the centuries so that an archaeological dig behind the church is not a surprise. A prehistoric camp is well-documented, as are the remains of a Roman villa just outside the town, but it was sometime later that the Scots raided the town in 1318 (and a great deal later before they got as far as Twickenham). The next skirmish seems to have been in 1826 when the Luddites set upon the cotton mills and destroyed the new power looms.

It is quiet in winter but is a pleasant change from the crush of Skipton if you want a pleasant walk and a comfortable pub at the end of it. Not that the "Gateway to the Dales" cannot offer a similar fare, it is just that everybody seems to know about Skipton, its castle, the shops and the market in the wide street in the centre. Gargrave is more conveniently positioned for walkers, boating people and for the driver who just wants to get away from it all. And I'll bet Skipton never had a character like Abe Beecroft. He raised a few eyebrows in Gargrave in his time and was in fact the last one to occupy the stocks outside St. Andrew's church after being caught downing a drop of the hard stuff during Divine Service. I've known a few sermons that might have tempted me too.

Lock and Pound, Leeds/Liverpool canal

The "Leeds – Liverpool" bit refers to the canal that runs through the Northern side of the town. It is open all the time and although there is hardly any traffic that isn't leisure boating, it seems to be active all the time. At a very sedate pace of course, which is reassuring after the hurly burly of the main road.

The town has an adequate number of shops and ample parking. It still has plenty of trees and green spaces within its boundary so don't be put off by the busy road. You will find there is a pleasant selection of pubs too, the Anchor Inn for the "boat people", the Singing Kettle in the High Street and the Mason's Arms near the start of the walk and opposite the church. Although there are good walks to the north and south of the town, the Mason's Arms, just south of the river is the one I usually visit, but there are others, most notable being the Old Swan on the notoriously bad corner as you come in from Skipton.

The Walk

The Route: Car park on road behind Old Swan- church – over railway – along Pennine Way – Bank Newton – return on canal-side path.

Map: O.S map 103.

The start and how to find it: Having driven here on the A59, take the right-hand turn (if you have come from Skipton), on the corner in the middle of Gargrave next to the aforementioned Old Swan. Within 150 yards or so you will find a free car park on the right. Park, and walk back to the pub to turn right and walk along the main road passing various shops (the newsagents sell Ordnance Survey maps) including an antique shop which opens when it feels like it or when an interested customer lets them know they are definitely coming. Map reference for start-point: 933543.

What the walk is like: Easy with mild gradients, field paths and canal-side towpaths.

Distance: 6 miles.

Walk along the road from the car park to the Old Swan until just after the phone box on the left and then see a sign pointing to the railway station you will be opposite a bridge also on the left. Go over that and head for the church. It is quite a nice one but can be looked at later as the route of this walk goes to the right just before you get to it. Then you are faced with the temptation of the Mason's Arms,

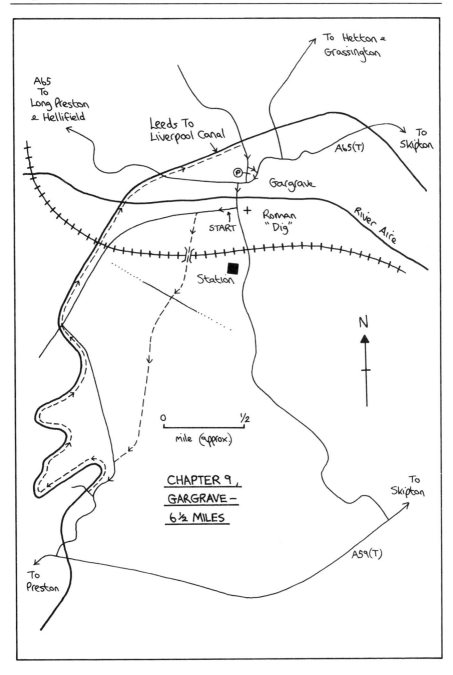

To Hetton & Grassington

A65 To Long Preston & Hellifield

Leeds To Liverpool Canal

A65(T)

To Skipton

Gargrave

River Aire

START

Roman "Dig"

Station

N

0   ½
mile (approx.)

CHAPTER 9, GARGRAVE – 6½ MILES

To Skipton

To Preston

A59(T)

and a drink and/or snack will perhaps depend on the time of day. Let's say that after a prayer for good weather and something to prepare us for the worst, we turn right off Church Street and go to the top of the incline in front. When you pass a house on your right that has a flag pole in the garden a path marker is very obvious on the left, so follow it.

You will find that you are on a well-used farm lane, tracks having been made at about tractor width, indicated as the footpath to West Marton. Go with it over the railway bridge and then through a gateway, across the cattle grid and follow the path markers that point a little way to the right. You should now be heading for a substantial piece of timber on the near horizon and which turns out to be a railway sleeper. Do not be misled by the cart track that goes straight on then down to a farm. Now you have it confirmed that you are following the Pennine Way. This is the point where you can turn around and see Gargrave church and part of the village nestling in the folds of this rolling countryside. Through a small gate next carrying on along the field edge with the wire fence and sheep netting on your right. Next comes an elaborate three step stile, cross this and go to the left to the bottom of the field and curve to the right, going along with the wooden fence on your left. A wireless or television mast is now ahead of you on a hill that is part of the horizon.

Next, at the end of the field, a thorn tree, another three step stile and a familiar yellow arrow. Over this one, go ahead to the stile on the left of the gate and after a short distance across the field another stile, this time on the right of a gate. After crossing that one, go round the right-hand edge being wary of the soggy patches that get quite big after rain. It may be necessary to move a few yards into the field away from the edge to find a better drained area to walk. You now come to a section that has a hill rising to the left, the foot of which also curves to the left. A wire fence is on your left for part of the way. That suddenly takes off to the left leaving you with a fence on the right to guide you.

Now although this is still the Pennine Way, you will need to keep your eyes skinned for a two step stile over that fence on your right which is apparently unmarked until you are about to cross it. Of course Wainwright was going south to north. When you are over, the path is half left and over a small hill. At the top there are two paths, one down to an old barn and one to the right. Go right and you will arrive at the road which you land upon after seeing a handful of path signs. Left along the road to a junction and a hairpin bend to the right. That's the one to take as it leads to a bridge over the canal. But just before you cross take the steps that go down to the towpath that are on the left-hand side of the bridge and at the bottom turn to the right and start to walk alongside the canal at Green Bank.

The snag here is that the canal is on high and rising ground, so to save money, time and effort it follows the contours, which makes for a meandering path. The good point is, being on high ground and following the sides of valleys, you get some pretty good views. The first section of the canal that you walk is part of a three mile, lock free stretch and includes a close up view of that television or radio mast. The locks soon arrive. First a few paces along the road after passing a farm house and then over the bridge to go down on your left, under the bridge and once again along the canal side and you are at Bank Newton locks, with its attractive setting of large pound on a gentle curve between the two locks and a house and garden that looks so purposefully placed. It is also the place where you will find out that the canal stretches for 127½ miles from the River Aire at Leeds to Stanley Docks at Liverpool. It also rises – and falls – 487½ feet.

From here it is just a matter of sticking with the canal, changing sides a couple of times, looking at the boats and enjoying the peace. It seems that in no time you reach Gargrave Locks where the path goes under the railway bridge to continue into Gargrave. I consider it rather nice that passers-by are reminded of the relaxed, unhurried manner of travel on the canals by a sign that says "Liverpool – three days maximum" At the bridge just after that there is a road that to the left takes the Pennine Way to Malham and to the right, down towards North Street and the car park from which you started.

Chapter Ten

Horton in Ribblesdale

Between the Three Peaks, plus a limestone pavement and a village from Norman times.

This village, set midway between Settle and Ribblehead, now with a station on the Settle to Carlisle railway line, is an excellent centre for exploring the limestone landscapes, climbing at least two of the three peaks and sampling a little of the Pennine Way. It has a fine, interesting church dating from Norman and medieval times and is unusual in having two lych gates, roofed with the enormous slabs found locally; similar slabs are also used for water tanks. This in an area where churches are a bit thin on the ground, mainly because of the state of the economy in earlier times. Upper dales parishes were always high on acreage, low on numbers of people. Aysgarth, for example, had one church to serve an area of 80,000 acres, Horton church would serve the whole of Ribblesdale and many villages still do not have an Anglican church. Perhaps that is why a bit extra was spent on things like the fine door. As Alfred Wainwright points out, don't blame the local ale if the pillars seem to you to lean to the south, because they do.

Progress has enlarged the quarries and has also taken another form. Car parks in the villages within the Dales National Park and some others, had honesty boxes. Now a pay and display machine gobbles up your coins and demands that you display the ticket that allows two hours for 60p or £1.20 for longer. Many might say that despite the gadgetry, the place gets too crowded and two hours is quite long enough to walk up Penyghent, look at the church and then go home. That would be unkind. First, you could come by train and enjoy the beautiful scenery that you will pass through. You could also have a meal and a drink in The Crown, which you cannot miss if you walk down from the station and cross the bridge over the river, as it will be right in front of you. You might notice on your map that it says "New Inn" – even Alfred Wainwright made the mistake of saying "The Crown Inn, formerly the New Inn." In fact, it has never been called anything else but The Crown, even when it also operated as a farm, reviving drovers and their animals. The owners told me that the map refers to a plot of land called New Inn, rather like "New Houses" further up the road. However, it is a good place for a meal and a drink and you can stay there too. The rooms are pleasant and the evening meal is good (so is breakfast) and you will be well set up to go on to Hawes or Middleham or Gargrave the next day. There is also the Golden Lion for a good pint and the cafe and information office. The cafe is worth special mention because of the continuing helpfulness of the owners, especially to walkers. They keep a log of people doing the Three Peaks Walk, give reliable information about the area, and carry a large number of books and maps. So the character of the place might not be what it was, but it remains a hospitable place throughout the whole year. Not that it was always so in this village – there was a time when Henry VI tried to take a break from the War of the Roses and was betrayed by a priest.

Ribblehead Viaduct, north of Horton in Ribblesdale

The Walk

The Route: Horton (The Crown) – Hull Pot – Limestone pavement below Dismal Hill – Top Farm – Sell Gill – Horton

Map: O.S. map 98.

The start and how to find it: Arriving by train, walk down to The Crown and turn right to start and finish at the car park. Anyone else – the car park! Map reference 808726.

What the walk is like: Moderate, can seem arduous in places after rainy spell. Not to be undertaken when mist is low (or when Penyghent is hidden).

Distance: 7 miles.

Come out of the car park and turn right. Almost immediately you will see a footpath signpost on the other side of the road. This track, which goes past the left-hand side of the house, is an old trackway that is now part of the Pennine way. It twists and turns for the first 500 yards and then is almost straight for over a mile. Finally, a sharp S-bend brings you to the top gate after which the Pennine Way goes to the right and up Penyghent, while your path is straight on. Clearly visible on its slope is the work that has been done to make a firm path. Before you say it looks awful, just remember that when a path gets muddy, people start to widen it by walking on the nearest dry edge. On the Pennine way, it gets positively bog-like in places and the hundreds that walk these sections can and have created a path forty feet wide. This stone is going to make it better for all, sheep included.

From that gate and junction of paths, 400 yards will bring you to Hull Pot, an enormous hole in the ground that has at least three waterfalls feeding it. Despite the vastness of it and the fact that streams are taking the water away underground, I have heard that it has filled completely to the top with water brimming over three times in the last twenty years. After a good – and careful – look, go the left. At the end of Hull Pot a path goes slightly right and up over the moor. well-trodden but sometimes difficult to see because the boggy bits spread themselves out in very wet weather. Both Ingleborough and Penyghent can be seen from here as you approach a wall. There is a stile of sorts although it is only just recognisable because part of the wall has been lowered. As you start to climb over

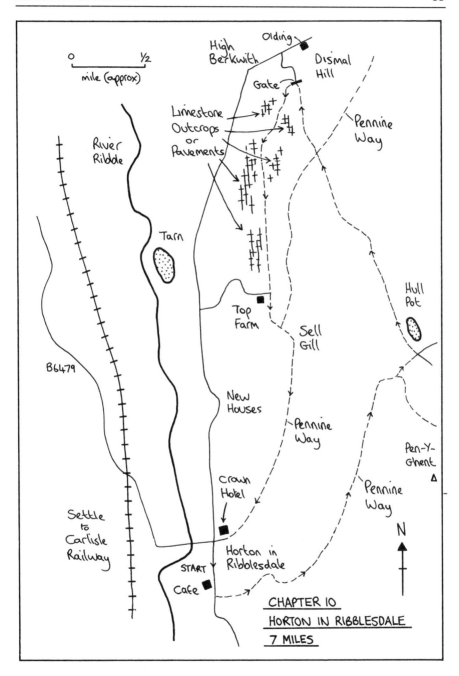

0 ½
mile (approx)

High Berkwith

Olding

Dismal Hill

Gate

River Ribble

Limestone Outcrops or Pavements

Pennine Way

Tarn

Hull Pot

Top Farm

Sell Gill

B6479

New Houses

Pennine Way

Pen-Y-Ghent △

Pennine Way

Settle to Carlisle Railway

Crown Hotel

N

START

Cafe

Horton in Ribblesdale

CHAPTER 10

HORTON IN RIBBLESDALE

7 MILES

it you realise that stakes have been driven through the wall as, I
hope, a temporary means of getting over the wall.

Once over, you have the consolation that the path continues its
wet, muddy way. Walk a line that is parallel to the wall on your left,
about ten to fifteen yards from it until the path is opposite a corner
of that wall as it turns left. Along this section you will be able to see
the Ribblehead viaduct with its twenty five arches and even though
the Lockwood viaduct has ten or eleven more, this one has the
advantage of being curved. That means that you can travel on the
train and take a photo from the rear coach of that same train crossing
the viaduct. From there veer very slightly towards the left, more to
make sure you do not wander a little to the right which would bring
you to a passable wall that crosses your front. You must cross the
wall on your left after which you go over the left-hand slope of a
small hill to arrive at about the centre of a length of wall that is now
on your right. When you cross that wall, the path that is fortunately
obvious as the Pennine way crosses 300 to 350 yards ahead. You can
shorten the walk if you wish, by a mile, if you turn left here and
follow the path down to Horton. Carrying on by crossing the Pennine
Way, you can examine the limestone pavement that is ahead, the
cracks of which offer protection to many wild flowers. Now, by
walking alongside the wall on your left and going on for another half
a mile, you will see a cart track going down hill towards a gate and
a building just visible downwards and to the right. Turn almost
completely around, to the left and walk back to where a wall and
gate lets you into an area just below the larger limestone crags.
Remember that the path is the one that has the wall on your right
and that if you want to examine or walk on part of the pavement to
see the flowers, you must return to this point. Going further on,
hoping to rejoin the path will expose you to the risk of slipping on
some of some of the smoother sections which happen to be near the
right-hand edge. Further on, this has a twenty-foot drop – and the
landing looks none too comfortable.

This is the Ribble Way and will take you to another gateway after
which the wall is on your left-hand side. When the wall stops, the
path continues to be obvious for another half mile along a section
where you get a view of the Tarn down in the valley on your right
and then joins the Pennine Way again at Sell Gill. On the left and
right as you cross over the natural bridge are deep holes with streams
disappearing into the ground. These pot holes are not easily acces-

sible and need the proper gear to enter them so why not just turn right and continue the walk down into Horton? This old pack horse trail and drovers' road is supposedly a nice easy section but not one to be hurried as the path is quite rocky and needs a bit more attention than you might be tempted to give considering the tremendous views from here. Once at the yard in front of the Crown, you know you are less than fifty yards from your car and might be considering moving it before you have a drink or a meal or arrange to stay the night. In good or bad weather, the place grows on you, doesn't it?

Chapter Eleven

Hawes

Not quite the market town it was, but the tourists still like it.

Despite being such a popular place and no secret to walkers, a good reason to include Hawes is that you will be able to compare it with Driffield, its East Riding counterpart described in a later chapter. Both are known as the market town of their area, but each is very different to the other. Few places can compare with Hawes as a centre for gentle walks with a few that are a little bit of a test – the Pennine Way goes through here. Nonetheless, it is rumoured that it was a Hawes farmer who remarked to a friend, on seeing a group of back packed walkers cross his fields, that he thought it was a rum sort of thing to be doing for pleasure.

The falls at Gayle, near Hawes

Perhaps Driffield still has the feel of a farming centre about it and has the accompanying bustle all the year, while Hawes puts on its special air of sophistication to please the visitors who pack the place for six months a year. You must judge for yourself. A walk along Hawes main street will give you some idea of the places to eat, drink and stay, there being no shortage of hotels, guest houses, restaurants, cafes, caravan sites and pubs in and around the town. Perhaps it is just a first impression that the town has turned itself into a piece of costume jewellery to persuade the visitor to buy some bits of gimmickry that at the time they are convinced they need. As a main street it does seem to lack shops that sell the basic essentials of everyday life.

Of much more credit to the town is the fact that they still produce the finest Wensleydale cheese. The business was established by one Kit Calvert who, after recovering in Leeds General Infirmary from a farm accident when he was a hireling at a rate of £1 per week, came home to Hawes and took the tenancy of some land. This was 1931 and he was happily, and profitably, able to sell milk around Hawes, the surplus going to the local creamery. The latter was unfortunately "banked" in 1932. His creditors, who included Kit, pulled the creamery through only to see it fail again in 1934. This time they decided that it would be safer if run by themselves as a committee with Kit holding the reins. He did well and eventually it was sold to the Milk Marketing Board in 1966 for £500,000. Going back to private ownership, it went fairly well for a few years until ambition overtook practical ability. This time a management buy out saved the day, which enabled the company to go on producing the real Wensleydale cheese. The cheese has a distinctive but subtle flavour that only Hawes can produce, due to that mix of grasses and herbs that make up the local grazing.

Hawes also has a fine bookshop. Hardly clinical in appearance, but I should think that that is planned, as it begs you to browse. And its name? Kit Calvert's.

There is still an Auction Mart with a respectable throughput, and the open market is worth a look, (market day, Tuesdays). The charter for the market was granted in 1699 which makes the town fairly modern when compared to others in this part of the world, although it remains the highest market town in Yorkshire at 800 feet above sea level.

Hawes is a maze of narrow streets with a Folk Museum, a rope works – or is it a rope walk? – and until quite recently, it was also known for its mole catcher who once recorded a catch of three hundred and eighty five in one day. There are potteries to visit, waterfalls to look at, antique shops and specialists in outdoor wear.

The Walk

The Route: Hawes Museum – Church – Gayle Beck – Thorney Mire- Hard Raw – Hawes

Map: O.S. Landranger series, 98

The start and how to find it: Roads come into the town like the spokes of a wheel, or go out of it if you like, and I once read that the road to Buttertubs and Thwaite was like an attempt to drive up into the sky. Go down to the old station yard and the large car park. Map reference 876899. Parking is currently 60p for three hours, which should be long enough for the walk and a short stop at Hardraw.

What the walk is like: Easy.

Distance: 5½ miles.

Come out of the car park and cross the road before turning right to go the right way down the one way street. Go over the bridge that crosses the beck and take an acute angled left turn at the opening in front of the church. Go up the roadway curving around the left side of the church and then through a gap the in the wall and its gate. Ahead of you stretches a paved path across the fields passing through another gap in a boundary wall and by some farm buildings on your right, until you reach the road. Then turn left and walk down to the bridge for a view of the waterfalls. When you have seen them, turn back and go to the first turning on the left, turn into it and walk along the lane past Beech House and then a bungalow on your right which has a footpath to follow immediately after the garden. The sign post says to Mossy Lane and it takes you first into the left-hand field at the bottom of the path so that you can then aim for the barn and go through the gap in the wall to the right of a large tree. This path is also paved, a fact not easy to notice as so much of it has been covered by grass.

Just after the barn, go round to the right to a gate and a rough track

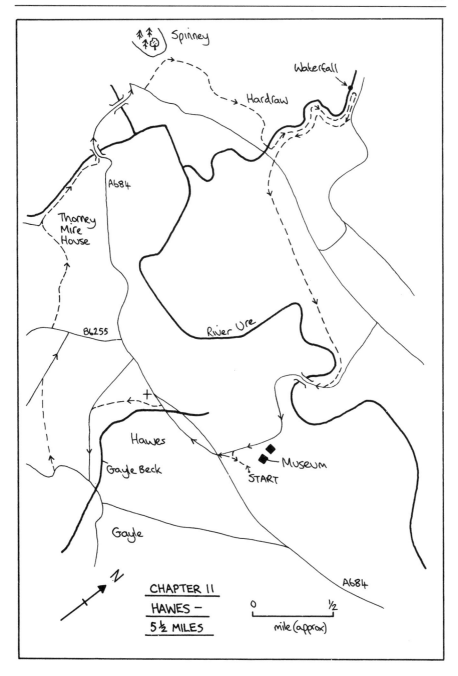

Spinney

Waterfall

Hardraw

A684

Thorney Mire House

B6255

River Ure

Hawes

Gayle Beck

Museum

START

Gayle

N

A684

CHAPTER 11

HAWES –

5½ MILES

0   ½

mile (approx)

bringing you to the stream that runs to your left. Go along the
left-hand bank, down the wall to the edge of the stream, forward into
the field and the apparent end of the stream. Walk across to the
wooden barn that is next to a stone one, then along the near side to
the corner on your left. There you will be able to go through a gap
and land on Mossy Lane. Turn to the right and keep on to the road
junction. You can see part of Hawes from this bit of the lane.

In front of you is a caravan site and this is the place to turn left
along what is the B6255. After 200 yards or so, turn right at the
footpath/bridleway sign and go down the edge of the field with the
stone wall on your right. At the brow, a wide vista of the dale appears
before you to right and left. From here walk over to the left as you
go downhill. The path goes above a small tree and a large tree and
you can see Thorney Mire House to the front and a little to the right.
Follow the trace of a path but, where possible, keep away from the
right-hand wall as it is even muddier there. Fortunately, it isn't far
to the road and when you reach it, turn to the right.

Now it is a stretch of lane walking for just over half a mile, along
a nice quiet lane of the type that is getting more and more difficult
to find these days, unless of course you are a regular reader of the
walking books published by Sigma Leisure. Along the way go under
a railway bridge left from the old, dismantled railway line – those
Victorian engineers must have been pretty good – and then at
Appersett, turn left to go over Widdale Beck, then right and left with
the road, crossing the River Ure between the two. At the place where
a road joins from the right, turn right and cross the road to the
footpath, signposted, going from a gap in the wall and straight ahead
at right angles to the road. Before you get to the first gate you will
be able to see the second one, higher up and to the left. You will be
going through that one but must first negotiate a very wet bit of
ground after the first one. Go which ever way looks best as you know
where your next point is. When the second one is passed look up to
the top of the small hill in front of you and walk towards the marker
post that is clearly visible there. After that, two more will come into
view. Go for the first one by going down into a gully and up the other
side and turn right when you reach it. To get over the wall that
appears to bar the way, go over a curious step arrangement of flat
stones thrust through the wall. Keep on the same line in the next
field until you are about 30 yards away from the next wall, when by
turning to the right a stile will be seen in the wire fence. Climb it

and then go to your left to the wall and climb over the ladder stile built over it. From here, walk ahead on a line that is halfway down the side of the slope that goes down into the valley on your left. Next, climb over the stile that is to the left of a gate. The same path can be seen to go towards a power line post at the far side that has a stile behind it. Cross that and you are in a lane which is part of the Pennine Way and which by going to the right, leads into Hardraw. Turn left at the road, over the bridge and you are at the Green Dragon.

A stop is essential at this point as you will want to go and see the waterfall, Hardraw Force and to do this you have to go through the Green Dragon – a small charge is made for admission. It is very impressive when the stream is swollen after heavy rain on Fossdale, the moorland above the force, but it is always worth seeing. As you walk up the ravine you will notice a raised stone and cement base encircled by a wall. This was the bandstand in the days of regular brass band competitions and concerts. I can imagine that it would be a wonderful sound in a place like this. On the bank opposite are the remains of some of the terraces cut out for seating – a natural amphitheatre. And then there is always a chance that just seeing the falls will make you feel thirsty, just when you are well-placed to solve the problem.

When you do come out, cross the road and go along the lane that is just after the telephone box. Then, after the farm buildings, go left, cross the farm track, go through a narrow gate and then follow a paved path. Two five bar gates with small gates for walkers on the left of them come up as you cross the fields. Then over a small hillock with signs of quarrying some time ago. There are also the remains of what might have been a sheep-fold or even a shelter for shepherds and a good sheltered spot it still is. Now onto the top, walking alongside a plantation that runs along the edge to the road onto which you step to turn right.

It is something of a surprise to find yourself on flat land again and even the river seems to meander as if lost. On one corner of the road, the river curves so close, that extensive work with boulders and concrete has been necessary to try and stop the river eating away at the road foundations. It is as well to keep to the road for the last part of the walk as nothing is to be gained by going into the fields. The car park is not far now and after you have passed the pottery on one side and a B&B, here is the main road. A left turn and you are back to where you started.

Chapter Twelve

Reeth

Lead mining and sheep, and the village is still going strong

You would do well to take the road from Marske to Reeth even if you have to divert from the A6108 five miles out of Richmond or take the top road from Richmond via Clapgate Bank. The reason will be stunningly obvious as you climb past Hardstiles Top, cross the moor below Cock How and take in for the view at Reels Head and down into Reeth by way of High Eremington. If this road doesn't impress you with its loveliness then I am going to worry about you. Throw out all your ideas about the people in Yorkshire wanting to tell you that every place they want to show you is beautiful, marvellous or the finest. Look at this, absorb it and enjoy it, because this is stronger than the South Downs, more gentle than any thing in the minds of the Brontës, this is a piece of England to treasure. The sort of place which you will remember and tell people, "we went over that bit of road from Marske to Reeth".

Reeth, itself is not a disappointment. There are times in the year when there are quite a few tourists, but many of them will be walkers, both serious and casual, who will be keen to get out to the hills.

The village has a market charter dating from 1695 which had the strange custom of being started by the butcher waving his apron, and no doubt a few other oddities but the key thing is its position. Strategically sited on the south facing slope of Calva's eastern spur it commands, the point where Swaledale divides, the main valley going to Muker, Thwaite and Keld, the other going north-westerly as Arkengarthdale.

It had an important market in the eighteenth and nineteenth centuries when the lead mining and hand knitting thrived. At the time of the re-organisation of local government in 1974, Reeth rural council looked after a population of about 1500 people, most of them

Reeth

in Reeth itself, leaving 74500 of the emptiest acres in the country. It is still a gateway to wonderful countryside and has old inns, grey stone dwellings and elegant Georgian houses that look across the large triangular green. The many Fairs have gone, like the weekly market, but there is still a popular Show in September and well-supported sheep sales in the autumn. The Methodist school-room has become the Swaledale folk museum and a further sign of the times is the fact that 75% of the population are incomers (the length of time it takes to be anything other than that seems to vary throughout the county). The result has been that the value of the cottages that sold for hundreds in the mid seventies has increased tenfold.

Lead mining dominated the employment and financial scene from the Roman times up to the mid-eighteen hundreds, when cheap ore from Spain began to price Swaledale out of the market. Before the decline, 4000 men were employed in this dale and they would produce over 40,000 tons of lead a year. The end might have been stretched out a little longer than the end of the coal industry, but the effect on the area must have been even more traumatic. Reminders of the industry abound, especially in the form of collapsed shafts to old, underground workings. The supports of the upper walls were usually wood which in most cases has rotted away letting the top, circular wall fall in and then the earth around it "runs" so that a cone shaped depression is formed. **Beware:** too often the debris is trapped at the top of the shaft and any sudden movement or shift in weight may cause a further collapse at any time. Far better to keep away from them.

As you wander around these lanes, you might consider their other industry, knitting. It is recorded that in the early part of the 19th century, £40,000 worth of hosiery was produced each year. That must be very near the amount produced by the "demon knitters of Dent".

The area around Reeth has still a small scattering of hamlets, some with names that are likely to be remembered, like Whaw and Booze. The latter is high up on the hillside with a road up to it more suitable for walkers than cars but with the same degree of disappointment for both, for despite its implied promise, the hamlet does not have a pub. It does have a few unusual wild flowers and I was told that one of them was a type of sandwort that also has the name "the mining plant" because it can tolerate lead in the soil.

The residents cannot eat the beautiful scenery that many walkers come here to enjoy and it was in the book "High Dale Country" by W.R. Mitchell that I read of a farmer from Booze had told the writer "T'living's aw reet; it's getting a living that's t'main worry".

The Walk

The Route: Reeth – Over Arkle Beck – along River Swale – Marrick Prory – High Fremlington – Reeth.

Map: O.S. Landranger map 98. As the walk continues on another map the larger scale Outdoor Leisure series No. 30 could be carried instead.

The start and how to find it: The Green at Reeth. Map reference 038994.

What the walk is like: Easy to moderate because of the fairly mild climbs – the first part can be very muddy in winter.

Distance: 6 miles.

From a place on or around the green at Reeth, walk down the Richmond road, over the stone bridge that crosses Arkle Beck and

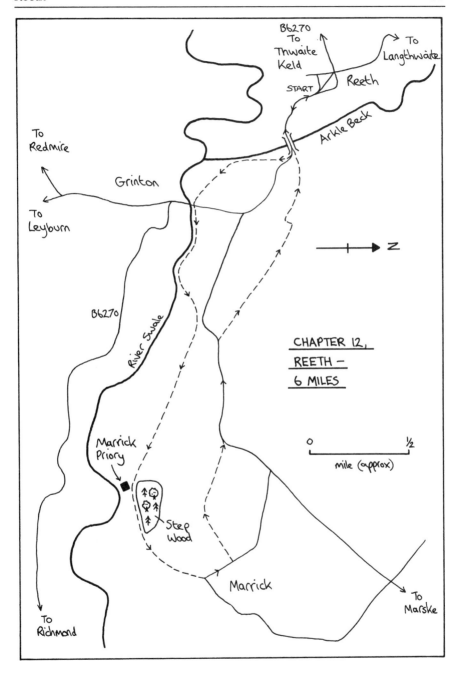

B6270
To
Thwaite
Keld

To
Langthwaite

START

Reeth

Arkle Beck

To
Redmire

Grinton

To
Leyburn

B6270

River Swale

N

CHAPTER 12,
REETH —
6 MILES

0   ½
mile (approx)

Marrick
Priory

Step
Wood

Marrick

To
Marske

To
Richmond

after 250 yards from that point, go through the wicket gate on the right. This path takes you along a short cut across the curve of the river to the road immediately before Grinton Bridge. Cross that road and join the path that is immediately opposite to walk along the bank of what is now the River Swale, for half a mile. A wood turns the path up the bank to the left to join a lane and this lane will take you to the right and Marrick Priory. The tower of the priory soon comes into view and by keeping to the path you will eventually find it adjacent to Abbey Farm. You will find that this old landmark was built at the beginning of the 12th century. for Benedictine nuns and is now a residential youth activity centre. This limits your exploring to a look at the outside before continuing. Do this by crossing the cattle grid near the buildings to a gate on the left and the path that goes up to and into Steps Wood. The paved path you will find going up through the wood was laid for the nuns to avoid getting dirty habits on their walk to Marrick village some way above. Coming out of the wood, the path is wide and clear, with a wall along your right-hand to lead you into Marrick.

Once there, take the left turn at the first junction, then onto the road, walking to the left, passing a farm before coming to the stile on the left. Cross it and follow the wall on your right until after about 150 yards a stile allows you to cross to the other side of the wall. Do this and now walk along with the wall on your left. It curves to the right and also leads to other stiles to cross before arriving at the Marske to Richmond road that was remarked upon earlier. Follow the road to the left as it descends. After a few curves, a path is marked to the left but go another 200 yards to where there is a sharper turn to the left. Almost at the apex, follow the path on your right. It is a straight path and although not as well-defined as earlier parts of the walk, is heading for High Fremlington which will give you an aiming point as well as four or five walls to negotiate, crossing a green lane and then joining a narrow path. At the end of that there is a lane to follow first to the left and then to the right. Then ignore the path that swings to the left and drops down to Low Fremlington. Go instead straight ahead, over a stile and then alongside a wall on the left. Two more stiles need to be crossed as you follow this path before reaching the fields. Crossing these fields brings two more stiles before coming to the bridge at Reeth. All you need to do now is cross the bridge and walk back up to the green.

Chapter Thirteen

Middleham

Castles, Kings and other thoroughbreds

I was first taken onto the Low Moor many years ago late in a summer when a horse called Dante had gone down from Middleham to win the Derby. In those days, Middleham was sometimes referred to as the Lambourn of the North, but as ruler of this kingdom, Matt Peacock, who trained Dante and many other good horses, wouldn't have cared what they called it. Peacock was a strong character whose owners occasionally raised their hats to him and seldom had the temerity to interrupt or disagree with his decision on where their horse should run or his riding instructions on the day. Since then I have come to enjoy the place more from mid-March up to mid-April, perhaps because of the horses, perhaps because the year ends and begins for me in a place like this and perhaps because there are very few visitors at that time. And visitors they do get – how could they avoid them with the wide open spaces of moorland on the doorstep? And the castle?

At one time in the main stream of English history, Warwick the King maker held his great feasts at Middleham castle, part of which still broods over the town. Then in 1471 Middleham passed to the crown and eventually to Richard the Third who loved the place and was loved in return according to local history – a rare opportunity to ignore what Shakespeare says. He did after all institute the system of bail for prisoners, extended the system of trial by jury and constituted the church collegiate (Charles Kingsley was one of the last canons). It is also popularly agreed that he learnt to ride here.

There have always been horses here. The monks, who owned most of Wensleydale from the Abbey at Jervaulx, were breeding them long before the thoroughbred appeared. But it was in the 19th century. that the place established itself as the training centre of the north of England. This was firmly cemented after the war when Matt Peacock ruled. Strict with staff and owners, he was also a generous host and the story goes that shortly after Neville Crump had started to train at Middleham, he was invited into Manor House for breakfast and told to tie his horse by the door. Breakfast after work on the moor was apparently a stiff whisky or two or maybe more, as Captain Crump was later seen walking his horse back to his yard.

After that and for most of the forty-odd years that Capt. Crump was the King, the village became an important jumping centre – when three Grand National and five Scottish "National" winners, were trained in his yard. There have been ups and downs of course and Mickey Hammond might be said to have taken over the mantle of top National Hunt trainer. Everyone hopes that training as an industry has been put on a steadier course by the young Scottish trainer Mark Johnston, who came here from a yard in Lincolnshire over five years ago, and made such good progress with the number of winners he has sent out each year that he now has 126 horses in his yard, 30 of which are owned by some of the Arab racing fraternity.

A qualified vet whose head lad attributes his guv'nor's successes to a good understanding of the horse's temperament, he won his first classic in 1994, winning over a million pounds for his owners in the year, and is always ready to tell anyone how much his family enjoy living in this wonderful little town. Quite inexhaustible, in one week he took a fancied horse to the Melbourne Cup only to witness a puzzling performance, flew back from Australia to Yorkshire in time to take a winner to Turin, then home again for a day and a half checking over his charges before saddling a winner at Doncaster. He then joined two more gentlemen, with the same enthusiasm for the town, in a presentation before the Minister for the Environment, to win a million pounds for Middleham to improve employment prospects and amenities for those who live there.

Fourteen trainers contribute to the surprising statistics that show on winners to horses run, Middleham has a 69.3% success rate. Their nearest rival being Newmarket with 57.6% for the 1994 flat season. That makes this small Yorkshire town the most successful training centre in England. Yes, you could say the village owes a lot to horse racing.

There are many other people here with the same keen desire to see the place succeed, and with its two squares, the three-storey Georgian houses and that underlying current that probably comes from the fact that it was at one time in the mainstream of English history, and may one day be there again, is definitely worth a visit.

A lot of walks start in and around Middleham, with Leyburn and Jervaulx Abbey to visit. There is also the small and pretty village of Wensley that gave its name to the dale. You would never think today that it had been the capital town of the dale, but it was until 1563, when it succumbed to the plague that almost wiped out the entire population.

There is the bridge too that will attract attention. Built where a ford used to be, it has enabled easier passage to Leyburn and I can only guess that the fortifications were built at the ends to reflect the spirit and character of the town.

But horses still rule, O.K? If you are not convinced by morning air filled with the sound of horses' hooves on their way to or from exercise, stay the night. But by staying, you will be sure to meet some of the characters that the racing game seems to produce in abundance, or hear some of the stories about them. Like the time when the outspoken – frequently colourfully outspoken – Captain Crump was asked by two Japanese tourists for directions to a village across the moor. He told them that as they didn't seem to have any trouble finding their way to Pearl Harbour, he felt sure that they could find their way across the moors. No prizes for guessing the missing words. And I am told that there is a local proverb which suggests that, if you shake a bridle over a Yorkshireman's grave in these parts, he will rise up and steal your horse – if it's good enough.

The Walk

The Route: Middleham – Tupgill – Spigot Lodge – Wensley – riverside path – Middleham.

Map: O.S.map Landranger series no. 99

The start and how to find it: You start in the larger of the two squares. It is a good place to park if you are here early enough (there are other places around the town if you are not) and you are surrounded by tea shops, inns, hotels and other handsome three storey buildings. Either Durrant's tea shop or the White Swan would be in my mental note book for refreshment upon return. Map reference 127878.

What the walk is like: Easy, with steady gentle climbs over the moor.

Distance: 7 miles.

From the square, head for the Black Bull and go along the road out

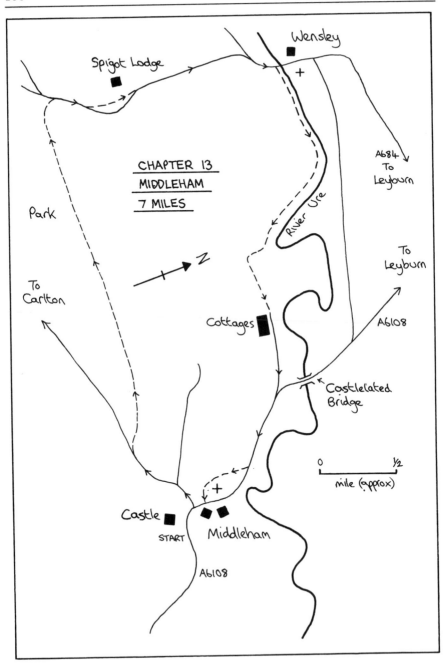

Wensley

Spigot Lodge

CHAPTER 13

MIDDLEHAM

7 MILES

Park

To
Carlton

N

Cottages

Castlelated
Bridge

River Ure

A684
To
Leyburn

To
Leyburn

A6108

0   ½
mile (approx)

Castle

START

Middleham

A6108

of the square at the top. That way, you go through the smaller square with its "ornament" built to commemorate Queen Victoria's Jubilee Year on your right and further over on your left, the remains of the Castle.

Exercise for the horses starts at the crack of dawn on most mornings from September to March but you will probably see some of the "strings" coming off the moor down this road, most of them turning left at the square, back to their yards. The second lot go out about 9.15 to 9.30, so by the time you get onto the Low Moor, you will probably have seen over a hundred racehorses walk or trot past you.

By keeping straight on along this road, you will first pass the start of a prepared gallop which disappears over the hill on your right. The path turns off to the right two or three hundred yards further on after the hill and slight bend ahead. It is a well-worn track and that takes you right up onto the top of Low Moor with one of the gallops on your right, marked at intervals by two white markers. Over to the left is Coverdale, with the road running along to the top of the dale near to Kettlewell. Ahead, there is a hill that looks like some enormous barrow with an extra hill at the end. That extra bit is called Heights of Hazely which is 552 metres high. The path then deteriorates slightly into a rough track along the level for a short way before it starts to drop in a series of up and down dips, little valleys running off to the left. After two or three of these, a rather posh gate and gateway appears in the wall on the left. It is not possible to see over the wall, but I believe it might still be Cotesque Park on the other side. It was in any case Armstron country, that well known racing family that trained here and from where a young lady came who eventually married Lester Piggott. Here a line of power line poles change direction and between the second and third pole in this line across the moor, where a view of a fine country house is possible. It might have been part of the estate at one time but now is another trainer's yard. The next dip reveals an opening and lane that goes down to the stables. Turn right and then left and go on along the wall that runs along on the left. A short way along that wall there is another gateway. This one is marked "Tupgill" and it is the place to turn right, walk along the road to the brow and go downhill through the gate at the bottom. A large barn on the right indicates the presence of more race horses while a little further along you will see the gates to Spigot Lodge Stables, once San Halls yard where Chris Thornton now trains 40 plus horses.

After the views down Coverdale and across the moor, Wensleydale reveals part of its glory and its valley with the River Ure. When you meet the main Leyburn to Hawes road at the bottom, turn right and walk to the bridge. From the near right-hand side the path continues to the right, but if you want to see a little gem of a village, cross the bridge and spend a little time to walk through the village and back. Back at the bridge, go over the stile and walk along the edge of the first field to the far gate. From there go left onto the river bank and continue the walk until the fourth gate has been passed. From here, go to the right, avoiding a lot of twists and turns of the river and go to the bottom of the field. Go over into the path-cum-lane that is at the foot of the embankment, turning left so that you now follow the path along the hedge that is now on your left. This ends at another gate which opens onto a hard surface lane.

A minor problem here is possibly caused by the gate up on the bank to your right. O.S. maps will show a path across the fields from here, but the path is neglected, wired off in parts, and generally difficult to follow. Perhaps a case of "out of sight, out of mind" as the farmer lives some way from these fields. I would advise you to continue to the Leyburn-Middleham Road along the lane upon which you now stand. Turn left and you will see the bridge and its turrets, turn right upon the road and follow it to the outskirts of the town. After passing St. Alkelda's Grove on the right, you will see a little way ahead that some steps jut out onto the path. It is here that you go right with the path at the top and finish up going left through the churchyard to the gate. Through that and down the lane alongside Kingsley House Stables before turning right on the road at the bottom, which brings you to the Market Place again.

If you can feel the friendly atmosphere that welcomes you in Middleham you may be interested to know that every Good Friday all the trainers throw open their yards for everybody to see what goes on and get all the answers from the helpful staff that are a lways around. A full days events are programmed but I advise an early start so that you arrive not later than 9.00am if possible.

For a wider view of this Dales town, come during the Middleham Festival which runs for seven or eight days at the beginning of July.

Chapter Fourteen

Middlesmoor

"Upstairs" via Little Switzerland

Lofthouse, How Stean and Middlesmoor are inextricably linked,
not just because they are grouped near the head of Nidderdale,
but because of old family links, farming associations, nicknames
and perhaps most of all, because visitors see them as one. They never
think of going "downstairs" – Lofthouse – without visiting "upstairs"
– Middlesmoor. The visitor may then decide to have a walk round
Little Switzerland and maybe have a cup of tea, which means a visit
to How Stean Gorge and the cafe there.

The road from Pately Bridge is pleasant enough, passing Wath
which boasts a waterfall and The Sportsman's Arms. A fine-looking
sandstone pub that has earned a reputation for good quality bar
meals, particularly fish; usually from the east coast, but frequently
local Nidd trout. Then past Gouthwaite reservoir, often mistaken for
a natural lake, perhaps because of its vast flocks of birds, and then
Ramsgill, possibly the prettiest village in the dale, which also boasts
a hotel, The York Arms. This is named after the once all-powerful
family that owned, until fairly recently, a large part of the surrounding countryside. Then it is on to Lofthouse, and the area of the walk.
Although it may seem strange to find a dale of this stature excluded
from the caring boundaries of the National Park system, it is even
stranger to discover that Bradford successfully put pressure on the
government to ensure that it was excluded from the Park because
they owned a string of reservoirs down the valley at that time.

At Lofthouse, you will find narrow roads, the road to Wensleydale, and an unspoilt pub, The Crown, which has its namesake
"upstairs".

It is convenient to start the walk at How Stean and take a clockwise
route and that is the order in which they are described. Having
reached Lofthouse from either Masham or Pateley Bridge, go
through on the road marked "Middlesmoor" and take the first road

Nidderdale from Middlesmoor church

on the left-hand side after passing the cricket ground on the right. At the bottom of that road, with the river in front of you, a car park appears on the left, or turn right, go over the bridge, turn right again and providing you intend to be a customer, you can park in the cafe car park.

How Stean Gorge, for which there is a small entry charge at either entrance – and believe me, it's worth every penny – was created by the fast flowing How Stean Beck that comes tumbling down from Riggs Moor and cuts through the limestone to a depth in places of 80 feet or so, creating a narrow canyon. A cliff edge path lets you walk along almost the entire length of it to see the waterfalls, the lichen and a wide variety of ferns and mosses, crossing rustic bridges to get different views. Many wild flowers have taken advantage of this sheltered setting but then the upper Nidd valley is well known for the comparative abundance of flowers. There are caves too. One, named after the highwayman Tom Taylor, who is supposed to have hidden in it, is quite safe and popular with children, especially the two who found 32 roman coins lying on a ledge in the cave in 1868. Other caves are there for the more adventurous but extra gear may

Scar House Reservoir Dam

be required. The cafe is pleasant and serves good food having a large menu board outside, on the wall.

A steady ascent from here will bring you to Middlesmoor, the village at the top of the dale with those commanding views. It is 1000 feet above sea level and perhaps that has something to do with the atmosphere of total peace. A seat in the graveyard by the church is a good – but sometimes windswept – spot to stop and have those sandwiches you brought; the view from there takes some soaking up. The church, by the way, has a Saxon font and the village is on the site of an Anglo-Saxon settlement. Some of the inscriptions in the churchyard are unusual but next to the Post Office there is the recognisable friendliness of the Crown Inn, offering warmth and excellent refreshment, as well as accommodation.

You will eventually return via Lofthouse where the Crown, mentioned before, also offers accommodation, and it is a tempting to stay and walk another track tomorrow or even get an early start over that great moorland road to Masham. There are not a lot of houses here, but what there are look good and sound, with an impressive little group around the memorial cross to those killed in the war. An unusual feature of this memorial is the tap placed at a convenient height with an inscription at the side to tell you how good it is for you to drink from it.

Some books may try and tell you that the railway spur line stopped at Lofthouse where there is indeed a building that was once the station. In fact the spur was mainly for the materials required for the dam at what was to become Scar House Reservoir.

The Walk

The Route: How Stean Gorge – Middlemoor – Scar House dam – Lofthouse – How Stean Cafe.

Map: O.S. Landranger series No. 99. (Outdoor Leisure 30 also covers the area)

The start and how to find it: How Stean cafe: map reference 088736

What the walk is like: Moderate, care needed in places.

Distance: 8 miles.

Leave How Stean Cafe car park and turn right. Depending on the

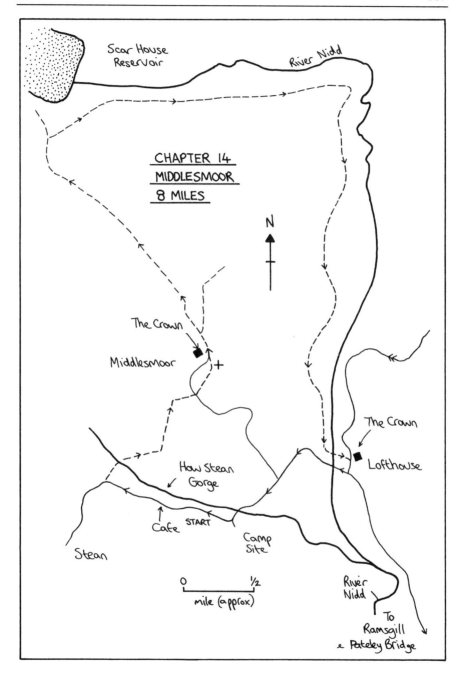

Scar House Reservoir

River Nidd

CHAPTER 14
MIDDLESMOOR
8 MILES

N

The Crown

Middlesmoor

The Crown

Lofthouse

How Stean Gorge

Cafe   START

Camp Site

Stean

0   ½
mile (approx)

River Nidd

To Ramsgill & Pateley Bridge

time of day, you will have decided to either complete the walk along all or part of the gorge before this start or will see how you feel on the way back. After a quarter of a mile walking towards the hamlet of Stean, you will come to a bend in the road going left. At this point the path goes to the right and is indicated by a signpost which says "Nidderdale Way". Go past a mobile home that is on your right and turn to the left, through a gap that is narrowed to "walkers only" dimensions, to go down hill. Down the stone steps also, to cross a bridge, then up the steps and through the gate at the top. From here go diagonally right to cut the corner of the field and through a gap in the right-hand wall, to turn left in the next field.

It is surprising to find that although the field is on a slope, it doesn't drain too well and the ground varies from slippery to muddy after rain. Twenty five yards later and it is through a gate and up the next field where at the brow the wall bends away left. At this point Middlesmoor comes into clear view. As you see you are approaching the top of the field, look to your right. How about that? What a marvellous view that is. And to think that when you get to the village and you will have the chance to see even more of Nidderdale from the very top of the valley.

Just keep going in the same direction and you will reach the road. There, turn left and follow the road uphill into the village. At the top you will see what appears from the outside to be a sympathetic and practical conversion of a chapel to a house. A nice touch is that the owners have been kind enough to fix a plaque onto the wall near their door, giving basic details that will be of interest to most passers by. When you are opposite the Crown, take the road that is in front of you and curves around to the right, behind the houses and then down to the left and into the churchyard and church (unless you want a drink in the Crown before your sandwiches) The interior of the church is peaceful as it should be, but it also feels as if it is used regularly. As if to confirm this you might come across a notice that says the kneelers have been worked on and maintained by local ladies aged from eight to eighty-nine.

Outside again and you will see conveniently placed benches to sit and admire the view. When you are ready, walk back through the gate and across to the left-hand side of the house you circled before and cross to the Crown. The path goes past the right-hand end of the building that also houses the Post Office. If you are ready, refreshed and suitably fortified, head up this road that takes you to the top of the moor and to Scar House Reservoir, two miles away. The climb is very gradual and the sign you pass that says that it is not suitable for motor vehicles refers more to the state of the track than to the climb. A gate and track to the left is passed after less than half a mile. After that it is just a matter of keeping on going. False hope may arise as you pass three beech trees on the left but you are only half way. Substantial looking butts stretch out to the right and for the four or five months from September the moor is usually well-covered by grouse. The colossal amount of money spent on breeding game birds and maintaining the moor must be of great benefit to the local economy. While accepting that the anti-blood-sports people are entitled to their point of view, many townspeople came to live in the country and then started trying to change the way of life which makes me think that they don't consider our views as much as we consider theirs. For now, enjoy the sight of the birds flying across your path.

On a clear day in autumn or winter I swear it is more enjoyable walking up here than on any summer's day. The sky is clear and with the right clothes you can easily keep warm on a path like this. And if you start to puff a bit, it's all good clean refreshing air, and like the Mackeson advertisement used to say, "by golly, it does you good."

Now, a wooden gate. Go through it and put it back on the sneck and then over what appears to be the final brow. It isn't, but it is the end of the climb and you can go forward, curving to the right to the next brow. From now on it zigzags all the way down to the bottom. From here you see most of the reservoir, a little lower and the dam is just below you, then the buildings to the left and on until you reach the bottom and go right towards the car parks (there are toilets too).

From here it is a case of following the road and watching out for all the signs of wildlife, of working life and the whole panorama. This dale is so narrow, even when it reaches Pateley Bridge, it is like have a theme park of a dale. Land slopes up to the right, down to the left and across the river to a patchwork of fields, a few barns scattered over the hillside and occasional farms. It doesn't reveal everything at once either, you go a mile and it bends a little to show a different pattern. Another half mile and the turn is nearly ninety degrees, then more trees start to appear. You may have noticed the old foundations of buildings that housed the men and materials to build the dam in 1907, and the closed ends of a tunnel cut through a spur jutting out from the right. This was for the light railway, the first to be municipally owned, which ran until 1929. After that, the track was taken up and replaced by a tarmac toll road from Lofthouse.

Half a mile after the tunnel end you go over a fast running beck and then pass a farm. If you look up to the skyline on the left, you can see the Shooting House, not as grand now as it used to be. From here it is about a mile to Lofthouse. When you finally arrive at the gate with the toll booth and parking ticket machine, turn sharp left and go over the bridge to turn right at the other side and walk up past the end of the house into what might be called the square, with its memorial cross. After a look around this pleasant spot, go down to the right passing the free car park, which is more than half full in winter, to the "Crown" – again. It is a good old unspoilt sort of pub, with a welcoming landlord. The beer's not bad either. Go down to the main road from there and turn right, carrying on and passing the cricket ground on your right. Next left, down the lane, over the bridge and along to the cafe on your right. Don't forget the walk along the gorge.

Chapter Fifteen

Ripon

Between Pennines and Vale

There isn't an easy tag for this area. When I said to a taxi driver "What is so special about this place?" he told me that there are things that are special, like the Cathedral and the race-course and, for walkers, the riverside or the park at Studley Royal – but that it's mainly the people.

Ripon is a good centre for touring without doubt, though you may think it hasn't many outstanding features at first glance. But the more time that you spend here, the more the city grows on you. And it is a city not only for the Cathedral, but also confirmed by Queen Elizabeth II at the time of the new charter in 1974, who deemed Ripon should forever retain the title and dignity of a city.

Standing as it does at the meeting point of the rivers Ure, Skell and Laver almost in the foothills of the Pennines and on the edge of the Vale of York it has always used its situation to advantage and even now claims to be the gateway to the Dales. Yes, another one, but I really like the place more each time I come here and I am sure you will come to feel the same. Perhaps for its quaint customs like the Horn Blower blowing his special horn from each corner of the obelisk in the market square at nine o'clock each evening, a ritual that has lasted uninterrupted for over a thousand years. This used to signal that the city was in the Wakeman's care for the night. This meant that he would have to catch any person who had burgled any property and pay compensation, which came out of his Wakeman's fees. Perhaps you like the many different shops and places of refreshment, or the walks, or just the people, a very friendly lot.

Incidentally, the Wakeman's house still survives in the south-west corner of the market square and on the south side, the creditable facade of the Town Hall with its linking quotation below the eves. Mentioning buildings demands notice of the Cathedral, but I cannot imagine how you would miss it. Parking in the car park mentioned, you have the chance to go and judge for yourself either before or after the walk and see what has survived a succession of ups and downs, quite literally. It appears to have had its final major rebuild from 1154 to 1181 by the order of Archbishop Roger of York, though claims are made that the first church was built on the site in A.D. 672 and indeed the Saxon crypt under the central tower does date from that time

A more attractive building is two or three miles out of·town at the far end of Studley Park. This is Fountains Abbey, with its lake and visitor centre. The latter might take more getting used to than the entry fee.

Ripon Cathedral

The Walk

The Route: Car park north of Market Place – Cathedral – Riverside – Low Lidrick – Studley Royal – Studley Roger – Ripon.

Map: O.S. map 99

The start and how to find it: take the A61 from Leeds, Harrogate or the A1, southwards on the A6108 or the B6265 from Boroughbridge or Pateley Bridge. The car park on the left after passing the Cathedral, travelling northwards on the A61, is the easiest to find and is at map reference 313713.

What the walk is like: Easy.

Distance: 7 miles plus 1½ miles to and from Fountains Abbey and the Obelisk.

Leave the car park from the entrance side and turn right. Walk along the road to the first junction and take the road on the left named Low St Agnes Gate, following its twists and turns and passing the east end of the Cathedral, then the end of High St. Agnes Gate to go down the right-hand side of the large house converted into houses, offices and flats. This brings you to the sturdy concrete footbridge that will take you over the River Skell. Turn right at the far side to take the riverside path behind the Vaux pub. On approaching the next bridge, you can, with a little care, follow the path under the bridge. Then comes Bondgate Bridge with the foundation Hospital and Chapel of St John the Baptist on the left as you face a road to cross. Not a very busy one and you will have no difficulty in seeing your way down to the path again at the other side. Now go along between the flats and the river and pass the end of a new bridge which is for traffic into the new blocks of flats. A little way after this, a gap in the wall and a steps give you access to the path under the bridge and takes you past the old varnish and enamel works, once famous in this area. After any heavy rain you will be thankful for "wellies" here and if you haven't any you may wonder if it is coincidence that the street you have just left is called Barefoot Street. You can, if you prefer, stay on the road, turn left along what is the A61 and take the opening and steps about fifty yards along on the right.

Still along the bank and a children's playground to be crossed. Through the gate at the far side, turn right and walk down the lane.

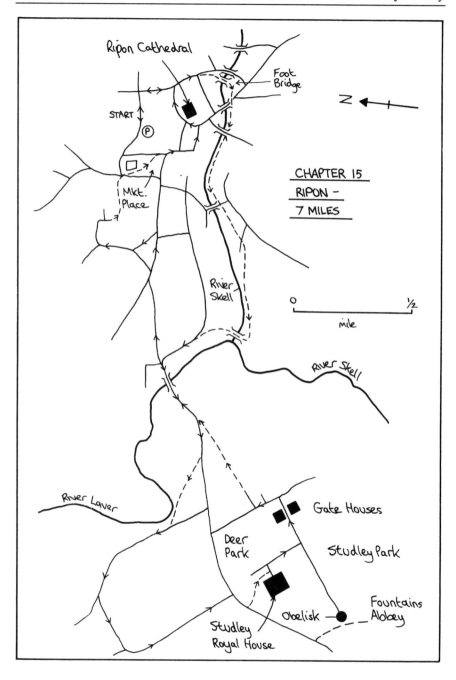

Ripon Cathedral

Foot Bridge

START

P

Mkt. Place

CHAPTER 15

RIPON –

7 MILES

River Skell

0   ½

mile

River Skell

River Laver

Gate Houses

Deer Park

Studley Park

Obelisk   Fountains Abbey

Studley Royal House

From the place where the tarmac runs out, it is only a short walk to the confluence of the Rivers Skell and Laver. Here there is a wooden footbridge to cross and gain entry to an open area beside the Laver. Follow the river's edge past what looks like a launching ramp, despite the apparent shallowness of the river, until you come to the road. Go onto the road and turn left so that you walk up to the B6265. Turn left, cross the road bridge over the river, cross the road to use the footpath and then after perhaps 200 yards you will see on the right, Garphy Lane and the public footpath sign to send you along it.

A gate soon blocks your way and it is here that you find a stile on the left to climb over and find yourself in a caravan park. The path proper goes along the right-hand edge of this property behind the caravans up to the top corner. There you will find a bank to climb and a path to follow behind a nursery and market garden until you reach a lane. This is a quiet road and goes through well-farmed land made more pleasant to the eye by the gently rolling hills and small woods and plantations. Walk for about a mile along to the right and you will pass a house on the left standing by itself on its own little hill and then, immediately before a bend, there is a slight incline and a lone old oak tree in the right-hand hedge at the top. Round the corner and three more oaks are stretched out along the hedge. At the third, take the lane on the left, opposite the lane to Birkby Nab.

When you reach the farmyard and farm house, turn left and stride out along a road through what was once part of the estate park. It will not be long before you spot the gate ahead. When you reach it, turn right along the road – the gates in front of you are often locked – until you spot a door in the wall on the other side of the road. It should have a National Trust sign on it and is the one to go through to get into the deer park. When you are in, head for the large house in front of you. This is Studley Royal House and when you arrive at the side gate you will see it is private so go left around to the front – not being able to walk through will not stop you being able to appreciate the building. At the front, turn about and walk down the drive. You must have seen the deer by now as there is a very big herd here with not all that big a park to roam and graze. Turn right at the T-junction and walk along it to the next one.

The scandal and general financial disaster of 1720, known as the South Sea Bubble, brought down the government of the day and caused John Aislabie, who was at the time Chancellor of the Exchequer, to retire to Studley and devote himself to creating a country park. This he did with style, even changing the course of the River Skell to provide cascades, a lake and ponds plus a number of bridges and sweeping embankments. His son was able to carry on, extending the project by bringing Fountains Abbey into his estate. In those days every estate had to have a ruin, but this must have beaten them all.

It is at this point you can go to the right and see the Obelisk, then Fountains Abbey and come back to here by way of the edge of the lake. From this point also, you turn left to return to Ripon; a fact underlined by the fact that the road points like an arrow through a line over the gate-house to Ripon Cathedral. Eventually you walk all the way along this avenue of trees, through the arch between the two gate-houses and then to the entrance gate. The old estate road is not part of the area managed by the National Trust, so is not open as a public footpath. So go to the left into the hamlet of Studley Roger in front of an impressive house, Lawrence House, and then the village hall. You might also notice that one house on the left has a lamp by the door that would appear to have been taken from either the Wakeman's House or the house of the Lord Mayor. After this ignore the first turn on the right and take the turn that is almost opposite the Bus Stop sign.

It is only a short lane and at the bottom there is a gate on the left-hand side of April Cottage. A rather twee name for a well-built brick house in mock-Georgian style but even worse to my mind was the stone plaque with that overused four liner that starts: "The kiss of the sun for pardon . . ." I spent a few yards of the path that goes straight ahead until it meets the road trying to decide whether this was better or worse than garden gnomes. At the road, turn right and go back over the bridge that crosses the Laver and keep straight on for the city centre.

You will pass tennis courts and the local dramatic society meeting place on the left, then the Ripon Spa Hotel and the spa gardens on your right followed by the Spa Baths with its fine Victorian entrance. Blossomgate then appears on your left, so turn left down here to see a variety of shops and unusual small businesses, such as ornamental stonemasons (a dying business?) and hardware of various types not yet absorbed by the giant DIY chains. On the right there is an excellent wine merchants called The Great Northern Wine company, with a very wide range of wines that will be able to satisfy every taste and pocket. It is one of the few that can challenge the supermarkets on price as well as range.

When you reach the Zion Baptist Evangelical Church, turn right down Westbourne Grove, follow the first turn it makes to the right and then cut across the car parking areas, right across to the other side. On your left, a brick wall that is the end of a building has two fire exit doors let into it. On the right-hand side of it is an alleyway for you to take, that comes out at the top north end of the market square. Walk diagonally across this which will give you a close up view of the obelisk which is given over to the ceremony of the Hornblower and was erected at the personal expense of some former M.P. Sounds a bit of an ego trip doesn't it? You also get a good idea of the city as you turn around to look at the different fronts on the buildings around the square. Now head for the Unicorn Hotel, stopping if you want before taking the next left down Kirkgate to the end, until you are face to face with the almost overpowering west front of the Cathedral. Go in or turn left again following the road and turning left again along St. Marygate and the starting place. Don't forget that the prison and police museum are opposite the car park if you are there between the beginning of April and the end of October – it is closed for the rest of the year. And if you want to wander around the town for a little longer, you can go through the other side of the car park, to investigate some of the other lanes or maybe the new and old bookshops and the bistros in Kirkgate. Enjoy yourselves.

Chapter Sixteen

Coxwold

History and literature in another beautiful Yorkshire village

Coming from north or south, the road to Coxwold starts in the middle of Easingwold, a charming little Georgian market town. The road goes off towards the east through a square that gives you a much better picture of the place than the one you get from the main road. But the place we are heading for is six miles further on.

Newburgh Abbey

The village of Coxwold, hidden away at the foot of the Hambleden Hills, may seem, on approach, to be a one street place. Being on a crossroads, it obviously cannot be. Nevertheless, nearly everything that commends the place is on this road that comes from Easingwold or Thirsk. If you approach from Easingwold, the first place you see on the very boundary of the village is Newburgh Priory, once the home of the Fauconberg family who have contributed so much to the history and well-being of Coxwold. One Lord Fauconberg fought bravely at Marston Moor as a faithful ally of Charles Stuart only to have his grandson marry Oliver Cromwell's daughter. This was allowed upon the condition that every one of the great oaks on the estate should lose their heads in lieu of the head of his Lordship. How petty can we humans be?

Not long after, in the scheme of things, Cromwell's body is said to have been replaced by the corpse of a lesser person and the Protector himself is believed to have been buried in a vault set in the front wall of the Hall by his daughter Lady Mary Fauconberg. No one has been allowed to break in and substantiate this popular story.

You then come to the crossroads (after passing a pleasant looking B&B and tea room). It's at this point the main street starts to open up. A wide street, cobbled at each side with grass banks and some parking places and lined with many honey-coloured stone houses, almshouses and cottages. A shop, as obliging as it can be, and the village pub, The Fauconberg Arms. This is a splendid pub; I like the beer, the food and the company, with its sprinkling of the slightly eccentric.

Further along on the opposite side is the church with its octagonal tower, some original 18th century glass and a breeches bible in a glass case made by "the mouseman" – Robert Thompson – whose business is still going strong in nearby Kilburn. And here the Fauconbergs come into the picture again. In 1760 the vicar of Sutton on the Forest became the most talked of man in London. He was entertained in the manner of the times by London's society, but Lord Fauconberg decided to do better than merely entertain this great wit and writer. He offered him the living of Coxwold, worth about £150 a year and Lawrence Sterne accepted. He went to live in the house that still survives with its massive chimneys, renamed by him "Shandy Hall". I don't think you would regret buying a copy of "Tristram Shandy" or "A Sentimental Journey" today, for both are a delight to read for the musings and for the characters. The writer knew the real meaning of the word "Shandy" in Yorkshire was contrary or eccentric, or in the case of a house, odd, for this house had 20 odd-shaped rooms.

The house is just a little way further up past the church, but is not always open to visitors so a phone call to the local tourist information office might help (Tel: Easingwold (01347) 21530). Try not to rush through the village because you can experience some-

Shandy Hall

thing very special here. The Circus may not visit anymore and the pub is no longer thatched, but the church clock still chimes on the hour, although in this place time is of little importance. You get to the feeling that little has changed for a long, long time.

The Walk

The Route: Fauconberg Arms — Shandy Hall — Angram Grange & Hall — Husthwaite — Newburgh Priory — Coxwold

Map: O.S. map 100.

The start and how to find it: The Fauconberg Arms; map reference 534772.

What the walk is like: The going varies but is never arduous, even though you walk along a high ridge with wonderful views.

Distance: 6 miles.

Walk up to the pub and then down the right-hand side of it, past and forward through one gate and on to a white one just a short

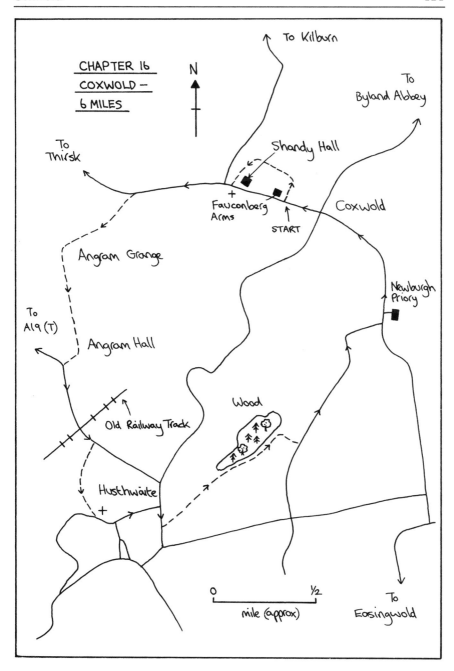

distance ahead. Go through the kissing gate to the left and across the field beside the hedge on the left and through the next gateway. Now veer to the right to cut the bottom left corner and then along the left-hand path going beside the Hawthorns. The church is now in view over on the left with its accurate clock on the octagonal tower. When opposite the end of the clump of trees also on the left, make a right angled turn to the left and go through the gate in the hedge that lets you out onto the road. The clump of trees turns out to be part of the gardens of Shandy Hall, the reason we have come to this gate. Walk down to the left for about 200 yards and there is the house where the Reverend Sterne lived and looked as quizzically at the world as his portrait in the church does today. Its large chimneys and solid looking gables may impress from outside, but inside the rooms will surprise you, not least the tiny study where he wrote "A Sentimental Journey".

Onto the road again and walk back to the gate. After the gate, keep going for three quarters of a mile, bearing left at the junction along the way. The road to the right goes to Kilburn where as already mentioned, Robert Thompson, the mouseman lived and worked and where his family carry on the business of making first class furniture, each piece bearing his signature of a beautifully carved small mouse crouched upon a leg or cross piece. When you do come to an opening on the left, you will find it is almost on the apex of a right-hand bend and is marked "Angram Grange" so turn in here and walk to the farmhouse. Turn right and go between the back of the house and the farm buildings, turning left after the house.

I was fortunate to speak to the gentleman whose farm this is, but who has retired now to let his son run the place. Naturally we talked of the weather and whether they were behind with getting the potatoes up or ahead with ploughing and also that he quite liked to see people walking through and that in any case the proper path that came from behind the sheds and other buildings was overgrown. "We get a lot goin' through in the summer" he said, "and most of 'em tell me what a marvellous place it is to live. Course, they don't see it when wind coming up yon valley banks snow up and we are cut off for a week". I could only suggest that it couldn't be all that bad and it didn't happen every year did it? "No, I suppose not and in any case I've lived here 78 years and I'm getting used to it".

From the far side of the house you can see a straight line that goes through two gates and points at the middle of the farm you can see ahead, Angram Hall. Make for the farm and on reaching the double width metal gates, go through, turn right, then left, then right again to come out onto the road. Turn left here too and walk along the road, passing on your right a large oak tree almost completely covered in ivy, even to the topmost branches. Then over the bridge that goes over the track of the now dismantled railway. Although it is a clear path nearly all the way to Coxwold using the track to the left, going right along the track is not possible. Instead, go on over the stream for about 150 yards to a gap on the right with a footpath sign beside it. Walk up the field beside the fence made from sheep fencing wire with a strand of barbed wire on top. The barbed wire is one good reason to stay on the left of the fence. The other reason is that you need to cross a stile at the top that lets you into an area beside the church. Head towards its tower and then, if you need some refreshment, go to the right when you have worked your way through the garages to the road. Along here you will find the Blacksmith's Arms, a Vaux pub.

The way out of the village is to the left from the church, but you will notice during the small diversion that there is quite a mixture of houses and cottages both old (one dated 1690) and fairly new. At the end of the village and at the T-junction, turn to the right and walk up the short hill to the gateway of Lists House which is on the left. There is a "private road" sign at the bottom of the drive, but do not worry, it is a public footpath and you should walk right up to the top, passing the house to reach a gate into a paddock. Now, to your left a magnificent view starts to open up, which includes the White Horse. This was cut by the schoolmaster Jerry Hodgson and helpers, on the flank of what is Roulston Scar at the wish of another local man who had made a fortune in London. He knew that Hodgson had experience of sketching racehorses at exercise and so got a figure that is over 300 feet long and 200 feet high at the shoulder. Unfortunately it is a long way away from the chalk hills in the East Riding and so has to be spruced up from time to time with limestone or similar material, with frequent weeding in between times.

I imagine this could be a bit of a burden for local people and serves no useful purpose except to show that perhaps some Yorkshire people are either stubborn or a bit daft.

Cross the paddock, go through the next gate and then into the big field, walking along with the hedge on your left. Keep going along the ridge, past a trig point and then through a gap into the next field. Now, as you walk along the side of the wood a farm comes into view. But you should now look over to the right, as at a point about 25 yards from the end of the wood on your left you should see a footpath marker post on the lane side at the end of a hedgerow. Go over to it and turn left walking down the lane to pass the farm. There is a footpath that goes down to the left across the fields but I strongly suggest staying on the lane. When you reach the road, turn left and in a short distance you come to the reason for my suggestion, Newburgh Priory, once the home of the Fauconbergs.

Now it is only half a mile to the crossroads and that lovely view up the village street to the church. Your vehicle must be near here, but try not to rush away. Let the atmosphere of this village get to you and see how much better you feel.

Chapter Seventeen

Masham

Here's health unto the family – and its black sheep

Pronounced "Massam" and with a market square much bigger
than that in the City of Ripon, Masham can boast a steady, solid
sort of background with a large number of families still living here
that can trace their ancestry back over 250 years. Their inde-
pendence lasted until the reorganisation of local governments in
1974. It must have been an expensive decision from the tax-payers"
view, as until then 11 councillors were there to serve the 1500
persons who lived in the nine parishes spread over 27,000 acres
surrounding the town. The town (which has an enviable village
atmosphere) only needed three full time employees who ran the
place with an efficiency other councils envied. Nobody owed money
on their rates and everybody knew everybody. This was just a part
of the caring community that didn't need a citizens charter, something that used to come naturally to rural communities.

Take the Theakstons for an example. They were here 500 years
ago and started brewing behind The Black Bull in Masham in the
1820s. You must have heard of the brewery, and no doubt of its most
famous brew, "Old Peculier" – not an odd sort of drink, but a good
beer that owes its name to the Official of the Peculier of Masham, a
Peculier being a parish exempt from the jurisdiction of the diocese
in which it lies, probably derived from the Norman word meaning
particular rather than odd. Although a Theakston still runs the
place, the company is now part of a major brewing combine.

The takeover was fortunate in one way, as it gave one of the
younger members of the Theakston family the chance to take advantage of the family's rights to use the brewery's spring water. And
because of that we now have The Black Sheep Brewery, operating
from nearby and producing two or three good beers. No-one seems
surprised to find that the new brewery looks as if it has been in
business for fifty years; the equipment is surely from a bygone era

and the brewhouse is built in the former kiln of the old maltings. As at Theakston's, tours of the brewery are available by phoning and booking. Phone numbers are: Black Sheep, 01765 689227; Theakston's, 01765 689057, Ext. 4317.

One other place you might like to visit is out of the town but associated with it, the Druids' Temple, built as a scaled-down replica of Stonehenge by a local man. It is situated in forestry Commission land accessible by a track to the centre from the Fearby to Ilton road.

The Walk

The Route: Masham Square – Church – river bank – Golf Course – Shaws Farm – Masham

Map: O.S. map 99

The start and how to find it: the market square, Masham; map reference 226807

What the walk is like: a short, easy walk for all seasons

Distance: 4½ miles

Starting in the market square, go to the church and go right to walk past the west door. A few yards further on, a gate in the fence on your right lets you out onto a path that goes left to the bottom right-hand corner where another kissing gate appears. Through that and along the top edge of the field (the boundary at your right-hand), through another gate and turn left to go down towards an old barn-like building and open gateway.

From here, the path becomes a farm track so that when you have turned the corner to the left, the track to follow sets off diagonally over the field on the right and the next field too. It is when you reach the next corner and go into the next field that you change your line slightly to the left to go straight down a line that is parallel to the left-hand side hedge, bringing you to the river. At the river bank, walk to the right alongside the river and at the right-hand bend, go into the wooded area by the steps fortunately set in this usually slippery bank.

You now continue along a riverside path but as you see, it is a different river. The River Ure has gone on to the left while we walk along the smaller and swifter tributary, the River Burn. After a short

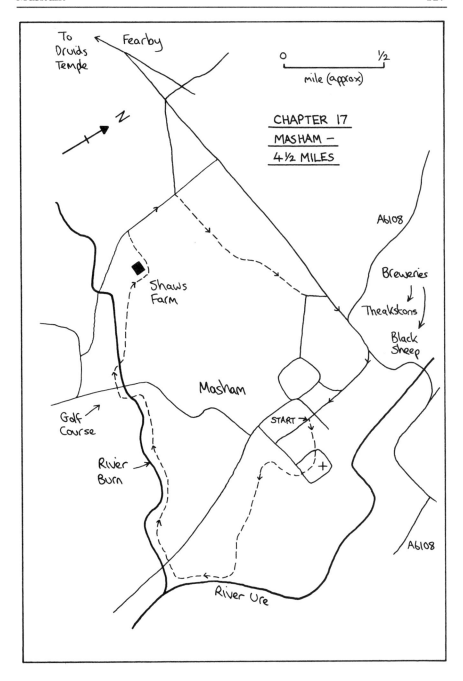

To Druids Temple

Fearby

0 ½
mile (approx)

N

CHAPTER 17
MASHAM —
4½ MILES

A6108

Breweries
Theakstons
Black Sheep

Shaws Farm

Masham

START

Golf Course

River Burn

A6108

River Ure

stretch through a spinney, the path opens out and you find you are on a tractor track. About here, the river divides to form an island with trees, coming together again just before the three arched road bridge. This is where you go onto the road through an iron gate and cross to climb over the stile at the other side. Once into the field you will notice that an old oak looks very like a poplar due to the fact that ivy covers it from near the bottom to the top. From that point walk along near to the river until you come to a stream with a bridge for you to cross. After that take a line half right that aims towards the left-hand end of a post and rail fence along the top of an embankment. This cuts across from one bend in the river going right, to the next one going left.

You will now be at the place where the path goes down to the very water's edge. Apart from one or two ups and downs it is an easy and safe path and before long it brings you to an open grass field. Ahead of you there is a post and wire fence and if you veer slightly to the right, a gate with a stile helps you to keep on track for the next gate which is where you go out onto the road, turn left and cross the bridge. You might also have noticed that there is a golf course on the other side of river.

Turn into the next opening on the right and walk a diagonal line to the right, making sure that no one is about to be hitting a golf ball in your direction, where you will find a footbridge to cross and continue the walk along the river to the left. Passing the thirteenth tee might remind you to keep an eye open all the way across this course although the superstitions associated with thirteen probably mean that an above average number of tee shots are miss-hit into the river. While climbing up from there, I was pleased to find that the description of golf as a game played by men with small balls was a nonsense as I saw a ladies' foursome approaching the tee.

Next is a seven bar wooden gate with a wooden stile beside it. A minor diversion may be necessary here to avoid the boggy bit by going nearer to the wall, then aim for the power line pole before going left, back onto the proper path. The path is now well above the river with a post and wire fence on your right. After going through a green painted metal gate, head for Shaws Farm and bear right to go around the back of the buildings. At the other side there is a silo and opposite the silo a gateway. The path goes from here, straight across the middle of the field passing the back of the farmhouse that is about thirty yards to the left. When you reach the road, turn right and walk along it to the junction of the road with a track.

At this point there is a footpath that starts on your right and goes alongside the left-hand hedge of the field. Turn right at the bottom and walk along the field boundary until you pass the end of the field that is on the other side of the hedge on your left. Now turn left and again walk alongside a hedge that runs along on your left. It is now a straightforward line for half a mile when you cross a stream and shortly after, join a lane that meets the Masham to Fearby road. When it does, turn right, straight on at the junction, passing the garage that is on the left just before Theakston's offices and then turn right again.

From this road you get a good view of the bridge and the river valley and also come across a very varied selection of shops before arriving back at the square with time enough, I hope, to visit the breweries and then take a stroll around the few streets of Masham.

Chapter Eighteen

Runswick Bay

*The place Neapolitans would choose to come and
see before they die*

It was a great temptation (resisted) to include Port Mulgrave for
this chapter. It is a place that has a bay and piers to show that it
really was a port at one time – during the boom in the local alum
industry – but it never developed, and is therefore attractive to some
for a nice quiet walk. But I resisted, mainly because it has only one
good walk and the bay has too much competition in this part of
Yorkshire.

Runswick Bay is a major geographical feature with Goldsborough
to the east where a Roman signal station was discovered in 1919 and

Runswick Bay

Kettleness, most of which slid into the sea in 1829. This fate was suffered by an earlier Runswick in 1682, so I hope that this one has had time to settle. Then there is Hinderwell a mile to the west, strung out along the road, but with a few more shops.

The bay below Runswick village is exceptional for its sands, its cliffs, for the wide sweep of safe summer sailing and swimming water. It also has a number of walks that can be linked together or walked separately, all bringing you back to a cheerful, hospitable village. How they remain so, I do not know; to be besieged from May to the end of September might be okay if you are in a business related to these visitors which makes enough profit to last through the winter. But it is not so good if you are young and cannot afford to buy a cottage in the place where you were born because the holiday home business has pushed the prices up.

There are still fishing cobles here that work for part of the year and the villagers are not as insular as they used to be, but still, few people live here the year round. So off-season is the time to come, when you can park easily, talk to local people and have a peaceful walk around the best small bay on the Yorkshire coast. It is sad just the same. These places, – Robin Hood's Bay and Staithes along with Runswick Bay – built sea walls after the last war. When a promenade was added, attracted more visitors came and was like a self-inflicted wound. There was nothing they could build that would protect their crumbling way of life. All we can do is admire those cliffs on the north side that have allowed toe-holds for so many attractive cottages that overlook the bay towards Kettleness and enjoy the experience.

Having mentioned safe sailing, it is only right to qualify that statement in case you are tempted to bring a boat here and do not take sufficient care. The tides have no worse effect than in any other bay and the approach to the beach is pretty good. But when the wind blows from the south the three valleys spread along the curve of the bay, can "gang up" on you. Sailing a dinghy across the bay can suddenly meet the spot where these wind chutes converge and only awareness and quick action will avoid a capsize.

Like many villages along this coast, it had a lifeboat which its record of bravery – and frequently a crew from Staithes – and it is a good place to search for fossils frequently exposed by the ever shifting cliffs. The remains of a plesiosaur and an ichthyosaurus were found here a mere hundred years ago. That should give you extra credibility if you have to force children (or grandchildren) away from their computer games and Jurassic Park.

The Walk

The Route: Runswick car park – beach – up third valley – along railway line – Runswick

Map: O.S. map 94.

The start and how to find it: you have the option (sometimes governed by the time of year and the number of cars parked here) to park either at the bottom or top of the cliff. In the latter case, walk down the one in four road and go down onto the beach; map reference 809161.

What the walk is like: Part beach, part stiff climb up out of the valley to the cliff top and part walk along the old railway track. This is the shortest of the walks available and clearly marked. Easy, with one short arduous climb.

Distance: Approx. 4½ miles.

Make sure you know the state of the tide and what it is going to do next, before you start. This first section along the beach going south is unlikely to take more than 20 minutes. There are steps at either end of the sea wall to help you get onto the beach. Now walk past the sailing club and go to the opening of the next valley. A path has been made here which goes along beside the stream until it is crossed by a wooden bridge. Now you start the climb up the flights of steps that take you to the top of the cliff and give you an excellent view of the houses on the cliff across the bay when you reach about half way.

At the top, a well-mown path takes you to the left and a stile at the corner of the field on the right. Climb over, once again follow a clear path and when you arrive at the railway bridge, climb over the wooden fence on the right. This lets you down to the track of the old railway line. Follow it to the right as it takes a big semi-circular route to follow the contours. Now you have the chance to admire sea views, the wooded valleys, the village at the top of the cliff and the wider view of green fields and farm houses

After going under a couple of bridges a metal gate needs to be dealt with. It opens O.K. but it is difficult to close with its spring-loaded bolt to engage while lifting the gate. Fortunately the next gate has a stile beside it. Soon you find you are crossing Coverdale Lane next to the old railway house and need to go through a gate that is at the other side of this house. Passing this house I recalled travelling on

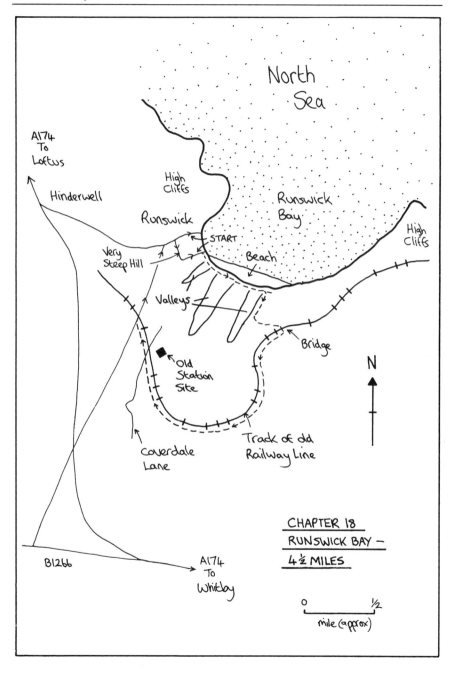

North
Sea

A174
To
Loftus

Hinderwell

High
Cliffs

Runswick

Runswick
Bay

Very
Steep Hill

START

Beach

High
Cliffs

Valleys

Bridge

N

Old
Station
Site

Coverdale
Lane

Track of old
Railway Line

B1266

A174
To
Whitby

CHAPTER 18
RUNSWICK BAY –
4½ MILES

0   ½

mile (approx)

part of this line, in 1952 or 1953, from Scarborough to Ravenscar, and then often along the beach to Robin Hood's Bay. After a sandwich and a drink, we would take the train back to Ravenscar. You can imagine the scenery on such a route running close to the coast from Scarborough, and on to Whitby and Teesside.

The cliffs come into view again and then the track starts to peter out as it first reaches the road, where you climb down and turn right to go along the tarmac towards the Runswick Bay Hotel, and then disappears in the fields at the other side. At the Hotel there is the steep hill on the right, down to the lower car park. If you have parked down there, take this opportunity to go to the top car park and have a look at the view from the edge on the left of the entrance. All that is left now is to walk down to the bottom and if you wish to explore take the bottom road on the left which will take you up to the pub and its well-sited patio that has a few tables and chairs and a view across the bay. And what a bay it is!

Chapter Nineteen

Flamborough

A walk around the headland, the bays, the village and that famous lighthouse

The road from Bridlington, the B1251 and the road from Filey, the B1229, meet at a point just before the solid-looking church with the squat, square tower that seems to indicate the sort of place you have arrived at. Flamborough is built on a headland that juts four miles out into the North Sea, and has a fine record of heroism in lifeboat rescue launches. The town has a tough but smiling approach to life that can be seen, winter or summer, when you walk down High Street and see the good selection of local businesses and meet the people who live here.

The lighthouse, Flamborough Head

The Vikings landed here over a thousand years ago and the area is known as Little Denmark. Indeed, some of today's inhabitants are said to be able to dance the Flamborough Sword Dance. The dance is also more than a thousand years old, although I'm not sure what that proves. And the earthworks that have been cut across the base of the headland from north to south, as part of the defences against marauders from the west, have been called "Danes Dike" but were built before the Danes came.

Firm, historical fact comes from disasters in the case of the lighthouse. Beacons were attended from the 21st June 1588 according to a list of instructions in existence, for positioning and action to be taken from that date, one month before the Armada was sighted in the channel. The Chalk Tower, built from chalk blocks cut from the cliffs, was built later, probably on one of these beacon sites, in 1669. However, it is believed to have been a look-out rather than a light tower and when the unlit cliffs claimed 170 ships wrecked or lost between 1770 and 1806, John Matson was contracted to build the present modern light. This he did in nine months for £8000 without the use of external scaffolding. As you will see, the stone, all white tower, 85 feet high, has an iron gallery 67 feet from the ground (which can be reached by 120 steps of circular internal stairway) and stands over 200 feet above sea level. For the first seven years after it was built, no ship came to grief on these cliffs.

A separate, large book would be needed to tell of all the deeds of the lifeboat crews here and a plaque in the village tells of the sacrifices of fishermen when their fleet, before the days of gale warnings and diesel engines, was caught in a gale and all but one managed to get in to the North Landing, and of how the coble "The Two Brothers" went back to their aid, only to perish after picking up the other crew. Men like this still fish here and still man the lifeboat even though the boat-houses at North Landing and South Landing with off-shore boats have been reduced to an inshore boat at the South Landing.

North Landing, Flamborough Head

The Walk

The Route: Flamborough – Thornwick Bay – Cliff Top walk to South Landing – Information centre – Flamborough

Map: O.S. map 102

The start and how to find it: There is no better way to get the feel of the place than to walk around it. In this case, a cliff top walk to see the four main bays, the point and the village. So start from near the cross roads at which you arrive after passing the church, the cenotaph and the Sea Birds Inn, that has the Post Office at the corner on your the right. Most days you will find parking to be easy along either side of this street. Map reference 227703.

What the walk is like: Easy to moderate – but exhilarating.

Distance: 6½ miles.

First, walk along the left-hand side of the wider street that passes the Victoria Institute and Club out of the village. After the Flaimburg Hotel and the last house along that side of the road, turn left to take the path that goes alongside the left-hand hedge through the green wide open space. At the holiday camp, go in by way of the path in front of you and then bear right toward the white gate on the right of the house in the far right-hand corner. Here you will find a fenced path to the right that takes you towards Thornwick Bay. Here, like many of the parts of Yorkshire that this book visits, you must decide between following a fine scenic walk as easily as possible or making a little extra effort to see as much as you can. Thornwick Bay's temptations are a number of large caves, an archway in the cliff, a shingle beach – and if the tide is right out – the chance to walk round into other, smaller bays. So at the end of the fence, the path goes on around the top end of the ravine, or it will take you to the left, a signpost, steps and a track down the ravine into the open area of the bay. If the tide is at its highest there is still the arch and a cafe. Back up to the path at the top and to the left in front of the three bungalows, taking care to respect the warning signs that advise you to keep away from the cliff edge.

The bay at North Landing is quite near and still has a few fishing cobles, some of which take out fishing parties during the summer months At the stile, climb over and cross the corner of the field and then head for the car park and cafe. The way down into the bay (and

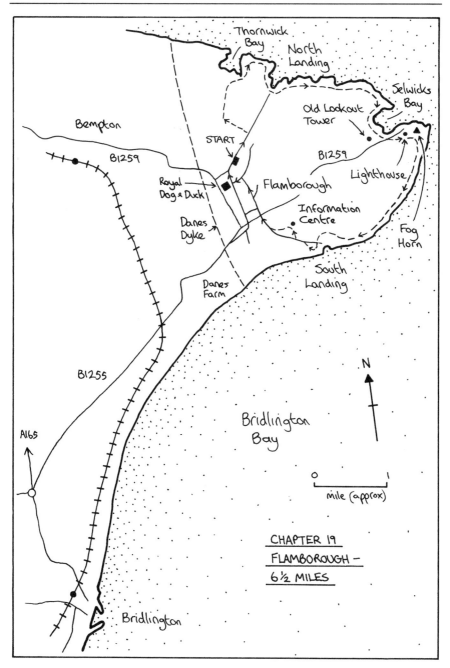

Thornwick
Bay
North
Landing
Selwicks
Bay
Old Lookout
Tower
Bempton
START
B1259
B1259
Royal
Dog & Duck
Flamborough
Lighthouse
Danes
Dyke
Information
Centre
Fog
Horn
Danes
Farm
South
Landing
B1255
N
A165
Bridlington
Bay
0   1
mile (approx)

CHAPTER 19
FLAMBOROUGH —
6½ MILES

Bridlington

up again) is easier here. There is also a ramp for the boats and a steeper one to the old Lifeboat house. There is also a bit of beach here and with good planning to give you plenty of safe time between tides, this is a great place for a swim, picnic, and general loaf around, investigating rocks and pools. It makes the perfect picture postcard scene, especially when the bright sun is reflected from the chalk outcrops under the water to give a luminosity to the sea. If the tide is in, take a short trip in a coble, as it is definitely the best way to see the cliffs and smaller bays. Another day perhaps, as only a small part of the walk has been covered.

At the cafe, turn left to go out to the Headland again. A pleasant enough ambush awaits you a short way ahead and might raise a smile or two, hopefully raising a bob or two for charity as well. When you have finished rolling around, or trying to remember some of the jokes to repeat later, walk along the cliff and (if you haven't already), start to notice the sea birds. Not the variety of Bempton that is a couple of miles north of Thornwick Bay – it is claimed that there are 33 different species of birds breeding there – but here, razorbills, many types of gull, fulmar, gannet, guillemot and even puffins can be seen.

Do take care. The cliff top here is not as crumbly as some parts, but you do pass many intriguing small bays and cliff shapes and pinnacles which might cause you to get a bit near to the edge for a better look . . . "I wonder if he used his camera on the way down?"

Briel Nook, Cradle Head and Stottle Bank Nook are all along this part of the coast and usually offer a view on approach or looking back. In Stottle Bank you might notice a pinnacle with a sharp point in the mouth of the bay. Sharp or not, it usually has a nest on the top. You will now be able to see the golf course; in fact, you walk right up to the 17th tee. An oddity here is the seven step high platform which I imagine is to let you get a view of the place to which you are meant to be sending the ball. Walk some way around the edge and you will see the old chalk tower that was used as a look-out (the hole that it stands near is named after it). You will also notice on this high part of the path, three stone slabs with an iron ring in each. These secured the ropes when men used to go down the face to collect eggs. This breathtaking act was done – most famously on Bempton's 400 feet cliffs – for about 250 years until the mid-Fifties. Apparently, it didn't reduce the numbers of birds, even though as many as 150,000 eggs were collected some years. These, except for a few that went to supplement the diet, were sent to Leeds for the tanning of leather. Then the big bay on your left is Selwick's Bay, pronounced 'silecs'. This is the stage setting for the headland and the lighthouse and is where the agile get the best value by going down the footpath on the side of the cliff and the steep steps near the bottom. But when you get there, walking below the headland, getting close to the white chalk stacks and rock pools, you will really feel pleased with yourself. Here is another world, part fantasy, part lunar, next to the ever-changing sea.

When you return to the top, you will find a licensed restaurant and also a toposcope, mounted on top of a low column of coloured stone which shows the direction and distance to places from where you are standing. In particular it points to where the American "pirate" Commodore, John Paul Jones beat the two British Navy ships escorting a Baltic merchant fleet before his own ship sank. Can this be the man with a dance named after him? Incidentally, the headland is equidistant from Land's End and John O' Groats, 362 miles. Now start to walk from the seaward side of the lighthouse, down towards the fog horn station and then when halfway there, turn right along the path to South Landing. The cliff are higher on this side with fewer bays and. it is usually a breezier walk too, from High Stacks onwards.

Besides the sea birds and local views you will soon get a view down the coast past Sewerby where the cliffs run out into the sands of Bridlington Bay. If you are walking here in the middle of August you might also see some fairly big fleets of yachts racing in the bay as this is when the Royal Yorkshire Yacht Club hold their annual regatta week. Note the "Royal", recognition of the good sailing to be had in these parts. At the same time it must be said that sailing around the head is not so easy with strong, treacherous currents, especially when the tide is on the turn.

Ahead of you is straight-forward walking, with a couple of small ravines and one steep-sided one, fortunately stepped. Then after a particularly good viewing point overlooking the South Landing, the path goes right and you can see the slipway and lifeboat house as the path goes to the left and then right, past picnic tables and to some steps on your left. Down these to the bay and the road that goes to the right, heading for the village. The bay is not one I would choose to swim in as it is rocky with a shingle beach, but there are some pleasant places to sit in the sun against the cliffs which reflect warmth. The local fishermen, I am told, used to keep a boat here and also have one at the North Landing so that they could launch whichever way the wind blew. But now to the return leg. Up the hill that passes the information centre which has a well-illustrated map on the wall and also reports that the South Landing was, between the 14th century and 16th century, a port and that in 156, Mary Stuart, on her way to Scotland to claim the crown as Mary, Queen of Scots, anchored there. The foundations can still be seen at low water.

I don't think Flamborough can be called a pretty village, although along this road there are some quite pleasant looking houses, bungalows and later, cottages, but it has got some character. Also along this road you will pass the entrance to what was called "Cliff House" and has been renamed "The Timoneer" as an Inn. Curiously, the sign board is painted in Gaelic characters although the name is an old English word for a steersman on the old sailing ships. After the football and cricket ground go straight across at the crossroads. It was here that I heard two ladies talking about some people "from the West Riding". Thank goodness the Ridings still live, even if at this time it is only in the mind.

Now in South Sea Road, go left at the village green and left again at the T-junction that has the Rose and Crown on your right, to walk along High Street. Plenty of shops and life here. At the end there is The Ship on the corner and ahead of you, Dog and Duck Square, which has by chance, The Royal Dog and Duck, a public house to enjoy food and drink in if ever there was one. Otherwise, turn right before it, right again at the Post Office and in a few yards, you should be at the place you started from. And with all these cliffes around that are made of chalk, would you believe that there is a rocks works here? Yes, it is Boro Rock Works, the boiled sweet, name of the town running throuigh the middle, kind, of course. But if you don't care to stop at the pub (is it something I have said?) turn right before it, right again at the Post Office and in a few yards, you should be at the place you started from.

Chapter Twenty

Burton Agnes

A Hall that proves biggest isn't always best

Burton Agnes is on the southern edge of the northern part of the
Yorkshire Wolds and clearly dates back to 1173 with the lower
chamber of a Norman manor house still remaining next to the
present Hall. With a stream and possibly a low road to the coast and
port (the high road being the Roman road that runs east from Kilham
up on the wold) it must have seemed as good a place as any to farm
and to accommodate one's labourers.

In the village now, there is little of special notice. It has a most of
the essential elements of a village – church, pub, pond, post office
and shop, cricket ground and football pitch and most of the farm-
houses are situated in the village, but I admit that the reason for
enticing you to this place is essentially the Hall. Currently owned
by the Cunliffe Lister family, it has never been sold, only changing
direct family inheritance when the male line "ran out". Its rise to
fame in modern times is due to the Wickham Boyntons and in
particular to one man, Marcus Wickham Boynton.

When you start to look around the inside, the feeling of stately
home cum-posh-museum is quickly dispelled as the house does
actually feel like someone's home. Perhaps the absence of roped off
areas and the fact that dining and sitting rooms are clearly used
helps, but so does the friendliness of the people who act as guides
or guardians.

The exterior may not appeal to you as beautiful, although that
might be due to the fact that the Tudor renaissance architecture is
less familiar. Certainly I didn't start to admire its symmetry until my
second visit. The gate-house is bound to impress you and you will
see how it sets off the south front of the house.

The inexpensive guide book is a must, providing background
notes, historical and contemporary. The fact that impresses me is
that this was the private collection of one man, a man who bought
and traded paintings, rare antique furniture, porcelain and Epstein

bronzes to better his collection as others might collect stamps. He must have been a remarkable man as he was able to breed thorough-bred race horses at his own stud and show a handsome profit, become High Sheriff of Yorkshire, and in 1977 was able to form a charitable trust to which he gave forty two acres of gardens and grounds, six hundred acres of good agricultural land and a substantial cash endowment to ensure the protection and the future upkeep of the Hall and its contents. A condition of the trust is that it must be open to the public for at least six months every year.

But the warmth of the atmosphere inside is not the only recommendation. There is the staggering array of paintings by English, French, Russian and other artists which enliven the rooms with the bright colours of Cezanne, Gauguin, and Matisse among works by old masters, bronzes by Epstein, 18th century furniture, lacquer panels and the sketches by Augustus John. And near to the end of a visit, it is a special treat to me to be able to sit in one of the alcoves off the Long Room, take a book off the shelves and read for a while about the artist whose work I have just been able to see. The Long Room itself is a master stroke of restoration work as it had to be taken

Burton Agnes Hall

apart, getting rid of seven bedrooms put there around 1810 plus an area left to decay. Then from a small fragment that remained, the barrel ceiling was also restored to its original state.

Realising that different visitors may wish to spend different amounts of time wandering around the house, the walk that follows has two options, option one is for those who want a view of the Wolds and an easy walk of moderate length – 7½ miles, or option two, an easy walk in level country around what is or was estate land, for 3½ to 4 miles.

The Walk

The Route: Hall – Farm road to Roman road – Thorn Holme – Harpham – Burton Agnes

Map: O.S. map 101.

The start and how to find it: The village is on the A166, half-way between Driffield and Bridlington. Map reference 103633.

What the walk is like: Nearly all on level ground.

Distance: 3½ miles or 7½ miles as indicated on sketch map.

Option one: Coming out of the gate-house at the Hall, walk down to the main road and walk just a few yards to a road that appears to go up through a farmyard on your left. Follow this to the top, turn right and keep to the road up to the junction. Turn right here and walk nearly one and a half miles to the Roman road that goes across your front at the top this lane and then go to the right again. A quarter of a mile along here from where you have splendid views, there is a grass track going down to the right. Walk all the way down this to the main road to Bridlington. Turn right, staying on the right-hand side of the road where there is a pavement. Walk out of Thornholme, first passing the petrol station on your left, a lane to your right and then, after the Burton Agnes sign, you can see a row of power line poles coming towards you from the short row of cottages on the left. Pass two then just before the third, there is a gap in the hedge on your left. Cross over and from this point, follow the route given from the beginning of the second paragraph in Option two (at the place marked ******)

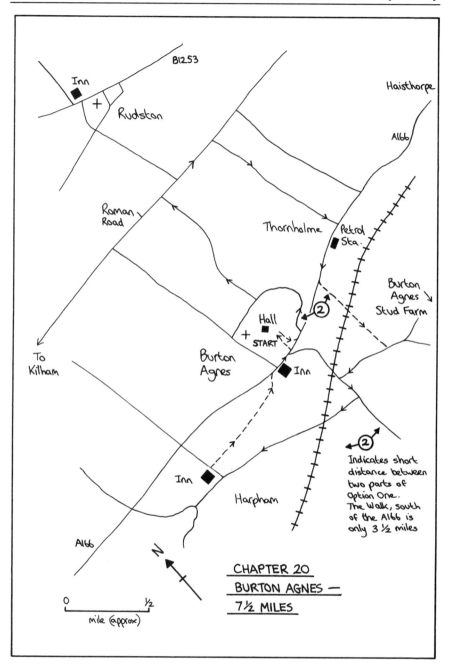

Inn

B1253

Haisthorpe

Rudston

A166

Roman
Road

Thornholme

Petrol
Sta.

Burton
Agnes
Stud Farm

Hall

②

START

To
Kilham

Burton
Agnes

Inn

②

Indicates short
distance between
two parts of
Option One.
The Walk, south
of the A166 is
only 3½ miles

Inn

Harpham

A166

N

CHAPTER 20
BURTON AGNES —
7½ MILES

0   ½

mile (approx)

Option two: Coming out of the gate-house at the Hall, walk down to the main road and go to the left, crossing the road as soon as you can see far enough ahead to make it safe, to make use of the footpath. Continue until after a short terrace of four cottages (one obviously the home of a keen chrysanthemum grower) to where the path stops and is continued on the other side of the road. Go along the other side of the road for a little way looking out for a footpath sign and gap in the hedge on the right-hand side.

** Go into and down the right-hand side of this field until at the bottom you need to go a few paces to the left to cross a bridge over a wide ditch on your right. In the next field a hedge starts about halfway across, going away from you. Go to the right-hand side of it and walk to the gate which is the crossing point for the railway. Cross with care. The path now goes straight across the middle of the field on the other side. The old Wickham Boynton Stud farm is to your right when you reach the road but there is little to see and in any case, it is now run as a separate business by tenants of the Estate. Going right along the road will bring you to a junction where you can, by looking right, see the level crossing. But here the walk goes left until the next junction on the right. It is marked as a cul-de-sac but this is because the crossing gates are chained and locked, opening only for local farm machinery, with a small pedestrians only gate at the side. Then it is on through the next field gate, along another section on lane where you will come across a protective wrought iron fence, inside which is a dome open on one side that appears to have been a well or the source of a spring. Continue into the village of Harpham, with its pub, just beyond the crossroads where you would ordinarily turn right.

Within 50 or 60 yards on the right-hand side at the end of the hedge and before what might have been the old school, take the stile and path by the side of the house. Take the next stile and go across the field towards the lone tree in the hedge at the other side. When you reach it, go over the stile on its right and follow the marked path. Your guide from this point is to aim for the middle of the village that is clearly visible from here on. I say this because although the path is a definite straight line, the crops in these fields seem to change and you may want to go around some instead of across them. Eventually you will reach a grass field that includes at the far side, farm buildings. You can go across this to the road or take the field on your left, crossing to almost the same point at the road. Walk to the right along the road until you reach the memorial to the dead of the last two major wars. From here you can go to the left and walk up to the church, gaining entrance once more to the Hall and old stable area or carry straight on to return along the drive to the gate-house where you started.

Sparing a moment to look more closely at the memorial, you will see that Major Henry Wickham Boynton, brother of Marcus Wickham Boynton was killed in action in 1942.

Anyone hungry for more points of interest – or just plain hungry – can take the road to Rudston, right at the main road, right again, follow the road round the back of the hall, then left and straight on. When a road goes to left and to right in front of you, go right and the next left. This brings you to Rudston with the grave of Winifred Holtby, authoress of "Land of Green Ginger" a place you can see in Hull and "South Riding", the Riding we never had, which has an open book as its tombstone. In the same churchyard is the monolith and in the same village, a pub that serves a fair meal and drink. Cheers.

Chapter Twenty-one

Thornton le Dale

That village with the stream, on the road to Scarborough where you always meant to stop

I do not know who makes these sweeping statements, but here is another village claiming to be the prettiest in Yorkshire. It is pleasant enough, I agree, but is a stream curving through, that has natty little bridges to the cottages on the other side, enough? Actually you cannot help liking the place with its quieter streets away from the main ones and sufficient shops and pubs to please most people. The 16th century, almshouses, with the taller grammar school building beyond are enough reason to stop. Certainly enough people stop to photograph Beck Isle cottage beside Dalby Beck to keep Kodak in business for a day or two. Add to that the pressure of a set of stocks and an ancient market cross to see at the end of the green and it almost outweighs the fact that there is an awful lot of traffic on the main road. Wander further and you will find a Tudor Hall set among splendid mature chestnut and copper beeches and there is still a cruck-framed thatch cottage. A couple of bits of unusual history too. One a trick of fate perhaps, in that a soldier by the name of Matthew Grimes fought in the Peninsular War and is buried in the churchyard here. It was a coincidence that he should also be a guard on St. Helena when Napoleon died and was there to carry the "Little Corporal" to his grave. Still, it is nice of the people of Thornton to remember him. From my brief experience, they are like that. As were those people who set themselves up as a commission of donors in 1781 to ensure that Thornton le Dale always had a bull. Sadly it was decided in 1960 that a bull was no longer needed and so they spent the money on street lights. Practical, but not half as good a story.

Another good point that is immediately practical is that there is a large car park if you turn down the same road as the stream. Go a couple of hundred yards and turn left, then follow the driveway and a large car park appears and only costs fifty pence a day. Not only that but the gateway near the top right corner leads to a path past the duck pond, over the stream and out at a point next to the main road. At this point, you have to admit that a place like this to start and finish a walk at the foot of the North Yorkshire moors cannot be such a bad place after all.

The Walk

The Route: Village centre — north towards Orchan Dale — Howl Dale wood — Hagg House — Thornton le Dale

Map: O.S. Landranger map 100

The start and how to find it: car park described above; map reference 835829.

What the walk is like: easy.

Distance: 5 miles

Go along the main road by the side of the stream and cross over when you are opposite the Almshouses founded by Lady Lumley in 1656, then at the end turn left up Brook Lane, going to the right a little at the top where it is marked as a private road and a public footpath. The road leads to an impressive large private house and the footpath continues up the left-hand side of the property. At the top of this, a white gate lets you out onto the road onto which you turn left to the junction with the road going uphill on the right. Walk up the hill and along this road for about a mile. It takes nearly half that distance to get past the high hedges and get any open views. They are at least rewarding when they appear.

There is a "Stag" sign on the roadside to use this time as a warning that the turn is near. First a farm track that you can see does not go far, then the next one on the left which is also a road open to vehicular traffic to get to Low Kingthorpe, although you wouldn't believe it unless you lived there. Walk down the lane which turns to the right after about a hundred yards and then as you are about to go under power lines, turn left and go under them, forty yards on, when on the footpath.

Follow this path to the end of the hedge and then turn right to head for the far corner of this field. There you will find a gap so that

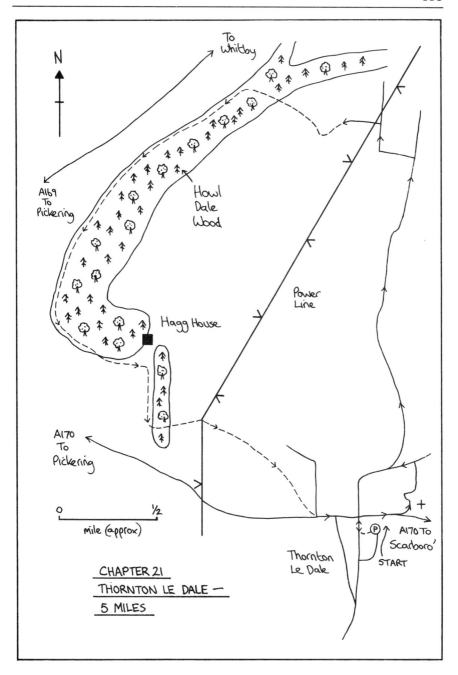

N

To Whitby

A169
To
Pickering

Howl
Dale
Wood

Power
Line

Hagg House

A170
To
Pickering

0   ½
mile (approx)

CHAPTER 21
THORNTON LE DALE —
5 MILES

Thornton
Le Dale

P A170 To
Scarboro'
START

you can walk along the edge of the first part of the wood (with it on your right) and continue into the second part, going right down into the bottom of the valley. At the bottom, turn left and start a very pleasant woodland walk of about a mile. There isn't so much ground cover here and you can see further through the trees, particularly on the left. This gives you chance to see more animals and birds. Then human animals as you come to an area where thinning is being done. I hope this means that if the Government continues its policy of selling off state forests, public footpaths through them will remain. I do not see why the two should not exist together.

As the path goes uphill, ignore the footpath sign and stile on the right. Further on at a place where a path goes up to the left, go through the gap on your right and then ahead again alongside the fence on your left until you are in the open area below the house. The path is a little confusing here as it seems such a busy farmyard. A path goes from it and through the wood to the right of the house, but I have marked a path lower down the drive to the same point at the far side of the field after the wood. So turn to the right and go down the drive until opposite a recently opened gap in the wood on the left. Go through the gap and at the other side take a path at an angle of 45 degrees to the left. You must have noticed by now that the area is laid out for Hunter Trials with some pretty formidable obstacles, but these need not be jumped on your way across this or any other field. A guide to the path is that you should meet the overhead power lines at the point where they change direction by 15 to 20 degrees. From that point walk across to the field boundary at the top edge of the next field which is two up from the road. After that point, the path is fairly clear over two stiles finishing with a diagonal line to the right over pasture to an almost hidden stile in the bushes at that bottom corner, through two or three yards and out onto the footpath of the Pickering to Scarborough road.

At the next lane to the left, cross the road to the right so that you have a footpath to walk on for the remaining hundred yards or so, back into Thornton le Dale.

Chapter Twenty-two

Lastingham

Challenger for the "most beautiful village" title

A quieter place than its very pleasant neighbour, Hutton le Hole, Lastingham is much smaller and, because of its situation, milder. True, it hasn't the craft shops or a mini-museum or a stream running down the middle of the village, but besides its beauty, it has charm, even if it is difficult to park. The pub and the church are opposite each other, which a long while ago was even more convenient than now as the wife of the curate bought the place and became the licensee to bolster her husband's stipend. Even the Bishop agreed that it was a good idea after he had been taken to the

Lastingham

Blacksmith's Arms to meet parishioners and test his curate's theory that more Christian work was done there than in the church.

History as well as beauty is identified with this village as it has been a major spiritual centre since St. Cedd of Lindisfarne founded a monastery here in the 7th century. Pilgrims from all parts of the world still come to visit his burial place in the crypt of St. Mary's, which just happens to be the only one in England with a rounded apse and was built about 1080, undecorated and springing straight from the ground. It is easy to see too, the restored steps to it, going down from the middle of the nave. More recent history you might note is that the Blacksmith's Arms was a winner in the Pub of the Year competition in 1993 and voted the "Best Ale House in Yorkshire".

As you take the walk from here you will see that it is in an almost complete hollow with a gap only to the east, although this is covered by the hills above Cropton. To the south, the hills are not as high and the rise more gradual. The result is arable land around more than half of the village and moorland to the north to keep off the Arctic blasts. This is ideal for local gardeners too, which all helps the village image. Sheep farming is, of course, still playing a big part in the local economy but doesn't employ a lot of people. Arable farming employs a few more but not a very big acreage is involved which probably means that the village is less likely to grow, which has its good points as well as bad.

The Walk

The Route: Lastingham Church – east to moor – Tranmire Plain – Camomile Farm – Spaunton – Lastingham

Map: O.S. map 100.

The start and how to find it: 3 miles north of the A170. Map reference 728905.

What the walk is like: Easy for most part, one or two gentle gradients and one steep short climb up to Spaunton.

Distance: 4 miles

Walk down from the church or pub (the latter on your left) and turn left at the bottom of the road and then left again into a lane with a

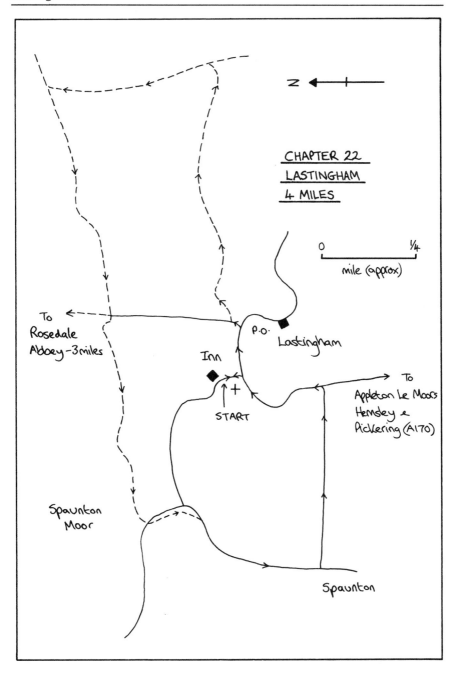

CHAPTER 22
LASTINGHAM
4 MILES

cul-de-sac sign at its head. After about 25 yards, follow the directions of the public footpath sign on your right, up towards a gate. To the left of the gate, go up the few steps, over a stile and along the path. A slightly gloomy start for all the promised beauty but the high hedges on either side soon stop at another stile where you go over and into the open. After the next stile the path now goes diagonally left towards a sorry looking tree that is to the right of a lone ash and has a post at its foot with familiar yellow arrow to send you on your way.

At the far side of the field there are two whitewashed posts to aim for as they mark the position of the stile, 50 yards down the hedge from the top left corner. Over that and the stout bridge that is on the other side and continue on a line parallel to the left-hand hedge. Then two stiles to cross within a hundred yards and again at the other side of the long narrow field that you are in now. There is a clear path, previously sprayed and in the next field it has resulted in a grass path through the stubble and leads you to a gate and another clear path to another stile. Go left a bit with the path in this next field, to a gate.

It is all around you now. Hills, valleys, woodland, green fields, cattle, sheep, the occasional house, farmland and moorland that changes colour with the seasons. All the best in Yorkshire countryside. It really does you good to be here knowing too that you can stroll around for miles over this part of the North Yorkshire National Park. Two tourists from Dortmund that I met walking across the moor told me that the area was so totally relaxing it had turned out to be the best part of their two weeks holiday in Scotland and northern England.

One more field and then a stile takes you into a plantation not long planted and the path which might become difficult to see, goes ahead for most of the plantation's breadth and then goes right to find a stile that lets you out onto the moor. Then turn left and walk along the wide grass track above the valley with its stream. Near the top, by the corner of a wall, the path goes left, go round with it and keep going until you arrive at a crossroads of paths. Left goes down towards houses, right to Rosedale. You should go straight ahead on the path marked to High Cross. Down into a little valley, over the stream and up the other side, past Camomile Farm on your left, over to the corner of the small fenced plot and then along side the fence that now runs along on your left and past the bee hives. Now you are near a wall, walk beside that and go past the gate that is part way along it on your left, keeping to the path that shortly after becomes a track more obviously used by vehicles. Follow its curve away to the left and down to a stile by a wooden gate and then to the road. Go to the left on the road and at the next junction go up the road on the right. I was along here once at sheep dipping time and kept seeing one of the farmers scurrying all over on a pony, trying to get flocks of sheep together. At the top of the hill I stopped to help while he went back for some others and then later saw him in the Blacksmith's when I was able to tell him that a hundred or more that had been split off by a barking dog had been recovered. This gave him time for another drink and a chat. The stories were good, but the remark that stayed in my mind was that although he realised that a Yorkshireman's steadfast belief in his superiority was based on confidence, this did not necessarily make him arrogant. Nevertheless it does no harm to accept that it is possible to be wrong, have good manners and remain tolerant. It was what he thought kept this community, with its wide spread of social backgrounds, together. I began to think that I might learn to enjoy living in this village.

However, you now go left at the point where straight ahead would mean a five bar gate, and through what is the hamlet of Spaunton. At the other end of which, the road goes downhill turning left at the junction, down into Lastingham. This is the place where you probably get the best impression of the village, as against the fence on the right-hand side you have a very good view of the houses and the church, And very soon you are there, ready to enjoy a drink of the pubs own brew and sit down to enjoy the atmosphere.

Chapter Twenty-three

Castle Howard

The big, big house

It may sound strange, but if it wasn't for the signs on the main York to Malton road, you wouldn't know it was there. You look at the Ordnance Survey map for signs of a big estate and even the name is camouflaged against the blue of two small lakes. Then as you start to go down Barton Hill, there is the sign. (If you reach Whitwell on the Hill, you have missed it). But that isn't all – the road bends and dips and crosses a crossroads so that you begin to wonder if you are on the right track. Just in time you see Whitwell Grange and shortly after, pass a huge monument. Another mile and over another cross-

Temple of the Four Winds

roads and then it is less than half a mile to the entrance with a wall
and towers on either side. But that turns out to be just the first one.
Another half mile of this roller coaster stretch of road and then
another gate-house – and you are still half a mile from the house!

The Walk

The Route: Gatehouse on main estate road – Pyramid – Ray Wood –
Coneysthorpe – Obelisk (house) – Gatehouse.

Map: On O.S. map 100

The start and how to find it: park about 75 yards before the second gate
by turning left onto a short track that goes into a walled area. Before the
opening into the yard, there is a grass patch, firm enough to park on and out
of the way of tractors on the right; big enough for two cars, maybe three,
without blocking any gate. Map reference 711695.

What the walk is like: easy to moderate walking in parkland: a short walk
that gives an overall view and, in any case, if you start by going round the
house and gardens you will be too exhausted to walk.

Distance: about 4½ miles.

From the parking place, walk through the gate-house arch and turn
right to walk along the lane marked private road. It goes to Gateley
Farm but is a public footpath and is the first point on the walk that
you see how every effort was made to impose some grandeur on the
place with, in this case, walls along the boundary with castellated
towers at regular intervals. Any building you pass looks solid
especially when a bit further on to your right you see the pyramid.
Down to the left, you can now see part of one of the lakes and then
a few yards later, a gap in the trees down on the left gives you your
first sight of the house of Castle Howard and to the right of it a bridge.

A hundred yards or so past the pyramid, turn left and walk down
the track to the bridge, a three arched construction built – like almost
everything else – on a massive scale. The path that leads you to it
also gives you a good view of the Mausoleum up on the right. Now
the bridge. I have seen less formidable obstacles on a tank testing
ground, but it isn't too bad as you get closer, and from the top you
do get a good view of the waterfall. Once over the bridge, walk
towards the building near the top of the hill on your left. This is the

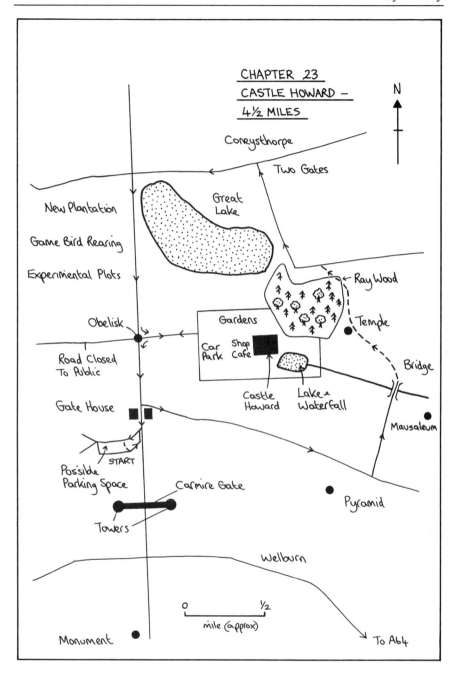

Temple of the Four Winds and certainly a little larger than your average garden pavilion. About now I think you will be realising that it is just as the guide book says, the house and the surroundings are one unit, each important to the other, impossible to imagine as separate entities.

Now go past the temple and over towards the wall and the metal gate. Through that to follow the wall downhill where there is the base of a tower. I am not sure if the stone is being taken away for other uses or being brought here to do a little building and "distressing". But go from here to the end of the wall to the gate and stile. At the next junction you come to, you meet the Centenary Way, (each rural council needing their own long distance path), and go left to walk along it for a short while. This will bring you to another path, the one to Coneysthorpe going right and passing a gate and section of wall that must have taken a vast amount of stone and a considerable amount of labour. When the first owner, Charles Howard, the third Earl of Carlisle, approached a successful playwright and a man of charm and wit, to ask him to design and build him a house, it must have been obvious that Carlisle was not trying to outbuild his contemporaries. John Vanbrugh had at the time not built a thing, but Carlisle saw him as a man of ideas, a man who could create for him the grand design. A partnership was then created by Vanbrugh with Hawksmore, so that his imagination could become reality through the training and experience of the latter. So with stone and labour, it came about, starting in 1700 and almost complete by the time of Vanbrugh's death in 1726, a fine Baroque castle. And they have been rebuilding and extending ever since (a large part was burnt down in 1940 and the library was only added in 1983).

After that wall and gate, turn right at the next junction walking along the right-hand end of what they call the Great Lake of which you might get a glimpse before the banking rises, by which time you have reached the edge of the caravan and camping site.

Keep going, there is fine open land to your right and gates in front of you. Aim for the gates and as you close up on them, take the small one on the left, go through it and walk down the road to your left. Here is the hamlet of Coneysthorpe, mainly a picturesque group of houses around a village green behind a War Memorial. That is to your right, further on, on your left, the entrance to the caravan site. After this you come to a cross roads and though it would be pleasant to walk around the other side of the estate, most of it is taken up with new plantings of rare trees plus a good selection of the less common English trees for use on the estate and areas set aside for game birds.

So turn left at the cross roads and walk down the wide grass verge to the obelisk. There is a large noticeboard at the side of the road there which tells you that Castle Howard is open from the middle of March to beginning of October. The House opens at 11 a.m. until 4.30 p.m. while the plant centre and gardens open an hour earlier.

To do both on the same day is a little difficult, especially if the weather is good and you want to walk around Ray Wood whilst many of the rooms are absorbing for the design or contents or both. It is big, that is really the main thing that makes it different to the other two great houses in this book and a quick tour of either inside or outside will give you reason to come back another day to finish the job.

Don't forget you have yet to finish the walk by going back to the obelisk, turning left and walking the half mile along the main drive to the gate-house and your car.

Chapter Twenty-four

York

No ghosts, just beauty from another angle

There are a number of ways to arrive in York. The Romans walked
in, the Vikings came up the river in adaptations of the longships
and being in the middle of the flat Vale of York people are still
turning up on bicycles. Very much a cycling city is York, but not
daft enough to leave them around for free use by anybody tried to
do in Oxford (that seat of learning) and had them nicked.

And you can still arrive by train. It is still one of the busiest
stations with trains coming and going from more than two directions. If that would have distressed Dr. Beeching, thinking of a
missed opportunity I would be surprised, as it appears that he closed
more lines of track in Yorkshire than in any other county.

There's more. Road of course, with a dual carriageway approach
on the main roads for bus, car and motor bike and by air too.
Certainly on every race day, jockeys, trainers and owners fly in to
the air strip at Sherburn, the old Eastern capital of the Brigantian
empire of Elmete, but they must then take a taxi for the last few
miles. It makes me wonder if, now that there is a 90% reduction in
military traffic in the area, York might consider special flight rules
for a limited number of days a year, landing on the Knavesmire. With
a grass strip it could only take light aircraft, and helicopters of
course. After all, they had flying races there as far back as 1913 and
flying training on a reportedly rough strip was based there in the 20s
and 30s.

The Knavesmire, on which the races are held, will be seen at
closer quarters later; for now let me say that while Ascot has
maintained the ceremonial side of racing together with some fairly
handsome races and prizes, York has always managed to provide
good racing for all those involved, with a good mix of tradition and
comfort. Regulars of this unique course will accept that, together
with Doncaster, the county has two of the best courses in the country

(and seven others that are not too bad). York offers good programmes, big races, excellent stands and a good view of the racing. Gentlemen are expected to wear ties in the County enclosure and the ladies look gorgeous without having to resort to silly hats. And the thoroughbred horses look O.K. too.

It has also had its share of good, old fashioned eccentrics. One I particularly like was a well-known peer who loved a gamble and not always on the horses. Towards the end of the 18th century, he bet a large sum to show he could send a letter fifty miles in an hour. As it was more than a hundred years before the motor car was invented, he had plenty of takers. He approached two cricket teams (each including 12th man) and with tape and markers positioned them to form a large circle on the Knavesmire. He then produced what looked like a cricket ball except for the fact that it had a hole drilled in one side. He asked the captains to witness the fact that he put in a letter and then offered them free ale for the night if they would throw and catch the ball under his direction for an hour. His calls of encouragement kept up the speed and towards the end of the hour, when no doubt the promised ale began to seem like an oasis in the desert, he saw that he had won and was delighted to call for the beer. I am pleased to be able to say he went on with his profitable wagers until he was 80.

The city is a delight for historians, artists, railway enthusiasts, boating people, racing types and tourists. Not many people live in York and it is easy to see why when the place is packed with people from every nation almost every day. Not that you can let that put you off; you have to go. It is such a beautiful city, it affords every amenity and above all, has atmosphere, nowhere more enveloping than when you are in the Minster. Go there and look. Maybe take a small pair of binoculars to look at the detail in the stained glass, then sit down somewhere and take some time savouring the feel of the place. Should you ever find yourself at 9.45 a.m. on a Sunday morning within 10 to 15 minutes of York Minster, get there for the morning service. Whatever religion you are – or even if you haven't one – sitting or standing there with the voices of the choir soaring above you, being with a group of people likely to be mainly Yorkshire people at their most gentle, you will experience an hour of happiness which I hope will stay with you.

How lucky we are in this county to have two Minsters, unequalled in beauty.

Now I have to admit that the walk I want to guide you along, does not include the Minster or the Jorvik experience or the Railway Museum or . . . well, let's say that it is meant as an appetiser and that you will keep getting glimpses of the reasons for spending more than a day or two here.

Restaurants here vary, but mainly in price, as none are less than fairly good and the pubs are first class, both for the comfort they provide and their beer. It is the accommodation that gets top marks. Despite the cynical being tempted to say it is a tourist trap, the same situation has, because of the competition, ensured good value for money, from the four- and five-star hotels to the B&Bs. There are too many good ones to make any specific recommendations.

Most of us will pick the well-known sights, but try to spare a minute for All Saints church on Pavement at the bottom of Parliament Street – a fine example of the Perpendicular – and the Black Swan, the black and white pub along The Stonebow, strong on history and a fine place to approach the horizontal.

The Gate House, Bishp's Palace at Bishopthorpe

The Walk

The Route: City Wall – Lendal Bridge – Skeldergate Bridge – Bishopthorpe – Knavesmire – The Mount – Micklegate Bar – City Wall – Lendall.

Map: O.S. map 105. The city map would be useful for future visits but not really essential for this walk.

The start and how to find it: There is parking, even if you drive into the centre of the town. Of course, a vast area of parking space is filled by vast numbers of visitors, so have a quick look at the mini-map of York, note the car parks, the bus station, the railway station, and where the cycle track comes in. Even better, if you are there any day, Monday to Saturday, make use of the Park and Ride. It is well-signposted as you approach the city and offers free parking and a low-price return ticket to the centre of town. Or come by train. In any case make your way to the front of the railway station. Map reference 597518.

What the walk is like: Level walking along city walls, the riverside, over the Knavesmire and back along the main street into York.

Distance: 6 miles.

Walk to the left from the station, past the Royal Yorkshire Hotel, down to the lights at the crossroads. Cross straight ahead and at the other side cross over to the right, passing the statue of George Leeman who was three times the Lord Mayor of York and then their M.P., to go under the arch in the wall. Once through, you will find steps on your left so that you can go up and onto the wall. This section stops at Lendal Bridge, so go down the steps, turn right at the bottom and go under the bridge. If you feel you need a coffee before the six mile walk ahead there is a very nice little coffee and tea shop at the other end of the bridge.

Continue the walk, by walking along the riverside, passing the insurance company offices and the hotel, until you come to Ouse Bridge. You might notice that the modern block you have just passed is skilfully designed to blend well with the smaller, older houses and cottage further along what is Wellington Row and North Street. At the bridge cross the road and then the river. The river is the Ouse of course and is the origin of the city's strategic importance.

At the other side, steps on the right go down onto King's Staithe and if you have timed your start to allow for an early lunch, here is a convenient pub, the King's Arms, which serves reasonable food at

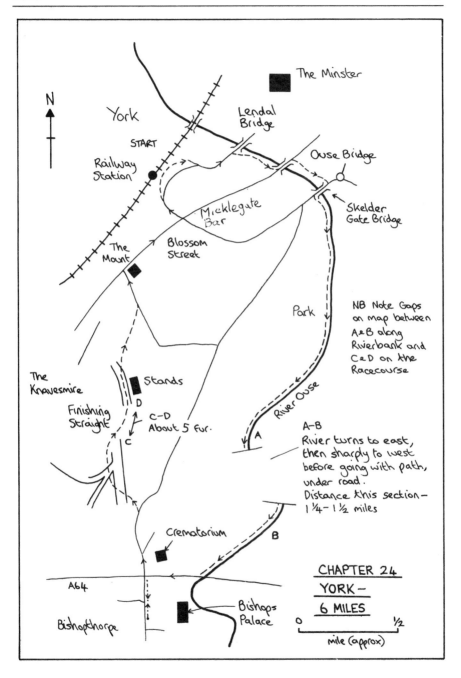

N

York

START

Railway
Station

The Minster

Lendal
Bridge

Ouse Bridge

Skelder
Gate Bridge

Micklegate
Bar

The
Mount

Blossom
Street

Park

NB Note Gaps
on map between
A&B along
Riverbank and
C&D on the
Racecourse

The
Knavesmire

Stands

Finishing
Straight

D

C-D
About 5 Fur.

C

River Ouse

A

A-B
River turns to east,
then sharply to west
before going with path,
under road.
Distance this section -
1¼ - 1½ miles

B

Crematorium

A64

Bishopthorpe

Bishops
Palace

CHAPTER 24

YORK -

6 MILES

0   ½

mile (approx)

reasonable prices with some good beer (and will let you see the height of the flood waters marked inside the building).

On the other side of the river you can now see warehouses converted into office blocks as well as old warehouses no doubt waiting their turn, also commercial barges whose only limitation on size is caused by the lock at Naburn just a few miles downstream. Big enough to allow what look like very comfortable floating homes, further downstream.

Next, after the boat hire points and the starting point of many river trips, there is St. George's Field on the left and then Skeldergate Bridge. Go up the steps onto the bridge here and cross the river once more before going down the steps at the other side that go down to the right. At the bottom, turn right and go under the span of the bridge and walk alongside the river for the next two and a half miles.

You start by going in front of two attractive blocks of flats, then along a road, which near the Rowntree Park, has bollards to stop vehicles going further than the Camping Club site. It then changes to part of the cycle track that goes to Selby, mostly along a re-surfaced old railway line but in parts, through fields by the river. It is a very pleasant walk, especially as although the first mile is still in the city, it is very peaceful with pleasant views, lots of trees and points of interest on the river such as the junction where the River Foss joins the Ouse (at the traffic lights) and the boat club, the flower gardens of the park and one or two impressive houses along the way – oh, and under the ring road.

Eventually you will arrive at the dreaded "Private Land" signs. A pity, as not long ago you could walk along the river to the other side of the Bishop's Palace but now you have to turn right and walk beside the grounds of the crematorium to the road. At the road, turn to the left for a look at the Palace, the coach house and the Brew house before turning round and walking back to the crematorium. Don't linger here. Bear left slightly to go uphill and over the bridge that goes over the ring road and cross the road when it starts to go downhill. It is here, when you are just past the blue boards at the end of the six furlong "chute", you will find a path down to the fence and a stile. Over the stile and walk over to the trackside rails.

Walk a little way to the cycle track that crosses the course and cross over with it. At the other side, turn right and go towards the five furlong marker on the part of the course that is coming from the left. Duck under the rails, cross, under the other rails and you are on the Knavesmire. It is public land with pitches for various sports, surrounded by trees and inside the ring of trees, is very flat. This land has cost a great deal of money for York to drain and the race-course has benefited too. However, although the race-course has also poured a vast amount of cash into improving the facilities over the last 16-17 years it remains a "flat only" race-course because of drainage problems that might occur in winter which have discouraged those with ideas to complete the circuit. So the course remains a very big horseshoe.

As you walk down the side of the finishing straight and before you come to the stands, you will find a small stile which lets you onto the course. So climb over, walk down past the winning post, out at the far end and over to the right and to the road whenever you feel like it. The objective is the Tadcaster Road that is way in front, which once reached is the place to turn right to walk back towards the city centre.

As you get nearer the walls, the pubs, cafes, sandwich shops and hotels begin to appear. After The Mount, the Bay Horse and then, at the crossroads, the Windmill, with designer bars and a restaurant. Another, diagonally opposite, has a pleasant little garden to drink in if the weather is fine. Go through the archway in front of you, which is Micklegate Bar, to find the Bar Hotel at the other side which starts a run of pubs all the way down Micklegate.

It is here that you cross the road and go up the steps to walk along the wall again, along what is the highest section above the road or outside land. Continue until just after Hudson House, named appropriately after the railway engineer and owner, like one or two places in York which still hang on to the railway city image, and then go down the steps that you used to gain access to the wall near the beginning. Go back under the arch and cross the road to the left. Walk past the cholera epidemic cemetery and you are back, opposite the railway station.

By now you must be wondering if it is safe to take my word, so let me quote King George VI, who said "The history of York is the history of England". And he should know, because he was the Duke of York before he reluctantly took the Crown.

Now a secret. Not many people know about the 17th century Treasurer's House behind the Minster, and it is one to add to your list of reasons for wanting to spend another day or two in York. Get there before everyone knows.

Chapter Twenty-five

Huggate

Still feels like the old farming village, with the best collection of Wold walks

You could say that four, five, or six roads fan out from Huggate, depending on whether you allow for roads branching off just outside the village. This gives you the idea that this village was a meeting point, the focal point of Wold village and farm life in this area. The village is small and the absence of any shop makes it seem inconsequential, until you see the size of the farms here. It does have a 14th century church, St. Mary's, that boasts a tower with battlements. The village green is quite large and has a deep well on one side of it.

The Wolds Inn, Huggate

It is obviously a central point for walkers even if the planners of the Wolds Way tried to miss it. All to no effect as every one that I have met who has "done" the Wolds Way has made the short detour, all of an extra half mile to Huggate. The only risk in such a detour is the possibility of picking the wrong yellow arrows from the dozens that seem to surround the village. Add to that the fact that the Huggate Dikes, earthworks outside the village, are believed to have been dug by Ancient Britons and that there is a very old well here that is 339 feet deep and you know that you are in a small community that is well able to survive the passing of time and cares not for change.

Any walk from here should start from the pub, now that it is open at lunchtime seven days a week. It is a friendly sort of place (and the landlord doesn't mind you parking there if you ask him). Besides which, the drink and the food is good. And if you think you cannot manage the large helpings in the evening and you are staying the night, the inexpensive red house wine in litre bottles is quite drinkable.

Actually, staying the night isn't always easy. During the fine weather months – don't ask me which those are as I haven't been able to work it out – the four bedrooms, which are very comfortable and all have their own bathroom, are usually booked in advance, so forward planning will be required.

Having said that – to the walk!

The Walk

The Route: Wolds Inn – Wold House Farm – join Wolds Way from Fridaythorpe – Northfield Road – Huggate – Wolds Inn

Map: O.S. map 106

The start and how to find it: the centre of the village; map reference 883550

What the walk is like: Mild ups and downs in open country

Distance: 6 miles.

From the Wolds Inn car park, turn right and right again down the village street passing the church that is over on your right and then pass the cul-de-sac sign. Then pass Southfield on your left and beside the gate just after Southfield, there is a stile. Climb over it

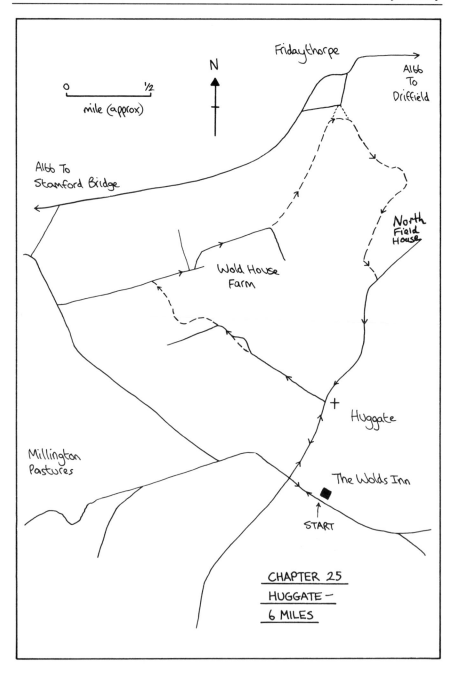

and walk towards Glebe Farm, the farm you can see near the top of the hill in front and slightly to your right. This line brings you to a gate in the bottom of the field and once through that, onto the road which you take to the left. When you come to the right turn that heads for the farmhouse, take the path in front of you. It is clearly marked and fenced and also cuts off just a few yards bringing you out onto the road again after the houses.

At the next bend in the road, signposts point to the left and also straight on, which is the one to follow. Keep to this bridleway with the hedge on your right all the way along until you come to a fence in front of you that runs along the top edge of the Dale down below. Walk along it to the left up to the point where there is a short section of wooden fence on your right which is meant to make it easier for you to get over and go down into the dale. It does to a certain extent but be aware when you are climbing over that the wire below is sometimes electrified. The path from that point goes down and to the left and after crossing to the other side passes two ash trees. Eighty yards further on, by a hawthorn, climb the stile to your right and then walk up the smaller dale or valley that comes into the one you have just crossed.

At the top, in the corner a metal gate is almost next to a wooden gate and between the two a stile that takes you onto a path to follow all the way alongside the fence and hedge until you reach a metalled road to Wold House Farm, so turn right. As you approach the farm you may see that the farmer is intently watching what is happening. Do not fail to greet him, he is the great uncle of the lady that now lives at the farm. That done, turn to the left and around the back of the buildings that are to the left of the farmhouse. It brings you into the old stackyard and as you turn right you have a Dutch barn on your left in the middle of an immaculate farmyard, that demonstrates efficiency and good management. Now head for the gap in the trees in front of you. Go through this gap and walk ahead, ignoring the turn to the right. You are now striding over Huggate Wold in the direction of Fridaythorpe, first through a gap in the hedge and into the second field, continuing along the track, then through the next hedgerow to turn left and go to the left-hand boundary of this third field. Now go right to follow the hedge that is on your left to a white metal gate. Once through the gate, a scrape of the ice age, downwards into the bottom of the dale, is an effective guide as to the path to take, turning right at the bottom to walk along what is a section of the Wolds Way.

When you think you are at the end of one valley and about to join another, a wire fence appears up the centre of the dale. Go to the left and do not be tempted to go right. Further on is the reason, the meeting of three paths and a stile at the left-hand end of some collecting pens. So over the stile and then turn right and after a short distance go left up the cut path that slopes up the hill, from about opposite the end of the pens. Just at the place where the dale below curves right, a path goes at a right angle to the left. Take it and go through the gap at the top, next to the ash tree. Use the gate, a gap, anything, just avoid the stile which has been very near lethal for at least a year now. Take the path across the field in front of you by following the hedge which should be on your right. Over on your left you will see woodland which is in fact that three sides of a square protection belt, that is so common around Wold farms. This one is around the house and buildings of Northfield House Farm. If you keep on going, the path will bring you to the farm road that comes up from Huggate to this Northfield. Turn right and walk towards the village. First a path will join you from the left, then as you go uphill, a road goes off to the right. But then at the top of the hill the village comes into view once more. And how tranquil it all is; what a lovely place to come home to. But all too soon, you are at the crossroads and a left turn has you back at the Wolds Inn in no time. I do hope they are still open.

Chapter Twenty-six

Great Driffield

Self-proclaimed capital of the Wolds, with cake shops that overcome your good intentions

This pleasant red-brick market town has somehow managed to keep its old fashioned air alongside all the usual amenities of modern living. It is a remarkable contrast to Hawes, seen as its counterpart in the North Riding. The most likely reasons are the type of farming that is and was so different in each place and the people who fill the town, more tourists in one than the other. Driffield had quite a few reasons for feeling that it is the capital, although it is only two hundred years ago that it was merely a large village with about a tenth of its present population of nine thousand.

Skiffs racing on the Driffield Canal

Solving the problems that beset the canal lock gates in 1772 was apparently significant. The place was already the collecting point for produce from the Wold farms making improved transportation to bigger centres essential. And it was at this time that Wesley preached here, encouraging the Non-Conformists take a bigger part in local affairs, the direct result being that they became a powerful force as trade grew. The town then got a post office, the roads grew with the town and finally, seventy years later, the railway arrived. All these improvements in communications not only made the town develop as a service centre for the farming area all around, it also became a dreadful bottle-neck for traffic and stayed like that until the mid-eighties when the by-pass was opened.

It is like Hawes in one respect especially. The market has shrunk in size, but here it is because there is less stock raising being done now and you don't take your cereal crop to market. But there has been some growth in agricultural engineering businesses. Not a surprising fact when you see the size and complexity of the modern machinery at work in the Wolds.

To see the town, the most convenient place to park is in the cattle market yard, which offers free parking on all days except market day, Thursday.

The Walk

The Route: Driffield – canal path – Wansford – Skerne – Driffield

Map: O.S. map 107.

The start and how to find it: The cattle market car park is approached on the B1249 from which there are adequate signposts and markers. Starting with a walk through the town, which will probably persuade you to explore further, later on, it then takes a short walk in the country. Map reference 026576.

Distance: 6 miles (total).

From the parking area, walk towards the covered area of the market and then down to the left to the bridge over the Beck. A twitch to right and left will have you walking up an alleyway called Providence Place that comes out on the main road at "Market Place", the section between Middle Street North and Middle Street South, next

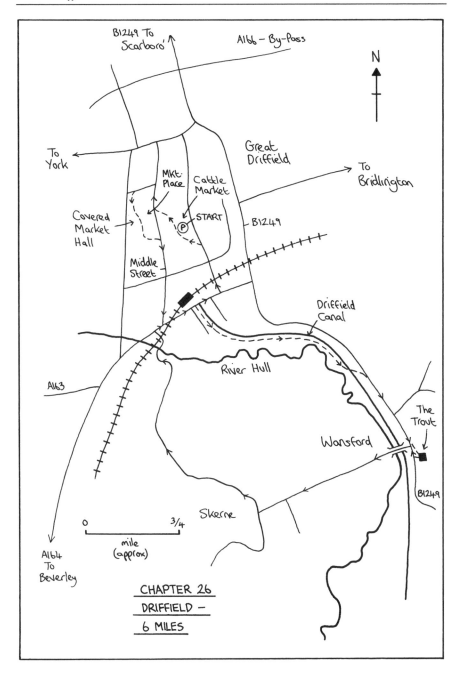

B1249 To Scarboro'

A166 – By-Pass

N

Great Driffield

To York

Mkt· Place

Cattle Market

START

Covered Market Hall

B1249

To Bridlington

Middle Street

Driffield Canal

River Hull

A163

The Trout

Wansford

B1249

Skerne

0   3/4

mile (approx)

A164 To Beverley

CHAPTER 26

DRIFFIELD –

6 MILES

to the Falcon Inn. You will see its front as you turn right and walk up to The Bell Hotel. This street is certainly the busiest but by no means the only street, as you will see if you turn left and cross the street to go up the road opposite, Mill Street, with first a charity shop on the left and a pub called the Full Measure, at the top. Opposite the pub and so on your left is the entrance to the market and library car park.

Next to the gate, the Information Board at the gateway on the right might interest you. It tells that what is now the town was situated where Turnpikes from Bridlington to Howden and Scarborough to Beverley crossed. It also repeats what I have heard said many times, that its Annual Agricultural Show is the best in the East Riding. So turn and go on to the market hall and see if that comes up to standard. Next, go left and walk down the row of shops under the arches to come out again on the main street with a greengrocers to your right, and walk back down the street to the end opposite the level crossing. You will have seen all the types of shops you might need, plus banks, estate agents and pubs and could not possibly have missed the baker's shops with such delicious cakes. Cafes are a little harder to find on this street but I can recommend The Bell for morning coffee in the open room in the centre. But now, a short walk in the country.

Go over the level crossing at the side of the station, having passed the Railway Tavern and The Sidings. After Halstead Printers, cross the road to the right so that as you approach Riverside court, you can turn right to walk along the front of the building. At the far end of what they call Riverhead and is actually the canal head you can start by walking along the edge, passing a hand operated crane which is still in good working order, before taking to the metalled road. A bungalow appears with what looks like its own dock and the path carries on to the right-hand side and then through a gate to walk through what is almost flat land between the canal and the River Hull which is on your right. Like the land between those water courses, the land immediately on the other side is for the most part grazing and after that arable land almost 90% cereal as far as you can see. With the trees in this shallow valley and the low hills at the start of the Wolds to the left, the effect is elysian, so acutely English, with almost total quiet.

Too soon, you draw near to the road and then a stile and a bridge which goes over a sluice gate. Due to some local difficulty, it is not possible to walk along the canal after the next bridge which goes to the left over the lock leaving you to go right on the Driffield to Skipsea road. You then walk the mile ahead to reach Wansford. Fortunately, it is not particularly busy, except at weekends and there is the attraction at Wansford of the Trout Inn. This is a pub that serves a very good lunch at a reasonable price and Theakston's Bitter, but has the odd distinction these days of having only a six day licence, not opening at all on Sundays. Wansford doesn't take much walking through, most of the houses being on the road to the left that goes to Nafferton. On the main road, which has a little bit of canal bank that you can walk on, you pass the Post Office and a road junction, cross the road to take advantage of the footpath and walk on through the next two bends in the road and you are at the Trout.

When you leave there, retrace your steps part way round the first bend in the road as far as the minor road to Skerne. It is now on your left and goes over the canal and the river before settling into a minor road saunter for about a mile to the small village of Skerne. On the way you will pass the farm at Golden Hill – I reckon there is about as much gold here as there are hills in the immediate vicinity. The village looks peaceful and neat, which probably means dull as it seems to be the only Yorkshire village that has no road through to anywhere of importance, but has three roads out of it. In addition, the pub doesn't open most lunchtimes. However, taking the first right in the middle of the village and the next left will get you back on track to the cosiness of Driffield.

A mile takes you to a right turn and three hundred yards more to the mill, complete with race. Does it still provide its own power from the River Hull? Regretfully not, which is a shame when the race is in good condition with ample water. Plus the fact that I know the owner of an abandoned mill who runs a large generator by the water power and sells the electricity to the Irish Electricity Supply Board. So far we have been idling through pleasantly relaxing scenery, now it is industry and you are suddenly back in town.

Then, regrettably, an abandoned factory and office unit. Not unusual in other towns but the first one to be seen on this route. Keep on to the level crossing and turn right after crossing it to the next crossing and right again. Yes, you did cross it before but this time go past the flats at the riverhead. Pass the Blue Bell Inn on your left, another mill of Bradshaw's that has been converted to flats on your right and then ahead, on your right, a period house of some prominence. Here you turn left into East Gate South, go along a little way and over the footbridge. You will come to a corner where it joins Albion Street and there go right and left to continue along East Gate until a lane on the left says it is Bridge Street and is fairly well-marked by The Mariners Arms opposite. Go down it, cross the beck, go right and by turning right again, cross the beck once more. There you see the car park is next to you on the left. The question is, have you enough time to go back into the Main Street and buy some fresh bread and cakes and then go through the indoor market to the streets behind to see a little more of Great Driffield, or do you chicken out and just have a quiet drink in the comfort of The Bell?

Chapter Twenty-seven

Beverley

Sir John Betjeman had it right when he said:
"A place made for walking and living in"

As soon a you start to walk around Beverley, you understand
Betjeman's feelings and find it easy to agree with him. The town
is busy but has a pace of its own; in the middle of a crowded and
busy day, a refuge is always at hand, a quiet lane, a peaceful garden,
or the wide spaces of the Westwood.

Beverley gets its name from the Beaver – or *beofor* – and *leah*, a
clearing in woodland, but that seems to have little relevance when
you discover that it was around 700 AD with direct connections to
the Minster and St John of Beverley that the town became well-
known and started to grow. St. John had retired and came to live in
the monastery here, bringing his reputation for miracles with him.
It was a reputation so widely known that pilgrims started to flock to
the town. Catering for the visitors' needs became a sizeable business
as the food and drink, plus most of the building materials required
to provide accommodation had to be brought to the town. Fortunately, the Beck and the River Hull were ideal for transporting the
bulk and gave access to the Humber, so Beverley became a port.

And while commerce flourished, so did the Minster (before
1066!); Beverley made cloth, tanned leather, and had a dye works
(thus Dyer Lane, between Walkergate and Saturday Market) and so
too, of course, did the population. In the late 14th century when
nearly 5000 people lived in the town, it was half the size of York
and twice as big as Hull.

The town did not have a wall but used a ditch as a protective
boundary with entrance and exit only via the Bars, or gates. Only
North Bar survives and that has been rebuilt a time or two. Outside
was pasture, but of the five or six main areas just the Hurn and the
Westwood remain. The Westwood also provided wood and clay for
brick making, as well as chalk and lime. And during this time of

South-side columns of the nave at Beverley Minster

steady development, the central feature of the town's history, the Minster, was burnt down and had the tower collapse. The rebuilt Minster that you now see was completed after 160 years of work, in 1395, but is still acclaimed as one of the three greatest Gothic churches in Europe.

The town that you see now really started in Georgian times when architects seemed to be trying to create a smaller model of York, even including Assembly Rooms and a race-course. It still has many elegant buildings and is one of the reasons that a walk around the town can be so fascinating.

The Walk

The Route: Beverley cattle market – St Mary's – through town (as sketch map) to Minster – Millitary Transport Museum – Long Lane – Westwood – Beverley

Map: O.S. 107, or the town map (free from the Tourist Information Office)

The start and how to find it: Car parking is not difficult. I suggest the cattle market car park by the side of New Walkergate, the main road on the west side of the town. All parking is free in Beverley, but this is the biggest parking area and you can stay all day. Map reference 037398

Distance: 4 miles.

On the pavement with your back to the cattle market, go to the right. You can see the bus station opposite, but go a little further before crossing the road so that you can see the old Regal cinema. Where the front of this building is now, once stood the Assembly Rooms which marked the centre of social life in Beverley. Assemblies were held fortnightly during the winter in the John Carr designed building. and those attending were asked to observe the strict rules of etiquette. Now cross the road and walk down Hengate. The first thing you are likely to notice is the sign of the White Horse, the inn known throughout the East Riding as Nellie's, after one of the sisters who owned and ran it for so long and who also refused to have electricity put in. I think it was finally put in when the lager "dispensers" needed it to pump out the drink many of her customers demanded. At the end of Hengate is a church so beautifully proportioned that sometimes a visitor mistakes it for the Minster. This is St Mary's church and if you want a closer look, there will be a better

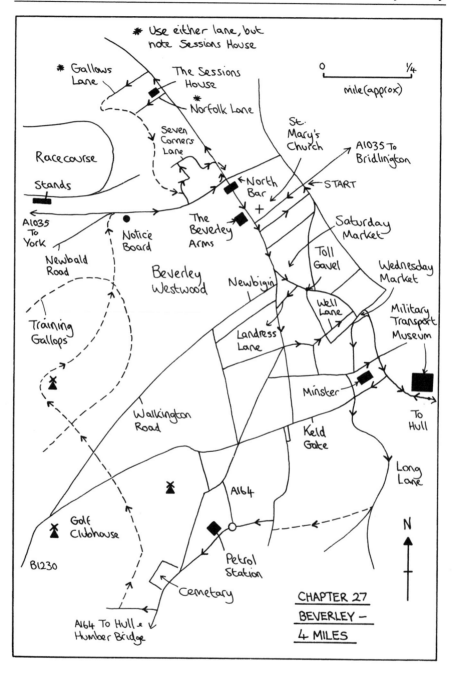

✳ Use either lane, but note Sessions House

✳ Gallows Lane

The Sessions House

Norfolk Lane

0 ———— ¼
mile (approx)

Seven Corners Lane

St. Mary's Church

A1035 To Bridlington

Racecourse

Stands

North Bar

START

A1035 To York

Notice Board

The Beverley Arms

Saturday Market

Newbald Road

Beverley Westwood

Toll Gavel

Wednesday Market

Newbigin

Training Gallops

Landress Lane

Well Lane

Military Transport Museum

Minster

To Hull

Walkington Road

Keld Gate

Long Lane

A164

N

Golf Clubhouse

B1230

Petrol Station

Cemetery

CHAPTER 27
BEVERLEY –
4 MILES

A164 To Hull & Humber Bridge

opportunity later as the route of the walk passes here towards the end.

For now, turn left and by walking down this short stretch of road, arrive at the Saturday market. There is a Wednesday market further along, but as the town expanded, most of the developing was done on the north side of town and so the market moved too, to keep up with the people. Here is the Market Cross, the second one to stand here and built in 1712. Keep going straight ahead, southwards, and there is a pub on the left called The Push. As it just isn't possible for you to visit every pub in Beverley during a short stay, I leave it to you to pick the one in which you take that drop of refreshment. Round the corner to the left you will see the old Corn Exchange, which is now a cinema. From there go to the top right-hand corner of the square where the pedestrianised area begins, noting the shops, cafes and bakers. This is Toll Gavel and along on the right is a small opening into Landress Lane, one of many lanes typical of the town's layout that has been preserved. In fact it is only recently that this lane has been restored. At the end of it, turn left along Lairgate passing some sound-looking smaller town houses until you come to the next turn to the left, Champney Road. Before turning, look over to the right. The big house set back a little is known locally as Admiral Walker House after the last occupant. Besides its fine exterior, there are some splendid rooms inside that may be visited by asking permission at the house, which is now the property of Beverley Borough Council. The dining room and the Chinese room should be seen, especially the hand painted Chinese wallpaper in the latter. Now go down Champney Road (the Library is on your right) cross Cross Street and go down the lane in front of you which is Well Lane. This brings you into the area called Wednesday Market.

Take the first turn on the right, Highgate, and walk down to the Minster. Tea shops and galleries are along this street, together with a bookshop and a Victorian style arcade. Very soon you are confronted by the North Porch of the Minster and inside it you will be able to obtain comprehensive guides to help you round this magnificent building. The proportions of the pillars down the nave are quiet awesome.

On leaving, turn right along Minster Yard North, turn right again and you are at the bottom of Eastgate. One of Beverley's more recent attractions is the Museum of military transport, on the site of one of the old tanneries, an industry no longer carried on in the town. The museum has a large array of vehicles with everything from dispatch riders' bikes to a Blackburn Beverley transport plane. To get to it, follow this road around the bend and you come into Flemingate. On the corner is the 16th century Sun Inn, reputedly the oldest surviving inn in Beverley, refurbished though it might be. Then on the way towards the level crossing you will see a part-timbered building next to the Nelson Inn. Opposite there is a garden with a spire, which is believed to be one from the Minster.

Should you have time after leaving the Museum, about half a mile further down Flemingate are houses numbered 56 and 58 which were originally one house. This is the site of the one time Bishop of Rochester, John Fisher's birthplace. He was executed in 1535 for opposing the religious policy of Henry VIII. The present house wasn't built until 1630.

Now retrace your steps all the way back to the Minster, but take the Minster Yard South lane and walk along the opposite side of that fine building to the one you walked before, going round to the west door to see all the carvings before turning left off Minster Yard South to go down Long Lane. Walk through the S-bend and you soon start to find yourself among fields to remind you that Beverley is a compact town surrounded on nearly all sides by countryside. Then, as Long Lane starts to make a turn to the left, there is the path to take on the right which starts in the driveway of a house. Go through this and continue on the lane ahead. To your right, an old farm building is looking the worse for wear in the middle of the field and is probably a sign that the developers are on the way. In fact after a stile the path that goes right has you walking alongside a fairly pleasant bit of housing development. At the end of Lincoln Lane, the path you have been walking along, turn and go up to the roundabout. Take the road to the left and when on it, cross the road. Pass the filling station, then the cemetery and go another 200 to 250 yards to a path that starts on the right and has a white house on the left of the opening. There is an open area on the right with a wooden fence along it and within 10 yards a gap to take you onto the path that goes to the right. It then makes a right-angled turn to the left and you are confronted with a stile. The path goes on along the hedgerow on your right and over the field to the gate at the far end. Turn right when you are through it and follow the path through the wooded area that surrounds an old quarry. Back on the field edge and to the next gate with a stile. Once over it, you are on the Westwood, go straight ahead (a path is faintly visible) with the Minster away on your right and the Golf Club with the tower of an old windmill in the middle of it, to your left.

As you near the road you can see, between the trees, another mill tower, so head for that. Over two roads, then up to the mill noticing, no doubt, the exercise gallop on the way. At the mill, you can see the race-course quite plainly and also get a good view towards the town with the tower of St. Mary's quite prominent. When you start to go down the other side, aim for the red roof of a house in the trees to your right and to the left of the town. This will take you over another part of the gallop which goes around the hill top in a complete circle.

After that the path is obvious and will take you, via tree lined roads and a very informative noticeboard with some of the history of this common pasture, to the very gates of the Westwood. On a wall by the gates, the Rules, By-laws and Orders pertaining to the grazing have been restored and refixed here by the Beverley and District Civic Society. The short length of York Road that remains at this point passes Pasture Terrace on the right and a new development of small houses on the left. Both places had racing stables not all that long ago. In the latter, Billy Hammett once trained, definitely on the list of Beverley's characters. Next, a timbered pub, the Rose and Crown. Turn left here and start to walk up North Bar Without. This road changes its name at frequent intervals and as you reach the Sessions House, the building currently being used as a Crown Court and local police headquarters, it becomes New Walk, a fashionable promenade in the 18th century.

Just after that, turn left into Norfolk Street. Walk to the end and you will be on the Hurn, an area of ancient pasture now part of the Westwood, so turn left again and walk towards the York road. Just before you reach it go over the stile on the left into Seven Corners Lane and go to the left following the footpath sign. The houses tucked away down here make it an interesting diversion and will in any case take you back to North Bar Without. Turn right when you get there and go through the Bar – notice the long thin shape of the bricks – and if you are on the left-hand side of the road you are about to pass Beverley's best ice-cream parlour. On the other side are Coronation Gardens and the Beverley Arms, the town's principle hotel.

Now comes your opportunity to have a closer look at St. Mary's; it is well worth any time you spend there. Its west front is similar to that of King's College Chapel, Cambridge but was built earlier. Inside, the proportions appear perfect. But spare a minute or two to look for the mouse and the white rabbit. On leaving, go left and down as far as Saturday Market to turn left and walk along Sow Hill to the bus station. Go right and cross the road and you are back where you started. All you need to do now is figure out how and when you can get back here to investigate the place in more detail.

Chapter Twenty-eight

Hull

. . . or Kingston upon Hull to give it the name it has
had since 1293, when created a port by Edward I

I spent my early years only a few miles from this city and thought
of it as the world's biggest fish and chip shop at the end of the
longest railway siding. The trawler fleet has gone, even if the siding
is still there. Hessle road will never be the same again although there
might be the odd fishing boat left. Most of the docks have gone and
some of the industries too and yet. . .

If it is your first visit, you might get the impression that this is a
modern town, but that is only because of the rebuilding necessary
after the Luftwaffe gave it a more concentrated pounding than either
Coventry and London. So you see a different city, a city geared more
to the people as the activities that drive the town now are no longer
the traditional industries. Visitors are catered for as never before and
although the place looks busy, a more relaxed atmosphere is apparent.

Stand in Queen Victoria Square and you feel more in the centre
of a city than any other I know. On one side the City Hall on the
other, Queen's Gardens. Between them the Town Docks Museum
and Whitefriargate. Opposite that, the latest pedestrianised shopping areas including the latest development of completely modernised shops in King Edward Street and Jameson Street. Near to
Prince's dock, with its fountains and hideous concoction called a
shopping centre is a large children's bookshop and then a jewel of
a gallery, the Ferens Art Gallery – certainly worth a visit.

Nearer to the river, the Humber dock is now a marina, well-run
and popular and now bordered by updated pubs and restaurants,
flats and boutiques. East from the lock gates will take you to the pier
from which the paddle powered ferries ran 'til the Humber bridge
was built. It is also the way to the parish church, the old town with

Civic Buildings, Hull

other museums, including the home of William Wilberforce, the slave emancipator, and the River Hull.

The people are friendly enough and have an easily recognised accent, their command of the language often being heard at its best when watching Hull R.L.C. or Kingston Rovers. But then they have an inheritance there as well, for the 17th century poet Andrew Marvell was born in Winestead and lived in Hull, the tradition he set – living on. Philip Larkin, though not born in Yorkshire spent most of his working life as Librarian of the University of Hull – and Huddersfield calls itself the poetry capital of the north!

Amy Johnson came from Hull, the woman who made the record-breaking flight to Australia in 1930. So did Tom Boyd, one of the heroes at St Nazarre, said to be one of the most daring raids of the 1939-45 war, the son of the founder of the Boyd line of trawlers. Ian Carmichael, actor, William Wilberforce, slave emancipator, and Sir John Hotham who laid plans with other leading citizens in the Old White Hart to deny entry to King James or access to its considerable arsenal. Didn't do him much good as he had his head chopped off by Cromwell's lads a couple of years later. And do today's customers find that the chocolate flavoured condoms on sale in the loo at that same pub do them any good?

This walk is also in danger of being classed as very difficult, or even dangerous, as in my long-held opinion Hull has the finest collection of pubs in England.

No longer does Hessle Road smell of fish and the smoke houses, but no longer can I describe the place as that biggest fish and chip shop at the end of a very long railway siding. The city has changed for the better and I'll bet when you see the place and walk around it, it won't be anything like the place you imagined it to be. You are going to get a lot of surprises, and all of them pleasant.

Hull lost its county cricket fixture and the council struggles on to stop it going back to the East Riding. I cannot understand the former as Anlaby Road is a pleasanter ground than the one in Bradford, and as for the latter, I have heard it said that they must be getting overpaid or they are barmy. Possibly quite a few in both camps. Nothing that can't be sorted out. So start, and try to finish, the walk and see the good points. More are sure to follow.

The Walk

The Route: Paragon Station – Queen Victoria Square – Marina – Old Town – Guildhall – Queens Gardens – Jameson Street Station

Map: Hull is on O.S. map 107 but the City map available from the tourist office and most stationers will give you the details.

The start and how to find it: From M62 & A63T follow signs to City Centre & Station. Parking 100yds on left. Alternatively leave car at Brough station taking one of the regular trains to Hull. Start immediately outside station. Map Reference 093288

What the walk is like: The walk is easy on level ground, but please take great care.

Distance: About 3 miles.

Start at Paragon Square, with your back to the Royal Station Hotel (it is conveniently close to car parks, the railway station and the bus station) and cross the road. Go right across the front of the two banks behind the Cenotaph, then turn left and go down Paragon Street. Immediately to your right is one of those pubs that expatriates try to copy in Spain, Malta or almost anywhere where there are a lot of Brits (bar Jeddah). It is called The Sandringham, is spotlessly clean but dark. One long room, a bare wooden floor, dark solid wood furnishings, pictures of Queen Victoria, mirrors and sepia prints. It has everything, including good beer. No food though, which at least gives me the chance to tell you about the Scotsman who went into a Glasgow pub and asked for a pint of heavy and a packet of crisps. "Crisps", says the horrified barman, "crisps, what do you think this is? A bloody restaurant?"

Outside again and you will see there isn't much modernisation here so a few old shop fronts have survived. Then having passed the Portland Hotel, the only totally new building here, some of us can mourn the passing of the Tivoli theatre that once stood here (and if anyone remembers Old Mother Riley, Arthur Lucan died in the wings there). Further on, on the right, the Paragon Arcade still survives with its specialist shops.

Now you come to the City Hall and the place where the old meets the new. Go across the Square, but stop halfway to turn and admire the front of the City Hall. Now go across to the right and note Ferens

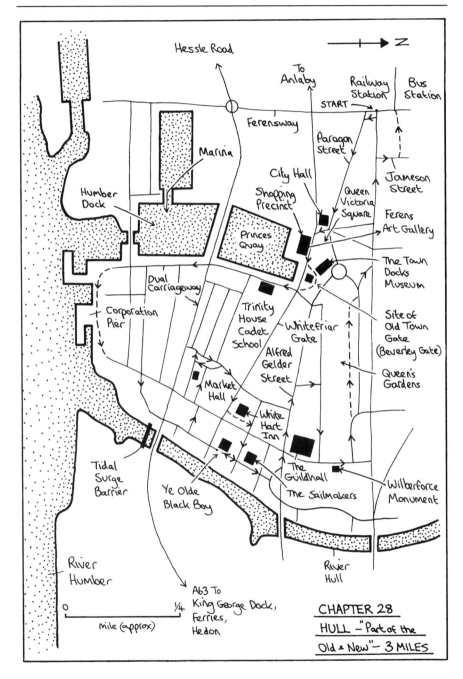

Hessle Road

To Anlaby

Railway Station
START

Bus Station

Ferensway

Paragon Street

Jameson Street

Marina

City Hall

Queen Victoria Square

Ferens Art Gallery

Humber Dock

Shopping Precinct

Princes Quay

The Town Docks Museum

Dual Carriageway

Site of Old Town Gate (Beverley Gate)

Corporation Pier

Trinity House Cadet School

Whitefriar Gate

Queen's Gardens

Alfred Gelder Street

Market Hall

White Hart Inn

Tidal Surge Barrier

Ye Olde Black Boy

The Guildhall

The Sailmakers

Wilberforce Monument

River Humber

A63 To King George Dock, Ferries, Hedon

River Hull

0   ¼
mile (approx)

CHAPTER 28
HULL — "Part of the
Old & New" — 3 MILES

Art Gallery. The shops between the Gallery and the iron railings of Prince's Dock once housed a fantastic wet fish shop, Monument Fisheries, who always had a wonderful display on a slab angled at about 30 degrees, and also "Our Maureen's Dad's tailor's shop" – the lady admired much more than the casual reference implies being the actress and comedienne, Maureen Lipman.

Opposite the railings is a protected site where the foundations of one of the old town gates, the Beverley gate, has been found, while in the dock where trawlers were once refitted, fountains play. So take the next turn on the right and walk down beside the dock, passing on your left the Trinity House Training College for possible future officers of the Merchant Navy. Then come places of refreshment, the Quayside and then the Waterfront Hotel, mere starters in temptation in a city steeped in seafaring of one kind or another and used to thirsty sailors. Then after a busy Posterngate leading to another shopping area, a dual carriageway to cross. At the other side, the old Spurn Light Vessel which you may inspect if you wish and the marina. By the size and the range of boats in this marina, Hull is not a depressed city and it does make you feel that things are getting better. Look to your left down Humber Street, centre of wholesale fruit and veg market, always busy, frenetically so in the early morning, and as colourful as Covent Garden ever was.

At the end of the marina dock (Humber Dock) there are lock gates and the management tower. There is also a flashy looking Cafe Bar and Restaurant. On the other side of the road is the Minerva. Turn left there and also note the small brewhouse next to the pub, the home of "Pilot's Pride" ale. This is Nelson Street and little remains of the pier where not long ago you could drive on or off the side paddle ferries that went from here to New Holland in Lincolnshire. "A foreign land", a local called it as we looked out over the river. Easy to agree when the river is fast flowing and two miles wide at this point. Just past the pier is a statue of Sir William Delapole, the first mayor of Hull between 1332 and 1335.

At the other side of the square, the River Hull joins the Humber. This was the centre of trade and wealth and called King's Town upon the River Hull, the port that traded with those across the North Sea and left the grid of narrow streets that is now the old town.

At the corner with the river pilots' offices, and opposite the statue, turn left and go down Queen Street. You can see Holy Trinity Church from here but take the first on the right, down the Eastern half of

Humber Street towards the Tidal Surge Barrier. At the bend in the road on the right you can see the "Manxman", the old Isle of Man ferry, now on its final mooring as it is fitted out to become a hotel and restaurant.

Follow the road to the left and go under the road bridge and take the next on the left, Liberty Lane. To your left at the end is Market Place, worth a walk down to see the gilded horse and rider. This is Hull's King Billy, William the Third, and whether they rode without stirrups in those days or the town just couldn't afford them, I couldn't say. The establishment opposite has been selling fine ales and porter since 1834 and is called the King William – what else? So cross the road and turn right passing a nice little pub, The Old Corn Exchange and then the Eastern end of the city's' main church, Holy Trinity. Even from the outside you can see that it has some fine old stained glass. After it, turn down North Church Side. On the right is one of the entrances to the covered market, another temptation for explorers. When you get to the end of this street, if it is between 12 and 4, you have a good chance of seeing inside the church by going left around the end to the south door. If not, there is a tea room in case all these pubs are worrying you, called the Trinity Tea Shop and in any case you need to turn right at the Kingston. It is very bad to find large churches closed. After all, the nave holds regimental colours from the area that recruited men to fight – and die – to maintain, among other freedoms, speech and prayer. So even if a charge for entry must be made (perhaps odd in a city where admission to all the museums is free) to cover the cost of the security that these times demand, it should be open at least in daylight hours.

The route is now a zig zag, which is simple if you note the names, clearly marked on the corners of buildings. First down Trinity Street to the junction with Whitefriargate and Silver Street, some of the big stores to the left, accountants and insurance offices to the right, turn right along the latter. Part way down, turn left down the alleyway marked Ye Olde White Harte, established in 1550 (info board at the entrance). In and out of the pub and to the other end into Bowlalley Lane where printers, estate agents lurk among other offices. Turn right, cross Lowgate in front of you and go down Bishop Lane that is opposite. A very typical old town lane, with the buildings in good original shape. Then turn right at the end. This is High Street.

First, I recommend a visit to Ye Olde Black Boy, even though this means turning right to go to it and then left when you come out to go back along most of High Street. Then, on the right, you might get a glimpse of the old Staithes onto the River Hull and on the left a popular family pub The Sailmakers built on the site of a ship's chandlers. Just after that the Maister's House, once the home of influential merchants, the Maister family, it was destroyed by a fire in 1743 in which the wife of the owner died. Rebuilt in 1744 it is basic Palladian at the front. Only the entrance hall and staircase is open to the public to see the rich ornamentation inside. The East Riding Museum is here, and further along is the Transport Museum and then Wilberforce House with two adjoining Georgian houses, making a fine showpiece. The main house, built in the 1660s, is the birthplace of William Wilberforce, a member of a leading merchant family and slave emancipator. Try and visit and look around so you can start to feel the pride that this man stirs.

Now take the road to the left with the big new modern block, Wilberforce Court on your right. This is George Yard, turn left at the end of it and you will see the eastern end of the Guildhall, Hull City council's offices, a most impressive building, almost overpowering. Is this why Betjeman and others have said it puts the Reichstag in the shade? In front of it is a statue of the first baron Nunburnholme, Charles Henry Wilson, whose family once owned one of Englands biggest merchant fleets. Now walk up the left-hand side of this outstanding building, along Alfred Gelder Street with the Post Office across the road and then on the corner of Manor Street, the Burlington Tavern, conveniently next to the offices of a firm of solicitors. The tavern is painted black and white, the offices, timbered black and white. In the 70s, the senior partner, the late Sir Robert Payne, was President of the Law Society. Next to those offices is a high modern block in vivid contrast, which I am sure wouldn't have worried Sir Bob whose open mind, dry sense of humour, ability to see all sides of things and persuade others of their proper order, won him the respect of many.

On that side of the road, Parliament Street is next along after those office and has a very well-restored Victorian terrace. While on this side, at the end of the Guildhall, turn right and walk into Queen's Garden which is ahead of you. Go along to the right, just for a good view of the Wilberforce Monument, which had to be moved when the roundabout it was on, started to sink. Can you imagine the job that was? After that, turn to the left and go down the shaded path along the other side of the gardens and head for the cafe. As you come out of the cafe, go to the right, passing the pond with some pretty big fish and out of the gardens at the corner there, over the car park, left past the Rugby Tavern, then right and left on Queen's Dock Avenue – a reminder that you have just walked across what was once a dock – and the end of Saville Street, to the point where George Street meets Jameson Street. From here you can see down Prospect Street to the Central Library. But your route is down Jameson Street on the left, through a quickly-changing shopping area that is also pedestrianised for safe walking around the city centre. When you reach Hammond's, turn and walk to the right and you can see the Prospect Centre behind the Star of the West, take the next turn left towards C & A and in a few yards you are back at the main road, Ferensway, and opposite the starting point.

Chapter Twenty-nine

Brough

Roman fording point and home of the Buccaneer

Although the flat land adjacent to the rivers that flow into the Humber would have absorbed a lot of the flood waters, there must have been at least one deep channel. And yet the Romans made the Lincoln to York road cross at this point. Not all of it was by ferry boat; indeed proof has been offered over the years to show that men marched and waded across to Brough on the journey north.

A camp was established here which grew in importance until in 160 AD. A theatre was founded, the gift of Marcus Ulpius Ianuraius and the site was later to become important enough to warrant a magistrate as shown by the large cut blocks with inscriptions that have been found. It was possibly the Parisi capital at that time and appeared to reach its heyday in the mid to late 2nd century, then declining even before the Romans left.

Around the 13th and 14th centuries, stone was used from Brough for the staithes and sewers of Hull, and no doubt the haven existed and brought more river borne trade. But it wasn't until the very early 1900s that the village was to regain fame, when the son of a mowing machine manufacturer decided to build and fly aeroplanes. In fact, Robert Blackburn was building aircraft in Leeds, transporting them to the beach at Filey, putting them back together and flying them with success. When sales began to look promising he was sent off by his father to look for an airfield. Young Mr. Robert found a good flat site with the possibility that the river that was next to it could be used, and the story goes that the fact that it had a good hostelry helped with the making of the decision. Although Blackburn mono-planes had been used as training planes in the First World War they were float planes and were based at Windermere, before the factory at Brough was founded. But by 1925 four aircraft were in full production here, plus two on the secret list for the Admiralty and in 1928 Brough was licensed as a Civil Aerodrome for all types of machines.

A Buccaneer aircraft at Brough

From then on, Brough grew as Blackburn's factory grew, although by the late 30s labour was drawn from a wide area. Many famous aircraft were designed and built here and although a number were considered too heavy for the power unit(s) others such as the Skua played a big part in 1939-45 war. After the war came their most brilliant design, the Blackburn Buccaneer, but regrettably it did not fly until shortly after the death of the founder in September 1955. Then Hawker Aircraft bought the company from the two sons and today it is part of British Aerospace, still keeping the village on the map.

Equally noteworthy are the two village pubs with their names from history, The Ferry and The Buccaneer; The Humber Yawl Club with its clubhouse and moorings at the Haven, and the golf club with its beautifully sited course and impressive clubhouse. The village may be a mixture of labour for local industry and a dormitory for those who work in Hull, but the western side of the village does have something of an upmarket air as you are bound to notice in the first part of the walk.

The Walk

The Route: Brough Station – Golf course – Elloughton – approach to Welton airfield – river bank – Haven – Station

Map: O.S. map 106

The start and how to find it: a good place to start is at the railway station whether you come by train, car or bike as there is supervised parking there, currently at 50p for 24 hours. If you come by bus, you will have the opportunity to see a little more of the village and the shopping area as you walk to the station. Map reference 939266.

What the walk is like: Easy going through village, golf course, airfield and riverbank

Distance: About 5 miles.

Go out of the station yard by going right with the road; pass the two pubs already mentioned and the newsagents, to arrive at the mini roundabout. There, on the left, two cottages have the road sign Old Haven Road and the date 1840. The road is now Station Road and the cottage is no longer a Toll House. Take the road to the left, a road with many pleasant houses, and walk past the golf club. Although I have played (badly) the only time I have been on this course was to watch an exhibition round by a foursome that included Dai Rees and Norman Von Nida – in the late 40s if the names puzzle you.

Take the second turning on the right after the clubhouse, which you will find is Mill Lane West. More pricey-looking houses and you will see the course is on either side of this lane and when you reach the lane that crosses your front, there is one lane that goes into the "playing area" which must be a bit hazardous at the weekend. Your route is fortunately straight ahead along a tree lined path that goes to the road to Elloughton and passes an unusual castellated house on the right and a house on the left with a beautiful garden, soon to be sold for development. A sign of the times, but a shame when our villages are nibbled away by apparent greed.

Turn left and then go along a narrow tarmac path that opens up about 20 yards along on the right (keep an ear tuned for cycles) that again takes you through to a road. This time turn right, crossing the road to take advantage of the footpath. Walk along it for three quarters of a mile and as you approach the hill that precedes the bridge, watch out for the footpath on the right. There is a wide gateway with an iron gate into which has been welded a most

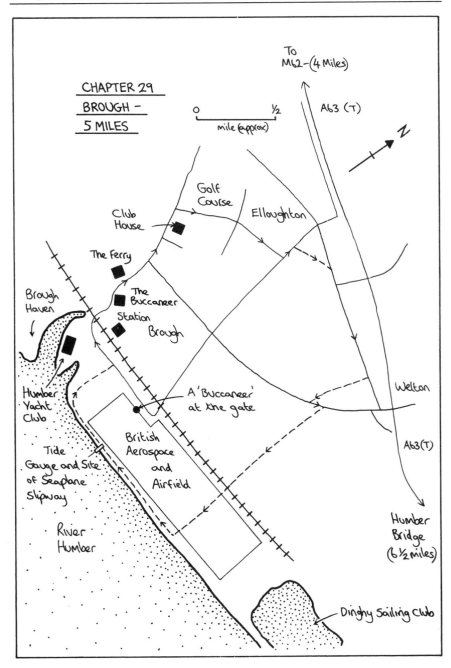

CHAPTER 29
BROUGH –
5 MILES

To
M62 – (4 Miles)

A63 (T)

N

0   ½
mile (approx)

Golf
Course

Elloughton

Club
House

The Ferry

Brough
Haven

The
Buccaneer

Station
Brough

A 'Buccaneer'
at the gate

Humber
Yacht
Club

Welton

Tide
Gauge and Site
of Seaplane
Slipway

British
Aerospace
and
Airfield

A63 (T)

River
Humber

Humber
Bridge
(6½ miles)

Dinghy Sailing Club

substantial looking stile, so you should not have any difficulty spotting it. Keep going straight ahead on through the fields. You will pass plastic covered hot houses on your right and then have the gable end of a house in front of you to aim for.

From this house, go to the right and walk along in front of the houses for about a hundred yards until you can turn left down Thorpe Road and walk to the main road at the bus shelter. Cross here and go to the left until you are opposite the end of Humber Crescent. There you will see a footpath sign to follow to the right over two fields to the railway line. Please exercise extreme caution as express trains·pass here. Fortunately the track is straight here so that you can see a fair distance. If you can see a train, even in the distance, do not cross as they go very fast along here.

When safely across, you will see that the path in front is taking you to an airfield. More warning signs here but less danger nowadays, although now that the Capper Pass chimney is down you might have expected more flying here. When the Buccaneer was being completed at Brough, it had to be towed to Holme on Spalding Moor airfield to fly as the chimney was too close to the flight path. This old smelting works had been operating for a long time and concern for local health was growing with many allegations regarding the effect it had on local children. So public opinion achieved what the aircraft industry could not. Now cross the airfield and the runways on a path that is well-worn and ends at the river bank. Here you can walk to the left or right. Go to the left and you will come to the old brick ponds where the dinghy sailing club is based, but you will need to retrace your steps. An odd piece of information that came to me via Humber Rescue, was that the Humber is second only to the Orinoco as the most treacherous river in the world. I would bet that is that it is definitely one of the dirtiest, so if you fall in you are in big trouble. If you open your mouth to shout you will be poisoned and if you don't, no one will know you are there and you will drown.

The route back is to the right and down on the water line you will see the old tidal gauge. This is where the slipway used to be, for the many flying boats and floatplanes that Blackburn's made. On your right, British Aerospace, but little to be seen. (there is a Buccaneer at the factory gates, which are to the right along the road you meet next). So by turning left at the road you go up and over the railway bridge, down steps on the right on the way down the other side of the bridge, through a yard by some cottages and out onto Station road, just opposite the Buccaneer pub. Turn right and you are back at the car park in just a few paces.

Chapter Thirty

Pontefract

Pomfret cakes, the hermit's cell and one hell of a finish

Strangely enough, I think I might owe my love of horse racing to "pomfret cakes". You see there used to be major manufacturers of liquorice and liquorice "sweets" in Pontefract. The business is still carried on but on a smaller scale, a business that is believed to have started when the Blackfriars brought the herb in the 13th century (incidentally, it is now imported in solid form). But then my father never missed a meeting at "Ponty", nor did he ever forget to bring me one of the green and gold tins of these little black cakes. It got the town off to a good start in my mind but it was some time before I grew to like the place as much for its places of interest as for the wide variety of little shops with their own specialities, some of them still surviving today.

But these delights do not reflect the rest of the town's history; in fact more gruesome events took place at Pontefract Castle than in any other Yorkshire castle. It was built by the Laceys, or de Laceys, and called at one time "the key of Yorkshire" and both Henry VIII and Queen Elizabeth I stayed there. Then it was reputedly magnificent with many handsome towers. But as centre stage in the power games of the time, less social occasions predominated. The "cast" in the history story included Thomas, Earl of Lancaster, beheaded after Boroughbridge 1322; Richard II, died in the dungeons of hunger, cold and thirst; and Archbishop Scrope, beheaded for taking part in the Pilgrimage of Grace. The duke of Orleans was imprisoned here for twenty years after Agincourt, 1415. Now it is a ruin, Parliament having ordered it to be demolished after the Civil War. The Royalists were besieged there three times and I can understand Cromwell's men being sick of the sight of it. Most of the stone was sold but what was left has been given a modest setting achieving an effect that manages to give an impression of the size and layout. The underground chambers still exist and can be visited, the graffiti written by prisoners still visible.

Nonetheless, Pontefract remains one of the least known of England's truly great historical towns and major Royalist strongholds of the Civil War. It was also Shakespeare's Pomfret, hence the name of the little black cakes.

Below the hospital off Southgate is a hermitage, hewn out of solid rock and founded by hermit Brother Adam in 1368. It has 62 steps to its oratory and living room. Close to it are the Friarwood Valley Gardens which were the home of the Blackfriars. Thankfully there are pleasanter things to find as in the Court Room of the old Town Hall in Gillygate, one of them being a plaster cast depicting a mortally wounded Nelson. The cast is one from which the panels at the foot of Nelson's Column are made.

I wouldn't say the pubs were particularly exciting. Perhaps for the most part adequate, with just a few that look good and serve a decent pint. Just at the top of the Shoe Market there are three that look O.K. and by the side of one of them, the Malt Shovel, a short terrace of ancient cottages with a rough stone bottom half and a plaster and

The Buttercross in Pontefract

timber top. It is hard to under stand how they have managed to stay up.

With Dick Turpin the highwayman being an incurable liar (a rope finally cured him) it is easier to believe that it was the local "baddie", a highwayman called Nevison who made the record ride from London to York. He also had a leap, across a ravine nearby named after him to suggest that he made it, on horseback in the 1670s.

Which brings us back to the race-course situated in Pontefract Park. In the park you will find a golf course, tennis courts, a boating lake which fishermen seem keen to use and a track that was enlarged in 1983 to make it a complete circuit of over two miles and a furlong. It is the biggest in Europe, which is a surprise to me.

The Walk

The Route: Racecourse – Museum – Castle – Football Ground – Park Lake – Racecourse

Map: O.S. map 105

The start and how to find it: Because the parking situation is a bit difficult in the town, it is convenient as well as pleasant to start the walk in the park. Drive into the gateway on the corner of the park, nearest the A639 that goes down to the M62, just a little less than half a mile from the town centre. Go through some old gate pillars and then park between the trees on the ground between the two stretches of roadway. Map reference 447223.

What the walk is like: Town and country, including a walk around the track

Distance: 4¾ miles.

From the parking place, walk back to the gate and using the pedestrian crossing, cross the main road on your left before walking to the right, going off Park Road and along Front Street. A railway bridge is crossed above Tanshelf station from which trains travel to Wakefield and Knottingley. As you start to go up the hill there is a road to take that goes off to the left and passes the Greyhound, The Green Dragon and the Blackmoorhead (such good landmarks in towns aren't they?). Almost directly in front of you is the Shoe Market, a short narrow lane and the one to walk down.

The next prominent building to pass is the parish church, turning left opposite the Beast Fair Vaults and go around the library to the

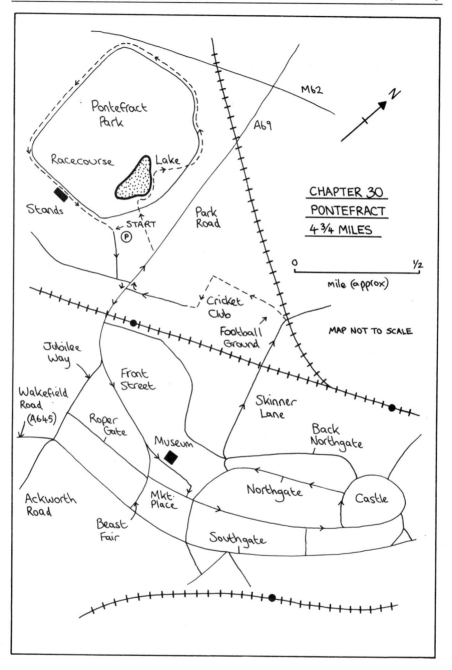

back and near the front door of the museum. A condensed history is in here and it will only take as long as you want to spend. From here go down the shopping street passing the back entrance to the Market Hall, to the wool market with a right and then left turn onto Bridge Street. It is here that I recommend a slight diversion by turning to your right and walking the length of the Market Place and back. Not only to see some of the smaller shops of good value (where shop assistants are still pleasant to customers) but, below the church, the open sided building that is called the Buttercross. This was erected in 1734 by the widow of Soloman Dupier who in 1704 was in the Gibraltar garrison and was suspected of assisting the enemy – an Anglo-Dutch force – to capture the Rock. Next to it is a somewhat dilapidated hand pump which has apparently been a source of water since Queen Elizabeth the First's reign. On the way back you will see the beast's head at the top of the arch on the front wall of the market.

Back at the junction of Bridge Street and Horsefair go straight down the road so that you pass the bus station on your left. Keep going straight down the road despite any name changes, finishing along the stretch of Castle Garth that is marked as a cul-de-sac and brings you to the Lodge House at the entrance to the Castle site. A walk around the perimeter and a little bit of nosing will only take 15 minutes and then, when you are ready, go back to the gates and walk to the first junction and turn right and then by turning left at the end of the lane, you come onto Northgate. Keep going until the supermarket is in front of you and the bus station is on your left. Diagonally across the road is a weird sort of castellated place, but turn to the right and the cemetery is on your left. So is the footpath. Upon that, walk down the hill on what is Skinner Lane, under the railway bridge and in about twenty yards go along the path that goes off to the left. It is well used, so a quick lesson on the local dialect might help: saying "good morning" to any one you meet (before midday) won't do any harm, but "ah do" will get a better response.

You will have noticed the slag heap by now. Years ago they were a blot on the landscape, but now they mean there is a pit about here that is still working and giving employment. This one is Prince of Wales colliery, which has been taken over by private enterprise.

The path takes you by the football field then the cricket field and then turns left towards a white building where you turn right and walk up to the traffic lights. There at the road go to the right until you can cross the road safely and walk down the roadside with the hedge on your left as far as the bus shelter, after which there is a gate to go through to get into the park by the tennis courts. Now head in the general direction of the race-course rails with the idea of following the track going right and then continuing anti-clockwise. As you approach the rails, the boating lake comes into view. A minute or two to divert, see the boating and the usually large group of enthusiastic fishermen and then sharp right to get back "on course". Now you are going gently downhill, but as you approach the bottom bend it is just a shade steeper in descent and you can imagine the horse feeling freer and gathering momentum as the bend starts to tighten up. Of course a jockey's experience will make him aware of all these possibilities, but as you walk around these two miles or so and see how the track undulates and gives very little straight anywhere except in a difficult bit before the last bend you will appreciate that this is a thinking jockey's course.

And then the finish. Less than two furlongs to the post, as you come into the straight, and it is still going uphill. It's not easy walking it either. But it is a pleasant place to watch the horses and see who are the better riders. So it is past the stands and Paddock and out, next to the laid track for cars to cross the course, and over to your right and the place where you started.

I couldn't help but bring up the subject when I stopped for a well-earned pint. I mentioned that Lester Piggott used to show a liking for coming up here to ride and got the reply I had expected. "Aye, he's a master of pace is that one and he could con the others so they be on a tired 'un when he made his move". His language was a little more colourful as he remembered some past excitement: "I've seen him holding his horse up as they came towards the bend and as if by magic he would be third or forth with a furlong to go. Then you see him change into that famous stance as he made his move to go on and win. You know there were times I thought he could ride a donkey to win round Ponty. It needs a bit of craftiness to get round here and by 'eck, it's a hell of a finish."

Postscript

An Outline of Yorkshire History

AD71	The Romans conquered Yorkshire and defeated the Brigantes, north of Richmond.
c.500	The Angles reached York. Squares sent south.
664	Synod of Whitby adopts the rules of the church of Rome.
665	Race meetings held on Sunday afternoons.
867	The Danes decide to capture York after getting bored with Lincolnshire.
876	Danes settled in the county and divided it into Ridings, thus creating countless experts who all know what Ridings meant.
919	Norwegian Vikings from Ireland capture York.
927	Norwegian Vikings hand York to King Athelstan rather than reveal the recipe for Guinness.
1066	King Harold defeats Norse army at Stamford Bridge, much further north than usual Chelsea ground.
1066	King Harold then goes to Hastings to get one in the eye. Army complains of exhaustion after first sponsored march, 280 miles south.
1069-1090	William the Conqueror harried the North Riding to subdue unruly peasants, wiping out two of every three villages.
1440	Peasants still unruly.
1460	Yorkshire "A" team beaten by Lancashire at Wakefield.
1461	Yorkshire first team win return match at Towton.

1483   Richard III sends scarves from Middleham to his
            nephews in the Tower. Damp accommodation blamed
            for fatal shrinking.

1536   Yorkshire rises against the dissolution of the
            monasteries, demanding compensation for consequent
            loss of brew-houses.

1590   Sir Walter Raleigh sails into Hull with dried leaves and
            subterranean apples. Cargo thrown into the river.

1591   Hull starts smoking fish.

1664   Parliament beats Royalists at Marston Moor.

1760   Beginning of Industrial Revolution.

1846   Thomas Cook starts package holidays for Parisians to
            visit Yorkshire.

1889   Start of Women's Rights Movement in Yorkshire.

1890   Glass balls appear on Christmas trees.

1891   Men-only cricket clubs opened.

1923   John Logie Baird, bored by Christmas, decides to invent
            something he says will make it better.

1994   Yorkshire Television prove him wrong.

We publish guides to individual towns, plus books on walking and cycling in the great outdoors throughout England and Wales. This is a recent selection:

More books about Yorkshire:

STRANGE SOUTH YORKSHIRE – David Clarke *(£6.95)*

SECRET YORK: Walks within the city walls – Les Pierce *(£6.95)*

YORKSHIRE DALES WALKING: On The Level – Norman Buckley *(£6.95)*

PUB WALKS IN THE YORKSHIRE DALES – Clive Price *(£6.95)*

PUB WALKS ON THE NORTH YORK MOORS & COAST – Stephen Rickerby *(£6.95)*

PUB WALKS IN THE YORKSHIRE WOLDS – Tony Whittaker *(£6.95)*

BEST PUB WALKS IN & AROUND SHEFFIELS – Clive Price *(£6.95)*

BEST PUB WALKS IN SOUTH YORKSHIRE – Martin Smith *(£6.95)*

Exploring the Lake District:

THE LAKELAND SUMMITS – Tim Synge *(£7.95)*

100 LAKE DISTRICT HILL WALKS – Gordon Brown *(£7.95)*

LAKELAND ROCKY RAMBLES: Geology beneath your feet – Brian Lynas *(£7.95)*

FULL DAYS ON THE FELLS: Challenging Walks – Adrian Dixon *(£7.95)*

PUB WALKS IN THE LAKE DISTRICT – Neil Coates *(£6.95)*

MOSTLY DOWNHILL: LEISURELY WALKS, LAKE DISTRICT – Alan Pears *(£6.95)*

LAKELAND WALKING, ON THE LEVEL – Norman Buckley *(£6.95)*

STROLLING WITH STEAM : walks along the Keswick Railway – Jan Darrall *(£4.95)*

TEA SHOP WALKS IN THE LAKE DISTRICT – Jean Patefield *(£6.95)*

CYCLING IN THE LAKE DISTRICT – John Wood *(£7.95)*

Further afield:

EAST CHESHIRE WALKS – Graham Beech *(£5.95)*

WEST CHESHIRE WALKS – Jen Darling *(£5.95)*

TEA SHOP WALKS IN CHESHIRE – Clive Price *(£6.95)*

TEA SHOP WALKS IN THE CHILTERNS – Jean Patefield *(£6.95)*

MOSTLY DOWNHILL IN THE PEAK DISTRICT – Clive Price *(£6.95)*
(two volumes, White Peak & Dark Peak)
HILL WALKS IN MID WALES – Dave Ing *(£8.95)*
WELSH WALKS: Dolgellau /Cambrian Coast – L. Main & M. Perrott *(£5.95)*
WELSH WALKS: Aberystwyth & District – L. Main & M. Perrott *(£5.95)*
WALKS IN MYSTERIOUS WALES – Laurence Main *(£7.95)*
RAMBLES IN NORTH WALES – Roger Redfern *(£6.95)*
PUB WALKS IN SNOWDONIA – Laurence Main *(£6.95)*
BEST PUB WALKS IN GWENT – Les Lumsdon *(£6.95)*
PUB WALKS IN POWYS – Les Lumsdon & Chris Rushton *(£6.95)*
BEST PUB WALKS IN PEMBROKESHIRE – Laurence Main *(£6.95)*
RAMBLES AROUND MANCHESTER – Mike Cresswell *(£5.95)*
LAKELAND WALKING: On The Level – Norman Buckley *(£6.95)*
FIFTY CLASSIC WALKS IN THE PENNINES – Terry Marsh *(£8.95)*
WEST PENNINE WALKS – Mike Cresswell *(£5.95)*
BEST PUB WALKS AROUND CENTRAL LONDON – Ruth Herman *(£6.95)*
BEST PUB WALKS IN ESSEX – Derek Keeble *(£6.95)*

More Pub Walks . . .

There are many more titles in our fabulous series of 'Pub Walks' books for just about every popular walking area in the UK, all featuring access by public transport. We label our more recent ones as 'best' to differentiate them from inferior competitors!

Cycling . . .

CYCLE UK! The essential guide to leisure cycling – Les Lumsdon *(£9.95)*
OFF-BEAT CYCLING IN THE PEAK DISTRICT – Clive Smith *(£6.96)*
MORE OFF-BEAT CYCLING IN THE PEAK DISTRICT – Clive Smith *(£6.95)*
50 BEST CYCLE RIDES IN CHESHIRE – Graham Beech *(£7.95)*
CYCLING IN THE COTSWOLDS – Stephen Hill *(£6.95)*
CYCLING IN LINCOLNSHIRE – Penny & Bill Howe *(£7.95)*
CYCLING IN STAFFORDSHIRE – Linda Wain *(£7.95)*
CYCLING IN THE WEST COUNTRY – Helen Stephenson *(£7.95)*
CYCLING IN SOUTH WALES – Rosemary Evans *(£7.95)*
CYCLING IN SCOTLAND & N.E.ENGLAND – Philip Routledge *(£7.95)* .
CYCLING IN NORTH WALES – Philip Routledge *(£7.95) ... available 1996*
BY-WAY BIKING IN THE CHILTERNS – Henry Tindell *(£7.95)*

Sport...

RED FEVER: from Rochdale to Rio as 'United' supporters – Steve Donoghue *(£7.95)*
UNITED WE STOOD: unofficial history of the Ferguson years – Richard Kurt *(£6.95)*
MANCHESTER CITY: Moments to Remember – John Creighton *(£9.95)*

- plus many more entertaining and educational books being regularly added to our list. All of our books are available from your local bookshop. In case of difficulty, or to obtain our complete catalogue, please contact:

Sigma Leisure, 1 South Oak Lane, Wilmslow, Cheshire SK9 6AR
Phone: 01625 – 531035   Fax: 01625 – 536800

ACCESS and VISA orders welcome – call our friendly sales staff or use our 24 hour Answerphone service! Most orders are despatched on the day we receive your order – you could be enjoying our books in just a couple of days. Please add £2 p&p to all orders.

IMAGES
of England

THE WILTS
& BERKS CANAL

A restored section of canal at Templar's Firs, near Wootton Bassett, in 1997.

IMAGES
of England

THE WILTS
& BERKS CANAL

Doug Small

TEMPUS

British Waterways – 2,000 miles of history

British Waterways runs the country's two-centuries-old working heritage of canals and river navigations. It conserves the historic buildings, structures and landscapes which blend to create the unique environment of the inland waterways, and protects their valuable and varied habitats.

As part of its commitment to the heritage of the waterways, British Waterways was instrumental in setting up The Waterways Trust, which aims to educate the public about the inland waterways and to promote the restoration and preservation of their rich architectural, historical and environmental heritage.

The Waterways Trust is a partnership between British Waterways, The National Waterways Museum at Gloucester, the Boat Museum at Ellesmere Port and the Canal Museum, Stoke Bruerne. The Trust cares for the National Waterways Collection, the country's pre-eminent collection of canal artefacts, documents and boats which are on view to the public at all the museums.

The Waterways Trust also manages the British Waterways Archive, a unique collection of inland waterway records dating back to the late seventeenth century and containing the largest documentary and photographic resource of its kind in Britain. Supported by the Heritage Lottery Fund, the archive is the subject of an ambitious project to make the collection available to all via the Internet. The new Cyber Archive will, for the first time, create a single catalogue of Britain's canal archives, revolutionizing research into the history of the inland waterways.

For more information about British Waterways call 01923 20 11 20 or visit the website at www.britishwaterways.co.uk.

For access to the archive, or to get up-to-date information about the Cyber Archive project, call 01452 318041.

First published 1999
Reprinted 2003

Tempus Publishing Limited
The Mill, Brimscombe Port,
Stroud, Gloucestershire, GL5 2QG

© Doug Small, 1999

British Library Cataloguing in Publication Data.
A catalogue record for this book is available from the British Library.

ISBN 0 7524 1619 7

typesetting and origination by Tempus Publishing Limited
printed in great britain by Midway Colour Print, Wiltshire

Contents

Introduction 7

1. Semington to Pewsham 13

2. Pewsham to Foxham 23

3. Foxham to Seven Locks 35

4. Vastern to Wroughton 45

5. Westleaze to John Street Basin 61

6. John Street Basin to Latton 75

7. John Street Basin to Uffington 93

8. West Challow to Grove 105

9. Ardington to Abingdon 117

Postscript 127

Acknowledgements 128

Useful Information 128

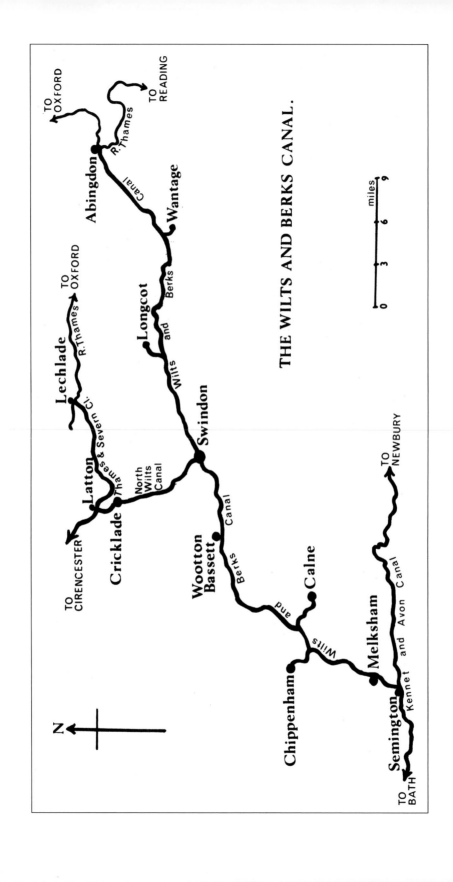

THE WILTS AND BERKS CANAL.

Introduction

Saved

Thanks to the curiosity of one man in the 1970s, the Wilts & Berks Canal has not been consigned to that depressing list of lost canals. In 1977 Neil Rumbol was engaged on voluntary work on the Thames & Severn Canal when he 'discovered', near Latton, the remains of the North Wilts Branch of the Wilts & Berks Canal. After further exploration, and a letter to *Waterways World*, a meeting of like-minded souls was called in 1977 and following on from this the Wilts & Berks Canal Amenity Group (W&BCAG) was formed. The modest aim of the Group at that time was simply to preserve what remained of the canal and its infrastructure. By 1987, with the upswing in the popularity of canals and the explosion in the number of waterway restorations, it was decided to change the objectives of the Group to one of full restoration using as much of the original line as possible. The restoration of the canal is now one of the major projects in the country and at over sixty miles one of the most challenging.

One other person deserves a specific mention and that is L.J. (Jack) Dalby. Eight years earlier (1969) he had spotted 'Track of old canal' on an OS map and then, after initial explorations around Wantage, he spent the following two winters walking the complete length of the canal including its branches. After extensive research in various archives, libraries and record offices he produced (in 1971) the first edition of *The Wilts and Berks Canal*. A second, revised and expanded, edition appeared in 1986 and this has remained the main reference work since. Always modest, Jack described himself as a 'non-expert' and preferred to call the book *The Story of…* rather than *The History of…*. Unconvinced in the early days that restoration was possible, he went on to become very supportive and eventually the first President of W&BCAG.

A Short History

The Wilts & Berks Canal was conceived late in the period now associated with 'Canal Mania'. The success of canals, both as commercial enterprises in which to invest and as by far the most effective form of inland transportation for bulk materials and goods, had been amply demonstrated elsewhere throughout England, particularly in the heartlands of the Industrial Revolution – the Midlands and Pennine flanks. By the late eighteenth century, the general fear was that the North Wessex area might be in danger of 'missing out' on the benefits of the industrial and transport revolutions. The discovery of exploitable coal resources south of Bath, in the Somerset Coalfield, proved the final justification for the formation of a company to finance the building of the Wilts & Berks Canal.

A committee of potential investors, formed in 1793, commissioned a survey of possible routes from Robert Whitworth and his son William, the former a pupil of the great canal builder, James Brindley. With a suitable route identified, the necessary Parliamentary Act granting compulsory purchase and other necessary powers was duly obtained in 1795. Work commenced at the southern extremity of the line later that year. Given the distraction provided by the Napoleonic Wars, it is perhaps not surprising that the fifty-two miles of canal from Semington Junction on the Kennet and Avon Canal to Abingdon on the River Thames Navigation took fifteen years to complete. The official opening ceremony was conducted on 14 September 1810.

The North Wilts Canal was nine miles long, and had twelve locks. With aqueducts over the River Ray and the upper Thames, and a short tunnel near Cricklade, it was opened on 2 April 1819, linking the Wilts & Berks Canal at Swindon to the Thames & Severn Canal at Latton. This provided an alternative route for trading boats enabling them to avoid the difficult Thames Navigation above Abingdon.

In addition to providing a route for coal to the immense London market, the W&B served to bring cheap coal to the market towns of Melksham, Calne, Chippenham, Wootton Bassett, Swindon, Farringdon, Wantage and Abingdon and to Oxford, while also offering economic transport for the regional export of agricultural produce and such locally produced goods as bricks, building stone, clay pipes, etc.

However, the W&B always proved of limited economic value. The Kennet and Avon, built as a wide canal offering passage for fourteen feet beam boats (compared to the W&B narrowboats with only a seven feet beam) provided a shorter, speedier and more economic route to the London market. The Somerset coalfield rapidly became worked out. Additionally, the rural nature of the region through which the canal passed provided little by way of high-value cargo able to afford the canal fees and dues necessary to repay investors and to leave a surplus adequate for the essential continual maintenance.

Ironically, the best times of the W&B Canal came in the 1830s, a mere fifteen to twenty-five years after completion – ironically, because peak revenues and profits for the W&B Canal company came about through Isambard Kingdom Brunel's GWR, the Great Western Railway. The W&B provided an efficient means of transporting the vast quantities of iron, brick, stone, aggregate and timber needed in the building of the railway which, apart from the eastern and western extremities, is never more than a mile or two away from the line of the canal. Thus did the W&B contribute towards its own eventual and probably inevitable downfall.

The rest of the nineteenth century is marked by the slow, steady and inexorable decline of the W&B. As more and more traffic shifted from canal to railway, tolls and fees tumbled, operating costs had to be slashed to match the falling revenues and the essential maintenance was cut back and back, in turn causing further problems for the few remaining operators. The last boat recorded into Wantage Wharf in the mid-1890s, for instance, was able to transport only seventeen tons compared with the designed limit of thirty-four tons, thanks to severe silting up of the channel through lack of dredging, reducing the available depth of water and thus the draft of the laden vessel.

By 1900, traffic had all but ceased on the W&B apart from a small number of movements along the south-western end of the canal, with occasional boats still making the journey into Swindon from the Kennet and Avon Canal. How long such traffic could and would have continued in its desultory way we will never know. One wet and stormy night in early 1901, nature, aided by the long years of neglected maintenance, stepped in to administer the *coup de grace*. To carry the canal over the River Marden between Calne and Chippenham, the canal engineers had built the Stanley Aqueduct, one of the few major structures on what was generally a somewhat unsophisticated canal largely lacking great feats of engineering. That night, an approximately four foot square section of aqueduct simply collapsed out of the roof of one of the row of arches, and like pulling out the bath-plug, the water from the canal just ran out, leaving the canal above Lacock literally high and dry.

With the canal all but useless, certainly for navigation, various parties attempted to officially abandon it and thus absolve themselves of their obligations and liabilities, but it was to be another thirteen years before the official Act of Abandonment was passed by Parliament, with the land on which the canal had been built returned or sold to the adjoining landowners.

Post Abandonment

After abandonment, the canal continued to degenerate as nature gradually reclaimed the work of man, aided in places by deliberate actions, such as the infilling with domestic rubbish of the locks in urban areas and even the use of the structures for military demolition practice during the Second World War. Urban development in towns such as Swindon, Melksham, Chippenham, Wantage and Abingdon has continued to obliterate parts of the canal line in these areas. Road improvement schemes usually called for the lowering of bridges over the disused canal leaving the water channel as a simple culvert in many places. Just south of Swindon, the M4 motorway crosses the line and in central Swindon the original route is entirely lost with the 'Magic Round-About' being on the site of Swindon Wharf. The branches to Longcot, Chippenham and Wantage are also almost certainly not restorable in the foreseeable future. Yet, despite much destruction, the canal remains in surprisingly good condition, particularly in the rural areas which constitute the majority of its original course, requiring little more than the clearance of choking undergrowth and some dredging of the accumulated silt of decades to restore the W&B to a fair semblance of its former glory. The major works required consist of the rebuilding of structures, locks, bridges, wharves, etc., including new ones to cope with the effects of developments undertaken since abandonment, such as the crossing of the M4. A serious consideration when discussing the W&B is the number of landowners (estimated to be about 200), all of whom have opinions and points of view which must be treated with respect.

Revival

Restoring over sixty miles of derelict canal is a daunting task for a small band of enthusiasts no matter how energetically they pursue their objective. From its modest beginnings W&BCAG now (June 1999) has a membership of around twelve hundred. Controlled by a council of management, eight branches administer the day to day business of their particular sections of the canal. A ninth branch (Bath & Bristol) being slightly remote from the canal line offers invaluable support to the other branches in innumerable ways, for instance in augmenting work parties, fund raising and attending publicity events.

Melksham Branch organises the very popular annual Semington Boat Rally, staged on the K&A at the original junction between the two navigations. They have also erected signs for the historic canal trail through Melksham. Although the new canal line around the town has not yet been decided upon, branch members have spent a lot of time identifying possible routes. Work has recently begun on clearing part of the old line into the town which might possibly be the new Melksham branch off of the new main line.

Calne & Chippenham Branch have restored 800 yards of canal from Calne Lock to the winding hole. Chaveywell Bridge has been renovated and the nearby wharf is used regularly as a boarding point for boat trips. Annual events here include the July Canal Day and in December there is the Santa Cruise which provides boat trips down the cut for youngsters to visit Santa's Grotto. The Calne Arm will make a very pleasant diversion from the main line for boats into the centre of the town. It is hoped that further clearance and dredging will take place in the near future. The only remaining tunnel is on this arm which takes the canal under the A4.

Foxham & Lyneham Branch have rebuilt Foxham Upper Lock which now only needs gates and paddles to become fully operational. Two lift bridges have been installed, one of which is in regular use. An impressive spillweir has been built and two accommodation bridges have been reinstated by the landowner. At Dauntsey, in co-operation with the Wilts & Berks Canal Company (W&BCC), two miles of canal have been dredged, two spillweirs built and Dauntsey Lock and the wharf next to the Peterborough Arms are being reconstructed. The Canal Company has also renovated the original canal cottages situated west of the B4069. These cottages, and the Peterborough Arms, were part of the original, thriving canalside community. The 'Seven Locks' area has not received any serious attention, but, as the longest flight of locks on the canal when restored, will be an outstanding feature.

The 1998 National Trail Boat Festival was staged at Wootton Bassett on the Templar's Firs section. Approximately fifty powered craft attended the festival which attracted several thousand visitors and proved a major boost for the restoration. An important achievement for the group was the successful conclusion of negotiations with Wessex Water who agreed to lower a sewer pipe, which crossed the canal at water level, to run beneath the canal bed where it is no longer an obstruction to navigation. A mile of canal has been dredged and is in water and a footbridge and a slipway have been constructed. Dunnington aqueduct has been partially repaired and clearance has started on the Dunnington Locks. It is expected that work will soon start on the next section along from Templar's Firs and it is hoped dredging will soon begin at Studley Grange where preparatory work has already commenced.

Swindon is at the hub of the canal and this branch of W&BCAG also takes in the North Wilts Canal. Moredon Aqueduct, a Grade II listed structure which spans the River Ray, has been rebuilt and the half mile of canal between it and Moulden Lock has been fully dredged and is in water. Restoration of the lock began in 1998 and further dredging towards Swindon is in progress. There is a further half a mile of canal in water at Westleaze and a successful Heritage Lottery Fund application means another half mile running back into Swindon should soon be completed. Plans to continue restoration towards the M4 are well advanced. The successful outcome of the navigable culvert negotiations at Latton on the Thames & Severn Canal secures the North Wilts' route to the upper Thames.

During 1998, Shrivenham Branch completed their Canalside Park, which covers almost four acres and is owned by the Group. It has been developed as an amenity for the local area and contains part of the canal line. With the assistance of WRG a slipway has now been built in the park area. Future work will include the reinstatement of the towpath through the park, grass-seeding and a major programme of scrub-and tree-planting. Plans for the future include more dredging, towpath clearance and the rebuilding of Steppingstones Lane Bridge.

An early indication that the idea of reviving the canal was not just 'pie in the sky' occurred in 1991 when the Waterways Recovery Group (WRG) decided to hold their twenty-first anniversary work camp in the Wantage area on various sites. The weekend attracted 1,000 navvies, the greatest number ever, who cleared many hundreds of yards of canal and swung much local opinion over in favour of restoration. There are now two lengths dredged and in water at Elm Farm and Stockham. Grove Top Lock has been partially cleared, the wing-walls rebuilt and the area landscaped. Grove Common Lock tail bridge has been rebuilt and clearance work has been carried out in several other places. Scrub-bashing and dredging on the East Challow to West Challow section commenced in winter 1998.

Drayton Lock, the main work site in the Abingdon area, had been totally infilled but is now being cleared. The line of the canal here passes right through the site of Thames Water's proposed new reservoir which will be a major consideration when planning the new route towards Abingdon where the canal will join the River Thames. The original junction with the Thames at St Helens Wharf is probably not possible but, as at Semington, alternatives are available according to the preferred new route. One thing is certain, boats from the Midlands, coming via the Oxford Canal, will one day have an easier and quicker route to Bath, bypassing as it does the Caen Hill Locks at Devizes.

The Future

1997 saw the formation of the Wilts & Berks Canal Trust. W&BCAG was a founder member of the trust, together with North Wilts District Council, West Wilts District Council, Swindon Borough Council, Vale of the White Horse District Council, Oxfordshire County Council and Wiltshire County Council. Since the reorganisation of the county boundaries carried out in 1974 the W&B canal no longer passes through Berkshire! One of the first actions of the Trust was to commission a feasibility study, the results of which were made public in March 1998. The positive results of this study have led to a Strategic Study being commissioned which is due to be published in mid-1999.

One further step forward has come with the formation of the Cricklade Corridor Trust which intends to combine the restoration of the North Wilts Canal and the Swindon-Cricklade railway into one integrated leisure amenity.

Since the publication of this book in 1999 much has happened. 2001 brought several changes to the structure of the restoration. The Trust was wound up and the existing members, plus many other organisations, formed a partnership which allows the restoration to proceed more effectively. The Amenity Group decided to rename itself the Wilts & Berks Canal Trust, as it felt this was now a more appropriate title. Currently several studies are underway and physical restoration is being carried out at many locations along the canal. The first major road crossing was achieved at Moredon with the construction of a navigable culvert under the Purton Road. Beavans Bridge has been completely rebuilt as a traditional stone arch bridge. Work at Wantage has progressed beyond West Challow Bridge towards Childrey. A second lift bridge has been built at Foxham. Work has begun at Steventon Lock, Kings Lift Bridge, Steppingstones Lane Bridge, Summit Lock, Seven Locks, Pewsham Locks, Forest Farm and the River Key Aqueduct. Extensive clearing and dredging is also underway. A major coup in 2002 was when retiring British Waterway Chief Executive Dr David Fletcher CBE agreed to become the President of the Wilts & Berks Canal Trust.

The original Wilts & Berks Canal Company Seal.

One
Semington to Pewsham

Joseph Priestley in his 1831 *Navigable Rivers and Canals* describes the Wilts & Berks thus:

'This canal, which is of great importance to that part of the country through which it passes, commences in the River Thames, at the south side of the town of Abingdon; thence passing in a south-westerly direction by Drayton and Kingsgrove Commons, to Breach Field, where a short branch proceeds from it to the town of Wantage; thence continuing westwards to Challow, passing Sparsholt and Uffington to Longcot Common, where there is another short branch to Longcot Wharf; continuing its course, it passes near Beckett House, Shrivenham, Bourton, Marsden, and Stratton, to the wharf at Swindon; a short distance from which is Eastcott, where the branch, originally called the North Wilts Canal, proceeds from it, and joins the Thames and Severn Canal near Cricklade; the main line, keeping its westerly direction, passes Chaddington, Wootton Bassett, Tockenham Wick, Lyneham and Dauntsey Park; then bending southerly, it passes Foxham, Bencroft, and Stanley House, a little beyond which is a branch to Calne; passing the river by an aqueduct, it then continues its southerly course, leaving Bowood, the Marquis of Lansdowne's Seat, to the left, to Derry Hill, where a branch goes off to Chippenham; pursuing its course it runs by Laycock Abbey and Melksham, to Semington, where it unites with the Kennet and Avon Canal'.

Priestley joined the Wilts & Berks Canal Company in 1810 and remained for about six years before moving on to the Aire & Calder Navigation.

Published by R. Wilkinson & Co., Trowbridge

When Reginald and Timothy Blunt were planning a holiday cruise in 1890, they were warned about the poor condition of the Wilts & Berks Canal. Undaunted they set out to navigate the ring consisting of the K&A, the W&B and the River Thames anticipating the popularity of modern day canal holidays. The local populace would no doubt have been as curious of their boat, the *Ada,* as they are apparently of the photographer here.

Having come down the K&A Semington Lock and turned right under the bridge at Semington Junction they would have immediately encountered the regulating lock. At a time (c.1890) when trading boat traffic on the W&B canal had dwindled to almost nothing a holiday boat would have been an unusual diversion.

14

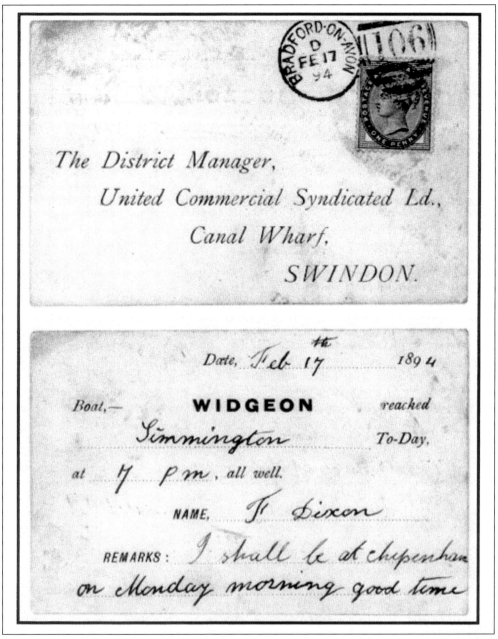

Some limited trading did still occur. This pre-addressed 1894 postcard from skipper Dixon of nb *Widgeon* is reporting his progress and his expectation of reaching Chippenham by Monday – a journey of approximately nine miles (about three hours travelling time under normal circumstances). Notice the spelling of Semington!

Situated above the lock was the toll collectors house and no doubt the early travellers would have had dealings with the incumbent. One wonders what financial arrangement would have been made. Given that theirs was not a trading boat it could not have been based on tonnage. A 1970 view.

The house still overlooks the walled-off entrance and the lock is now buried in the garden. This is a very impressive building and must have been in keeping with the importance of the toll collectors status.

16

This is a typical lift (lever) bridge although judging by the ivy and the twist in one of the beams it had been a long time since it was operated. A view from the 1920s, twenty years after closure.

Along the canal towards Spa Road Bridge, c.1920. Although the reeds are encroaching, the centre channel is being kept clear. Melksham wharf and rope yard were nearby so perhaps there was still the occasional boat movement.

One fully loaded boat and one nearly empty and nothing on Melksham wharf. Not a very busy scene at the end of the nineteenth century even through traffic was still possible.

Boat movements had by 1915 definitely stopped as indicated by the low water level. Spa Road Bridge has been demolished and a residential block has been built on the wharf site.

There are several explanations for the name 'Gallows Bridge'. The one I like comes from a letter to a newspaper from Nellie Irene Batty (*nee* Bolwell) whose grandfather ran boats on the K&A. According to her family, the bridge was used in the 1800s as a place of execution for sheep stealers.

On the *Ada* in 1890 the accommodation for the Blunt brothers was under canvas, while the crew used the small boatman's cabin during the day. It had a crew of three who, after safely mooring the boat and settling the boys in for the night, would proceed ashore to lodgings.

Just north of Melksham, Forest Lock would be the first real lock encountered. Modern travellers will not be able to enjoy this pleasant scene as the lock is now buried and the cottage was demolished in 1956. An alternative route for the canal could bypass the town probably rejoining the K&A below the Seend locks. A 1900s view.

Seen here in full working order c.1900 is Ray Mill Bridge, near Lacock. There was also a wharf nearby but no trace of either remains. A bridge of this type has been successfully reconstructed by volunteers a short distance above Foxham Top Lock.

The village of Lacock is still relatively unspoilt by modern incursions and is a pleasant tourist attraction. East of the town is the River Avon and running almost parallel to the river is the line of the canal.

Lacock Abbey is the former home of William Henry Fox Talbot, pioneer photographer and the inventor of the negative positive process 160 years ago. Now owned by the National Trust, the Abbey and the Fox Talbot Gallery are open to the public.

Perched precariously on the parapet of the unusually wide Double Bridge in 1970 is Jack Dalby, who, after the formation of W&BCAG, slowly became more involved with restoration and was eventually to become the group's first president.

Jack passed away in 1990 and, as a tribute, a replica milestone was erected as a memorial to him.

Two

Pewsham to Foxham

The Wilts & Berks entry in the 1904 Bradshaw rates very little space:

> 'Although the canal is not officially closed, navigation throughout the whole of the system has practically ceased owing to the income being insufficient to meet the cost of maintenance.'

In 1901 a section of Stanley Aqueductcollapsed preventing through passage and thirteen years later the canal was officially abandoned by an Act of Parliament. Although the abandonment had been actively sought after by many of the communities through which it passed it was not universally welcomed. Many landowners expressed concern that they would lose the water supplies which were essential for both their animals and crops.

It shows the resilience of rural canals that, eighty-five years after abandonment, most of the line of the canal in the countryside is still visible and in the majority of places easily recoverable. Although the Chippenham arm has suffered badly and been obliterated in the town, the arm to Calne has fared better and is ideally placed to tempt boats off the main line.

An early work party, c.1985, clearing the chamber of Pewsham Top Lock, less formal than nowadays when hard hats are compulsory. This was a flight of three locks coming up towards Stanley Junction with a total rise of twenty-eight feet and eleven inches.

Chippenham tunnel, opened in 1803, was ninety yards long, had no tow path and led directly to the wharf. The tunnel was filled in during the 1970s but not destroyed. Strangely the north end portal was built of stone while the south end was built of brick.

J.H. Brinkworth founded Brinkworth's coal depot at Chippenham Wharf in 1828. Thirty years later he was the mayor of the town which is when this photograph was taken.

John Trow, a resident of Chippenham, at the helm of nb. *Helen* at the Wharf in the early 1890s. Standing behind him is Mr W.H. Brinkworth (obviously a relative of the founder). The horse-drawn boat would collect coal from Camerton in Somerset, a return trip of two days

Best Camerton coal was being sold at the wharf for eighteen shillings a ton around 1880. According to Dalby the amount of coal coming to the Chippenham arm dropped from a peak of 9,587 tons in 1854 to 1,745 tons in 1878 when records ended.

The working boat at the wharf has now given way to the family row-boat. Since 1977 the area has been the site of the bus station and a car park so it will be some time before boats come back to the centre of Chippenham.

On 21 November 1901, the *Wiltshire Mirror* reported that, 'the aqueduct over a branch of the River Avon, near Calne was washed away during the floods of last winter, the shareholders not being able, or perhaps unwilling to repair it and restore through communication.' The east side of the aqueduct, *c.*1970.

Seventy years after the event, looking at the still substantial remains of the aqueduct, one suspects that this collapse was the excuse the company had been waiting for and that there was probably never any serious thought given to repair. The west side *c.*1970.

Only four years after the formation of W&BCAG these youngsters are clearing the accumulated debris from under Chaveywell Bridge.

A timeless winter view of Chaveywell Bridge, after restoration, looking back towards the main line. There was a tunnel on this three-and-a-half-mile-long arm which took the canal under the A4 and on to the two Conigre locks.

Another generation enjoying the canal. Raft racing was one of the many events at the annual Calne Canal Day. As well as the activities on the water, there were boat trips and lots of displays and stalls in an adjacent field.

Boats would lock through Calne Town Lock to the wharf on the River Marden which was a useful water supply for the canal. Part of the North Wilts River Route of the Sustrans (sustainable transport) cycleway system now runs on the far side; the towpath being in the foreground.

The lock, although derelict, is still basically intact. The Calne Arm will be restored and it is expected that boats will one day be able to lock up into the town which will be a pleasant diversion for travellers and an added local tourist attraction.

12 August 1984 saw Ken Goodwin (centre), the then chairman of the Inland Waterways Association, paying a personal visit to the canal. Relaxing here with him on Chaveywell Bridge, Calne, are Neil Rumbol on the left, W&BCAG founder, and Richard Porter, member number two.

Boats passing through the lock, onto the River Marden, would swing to the left and head the short distance to the wharf just beyond the bridge. The water level of the River Marden has been altered now and this will make it more difficult for boats to reach the original head of navigation.

The River Marden, Calne.

The end of the line was Calne wharf, on the left. As the river was not wide enough to allow boats to 'wind' they would either have had to come up the lock backwards or reverse down. The 'winding hole' is five hundred yards below Chaveywell Bridge. A 1900s view.

It is not difficult to imagine boats back at the wharf. This would be an excellent place to stop for shopping, but it will need some imaginative planning to achieve.

Calne wharf with the newly completed town hall, *c*.1886, on the right and, just beyond the wharf, the canal offices and warehouse.

It really has not altered much over the last hundred-odd years; the canal buildings still exist just beyond the new housing.

In 1991, more than 700 school children re-enacted an historic day of 1841 to see what it was like to live on or near the canal in early Victorian times. Much of this took place on Lord Shelburnes' estate through which part of the canal line runs.

The children also spent some time at Foxham, where the canal was still in reasonably good condition. It has since been the subject of considerable improvement by both volunteers and landowners.

Three

Foxham to Seven Locks

In *The Canals of South and South East England*, Charles Hadfield wrote:

> The development of the Wilts & Berks after its opening in 1810 followed a quiet pattern. Apart from coal, the principle traffic was corn and agricultural products collected along the line and moved towards Semington on their way to Bath and Bristol. The tonnage of this trade in 1843 was 11,740 tons. There had been for a time at the beginning an attempt to work up a through traffic between Bristol and London, but the longer distance, together with the maximum toll charged by the Kennet & Avon for goods passing over their line to enter the Wilts & Berks, made it impossible for the company to compete successfully.'

According to Joseph Boughey, Charles declined membership of W&BCAG because he was 'disappointed to find that the Group set full navigable restoration as a long term goal…' Charles died in 1996 just as the restoration was beginning to gain momentum. As he apparently placed the Wilts & Berks in the same category as the Thames & Severn and Huddersfield Narrow canals I'm sure that if he was to be asked to support the restoration today his reaction would be rather different.

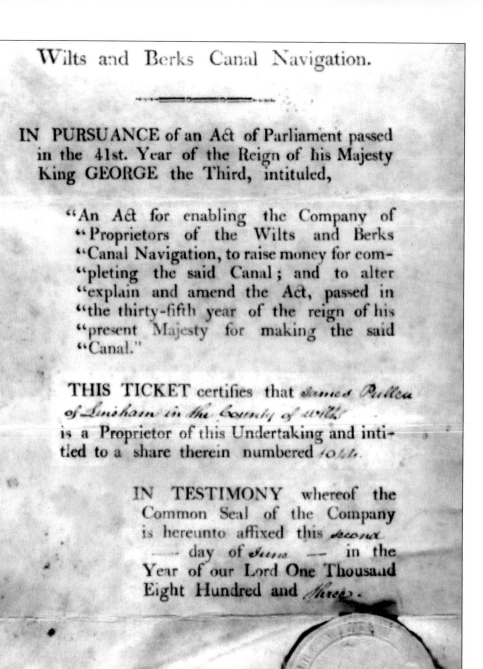

Wilts and Berks Canal Navigation.

IN PURSUANCE of an Act of Parliament passed
in the 41st. Year of the Reign of his Majesty
King GEORGE the Third, intituled,

"An Act for enabling the Company of
"Proprietors of the Wilts and Berks
"Canal Navigation, to raise money for com-
"pleting the said Canal; and to alter
"explain and amend the Act, passed in
"the thirty-fifth year of the reign of his
"present Majesty for making the said
"Canal."

THIS TICKET certifies that *James Pullen*
of Linsham in the County of Wilts
is a Proprietor of this Undertaking and inti-
tled to a share therein numbered *1044*.

IN TESTIMONY whereof the
Common Seal of the Company
is hereunto affixed this *second*
——— day of *June* ——— in the
Year of our Lord One Thousand
Eight Hundred and *Three*.

James Pullen was issued this share certificate in 1803, seven years before the canal was fully opened between Semington and Abingdon. It would have been many years before he would have seen any return on his investment. (British Waterways Archives)

Foxham Upper Lock has, with the exception of gates and paddles, been completely restored and will easily be made operational when the time comes. The section above here is relatively intact and will soon be restored to navigable dimensions.

Peglar's Lift Bridge is an excellent example of the type of bridge that was common to the canal. This one was built completely by volunteers and is in full working order.

This was originally a lift bridge but has been rebuilt as a fixed structure by local farmer Bob Kinch, one of the many supportive landowners. It will be raised when required to allow for navigation.

If you had been travelling east along the canal from Foxham towards Dauntsey during July 1998 you might have met a contingent of WRGies (Waterway Recovery Group volunteers) at a week-long work camp. As always, in spite of the hard work the WRGies always inject an element of fun as well as working to exacting professional standards.

The object of the work camp was to construct a new spillweir, which had been specially designed by Richard Hignett of Southampton University for the Canal Company that owns this part of the canal. The spillweir was of an unusual design but, when completed, fully lived up to expectations. The company's purpose-built work boat, *Peterborough*, was used to transport materials to the worksite.

There used to be a thriving community around Dauntsey Lock, but years of neglect took its toll as the sad state of these cottages in the 1960s shows. Fortunately help was at hand in the shape of The Wilts & Berks Canal Company (W&BCC) who bought the buildings and two miles of canal.

The canal in front of the cottages has been fully dredged. This is looking west from the B4069 road bridge under which the canal currently passes in a culvert.

The cottages have been renovated and are now inhabited. The towpath will be re-routed on the opposite side for a short distance to preserve the residents' privacy. This section is a reminder that the majority of the canal is, at present, still on private land and landowners rights must be acknowledged.

Behind the cottages lurks a weighbridge built by Bartlett & Son of Bristol. It has a six ton capacity and is complete with all machinery but not in working order. It is probably the oldest surviving weighbridge of this type in Wiltshire.

Troops resting in front of the Peterborough Farm House, c.1915. The present B4069 runs across the picture and Dauntsey Lock is just by the buildings on the left. There are now houses where the field was.

Until 1920 this was the farm house. Spotting a gap in the market the farmer then opened part of it as a public house and it is now the only remaining pub at Dauntsey Lock.

Dauntsey Lock looking east with the double bottom gates open waiting for the boat to enter, *c*.1880. The view beyond the lock, with the towpath on the left, gives a good impression on just how wide this 'narrow' canal was.

Looking back west at Dauntsey Lock, which is in its final stages of renovation, where the canal will immediately pass under the B4069 which is just behind the bottom gates. Part of the building on the right was the lock-keeper's cottage.

Two miles further on is 'Seven Locks', the longest flight of locks on the canal, seen here in 1910. They are all still there although usually hidden under the dense bushes. This is Bowds Lock (lock number 2) which had a lift bridge across the chamber.

It is well under a mile to the top of the flight and even with the dense undergrowth it is easy to visualise. The locks are in various states of decay. This is the top lock with one of the bottom gates still hanging open.

Four

Vastern to Wroughton

'A notice, signed by the Earl of Peterborough whose estate was at Dauntsey, appeared in the paper (The Bath Chronicle) on the 3 January 1793 calling a meeting at Wootton Bassett Town Hall to discuss the promotion of a canal from Abingdon to Bristol or to the intended Western Canal at or near Chippenham. This meeting was held on the 30 January with the Earl in the chair. A number of resolutions were passed. It was agreed that the proposed canal "will be of the greatest advantage to the Landed and Commercial interests of the County by opening a regular, safe and certain water carriage between all the towns and places near or adjoining such intended Canal from Bristol to or near Abingdon, and from thence (by means of the Thames) to London". Surveys were to be taken to decide the best line under the direction of the Committee appointed who were given full powers to employ one or more Engineers for the purpose. This Committee consisted of twenty-eight gentlemen, any five or more of whom were empowered to meet and act on all matters for carrying the canal into execution.'

From L.J. Dalby's book *The Wilts & Berks Canal*, describing the inaugural meeting held in an atmosphere of great expectation.

One of the few scenes available of the working canal is this view at Vastern Wharf in the 1890s. The buildings here include the managers house and a 'Tommy' shop where the boatmen could buy their supplies with 'company' tickets.

Gone are the boats and rapid decline has obviously occurred in this view of 1900. The site still continues as a wood yard to the present day. The road bridge has been levelled and filled. It used to carry the old A420 but this has now been bypassed by the A3102.

Dunnington Aqueduct, over Brinkworth Brook, still looking good in 1970 even with the trees growing up from the canal bed. Repairs to the structure began in 1995.

Cleared of all the ivy and with the brickwork repaired, the gentle curves of the aqueduct make a fine sight. Between here and Wootton Bassett there are two more locks.

Dunnington Top Lock and cottage looking west, c.1912. In 1925 bricks from here were used to build houses in New Road. Very little remains today of either this or the bottom lock although work has started on clearing the original sites.

The Bridge Inn was owned by Lamb Brewery Ltd. of Frome, in Somerset. The brewery closed in 1955, a year before this view was taken, and the building was demolished in 1987. This is now the site of a council depot.

Pioneer approaching a large sewer pipe which crossed the canal at water level on a newly restored section at Templar's Firs. This was to be the venue for the 1998 IWA National Trailboat Festival and the pipe was preventing full use of the length. BBC TV *Close Up West* reporter James Macalpine and cameraman were filming for inclusion in a half hour documentary.

De-watered, with the offending pipe exposed in preparation for its removal and lowering to beneath the canal bed. The work was carried out by contractors of Wessex Water on very favourable terms for W&BCAG and was completed in time for the festival.

An ebullient David Bellamy officially opened the 1998 IWA National Trail Boat Festival, after which he stayed on the site for several hours and was a most enthusiastic advocate of the project.

Audrey Smith, the IWA National Chairman (her description), relaxing at the festival with husband David. Audrey was present over the whole three days of the festival which, especially with so many other waterways events taking place over the Bank Holiday, was greatly appreciated by all the participants.

The sentiment on the BT hot air balloon *Investing in Our Future* really sums up the aim of W&BCAG. The balloon tethered here alongside the canal was one of several at the festival.

Looking west down the canal where there were about fifty powered boats moored along the towpath. The canal to the east is blocked for a short distance, but a new alignment is possible just to the north through the council depot.

David Smith (no relation of the IWA chairman) takes a peaceful evening cruise. When the W&B is re-opened boats will be able to use the relatively easy route from the Thames to the Kennet & Avon, bypassing the still difficult and unpredictable Caen Hill Flight on that canal.

Centre of attraction were the boats, many of which were from the Wilderness Boat Owners Club. The W&B had never ever had so many boats on the water in one place.

52

Another important contributor to the event was the Association of Waterways Cruising Clubs (AWCC) whose expertise in this type of event was of invaluable help. AWCC chairman Tony Mason, left, accompanies the Rev. Bernard Garrett on board *Pioneer* as he blesses the boats.

A conventionally shaped narrow boat of an unusual construction. This is the first Wilderness boat built of welded aluminium which makes it light enough to be towed. When it is launched, ballast tanks are flooded to give it stability. *Nonsuch* belongs to long time W&BCAG member Vic Miller and this was the boat's first taste of the water.

Luke Walker, who can be found working most weekends at Dauntsey, is instructing one of the next generation of navvies. Getting youngsters interested and involved in canals is a most important prerequisite of the Group.

This was one of three pedal-powered craft at the festival, the largest of which was *Escargot*, the Environment Agency's boat.

John Gould a vice president of W&BCAG taking control of *Pioneer* with Lee Caukwell, who was the trip boat commodore. John, a driving force behind the restoration of the K&A, was a regular attendee at W&B functions.

Always adventurous, on his second visit to the festival, John did not hesitate when offered a trip over the canal in a helicopter. Early in 1999 John sadly passed away.

Moving on from Wootton Bassett there are two more locks before the summit at Chaddington. There could be some confusion over the names of these locks, Chaddington Top Lock is sometimes referred to as Summit Lock. This is the lower of the two locks in 1914.

Nearly forty years later there is not much left of Chaddington Lower Lock and even these remains are now gone. However, as is true of so much of the W&B, the canal line is still plainly visible in this 1956 view.

Chaddington Top Lock (or possibly Summit Lock) *c.*1899. The lock keepers family pose in front of their cottage. The canal was still open at this time so the occasional boat probably still passed by.

It was a bit optimistic here having the bottom gates open as the balance beam on the top gate has broken off. The cottage was destroyed in 1978 and some masonry is all that remains today.

A look below the bottom gates of Chaddington Top Lock, *c.*1912, emphasises the lack of boats. Above here was the approximately six-mile summit level leading towards Swindon, where moves were afoot to secure the official abandonment of the canal.

An ignominious end for Chaddington Lock Cottage. It was eventually demolished in 1978. Oddly, looking at the previous pictures, it does not seem to have had any windows at the rear of the building.

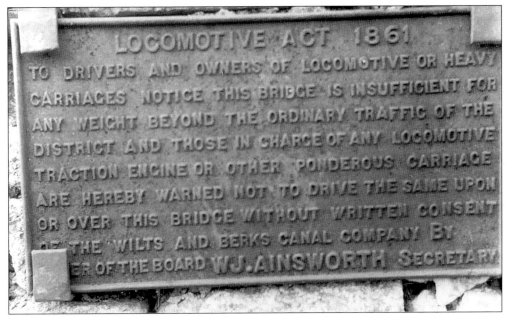

LOCOMOTIVE ACT 1861
TO DRIVERS AND OWNERS OF LOCOMOTIVE OR HEAVY
CARRIAGES NOTICE THIS BRIDGE IS INSUFFICIENT FOR
ANY WEIGHT BEYOND THE ORDINARY TRAFFIC OF THE
DISTRICT AND THOSE IN CHARGE OF ANY LOCOMOTIVE
TRACTION ENGINE OR OTHER PONDEROUS CARRIAGE
ARE HEREBY WARNED NOT TO DRIVE THE SAME UPON
OR OVER THIS BRIDGE WITHOUT WRITTEN CONSENT
OF THE WILTS AND BERKS CANAL COMPANY BY
ORDER OF THE BOARD W.J. AINSWORTH SECRETARY

Ken Buckland was unsure which bridge this notice was attached to. He suggested it was either
Costow or Berrywood. Costow was a Lift Bridge and in 1956 there was probably no trace of it.

This bridge, which is in very good condition here in 1956, is probably Berrywood Bridge and
the probable site of the warning sign. Some brick work still remains. A road now follows the
line of the canal here.

This imposing house is at Wroughton Wharf which is close to where the original line of the canal crosses the M4 motorway. To enable thrust-boring under the M4 to be practical a diversion will be necessary which means that this part of the line will probably not used.

The dry canal bed at Wroughton in 1970 before its burial under the M4. It is certainly fortunate that an alternative crossing of the M4 has been identified otherwise the canal would be irretrievably lost as has happened on the Northern section of the Lancaster Canal due to multiple M6 crossings.

Five

Westleaze to John Street Basin

In his book *Canal Days in Swindon*, Dr Eric V. Tull describes how Swindon Corporation spent £1,500 in 1908 dredging 3¾ miles inside the borough but it was soon choked again with weed, mud and rubbish. The Royal Commission on canals and inland navigations presented its report in December 1909. It commented on the Wilts and Berks:

> It was largely used within living memory for the transport of coal, corn, building and road making materials. Now it is absolutely unused and its banks are dilapidated. The company which owns it makes a small revenue, insufficient to meet expenses, by the sale of water. The stagnant condition of this canal makes it offensive to the people of Abingdon and Swindon and a desire has been expressed in these towns to close it altogether and fill in the bed. This closing is, however, opposed by the landowners for certain reasons, including the fact that their tenants obtain water from it for their cattle'.

Swindon and Abingdon eventually got their way, leaving Swindon as one of the few major towns without a waterway, a situation that W&BCAG is aiming to rectify.

Looking south over Swindon in 1958. The canal line worms its way down from the top right-hand-side to the junction in the centre of the lower half. The main line continues out of the bottom of the left hand side and the North Wilts canal line goes off on the bottom of the right hand side. © British Crown Copyright/MOD

This length of canal west of Swindon has been restored by the local farmer and stocked with fish. The building on the hill is Swindon Hospital which will be quite a landmark for approaching boats.

A further sixty miles of fishable water, which will available when the canal re-opens, will no doubt be most welcome to the thousands of anglers in the country. This is looking towards the west from Westleaze in 1997.

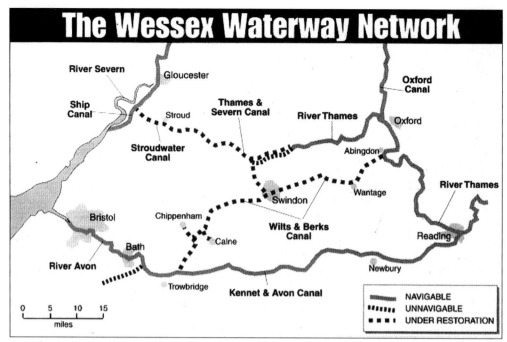

The Wessex Waterway Network

Swindon is not only halfway along the canal, but is strategically placed at the centre of the Wessex Waterways Network. When the network is fully operational it is quite probable that many hire fleets could operate from the area offering a variety of different cruising rings.

The aqueduct over the River Ray in 1970. There was also a winding hole just above here. In the background is the bridge of the old Midland & South Western Junction Railway.

The canal under here will be restored taking it as close to the town centre as possible, but it will be a dead end. The new line for the canal south of Swindon will almost certainly leave the original route before reaching here.

Attempts to have Skew Bridge (sometimes known as Rushey Platt Bridge) made a listed structure have not yet been successful, but, as it is now a cycle way connecting Old Swindon to New Swindon, its future is reasonable secure.

After the W&BCAG came into being it was essential that work should be started to preserve the canal. Early work parties, such as this one in 1980, usually meant getting stuck in with a spade clearing the accumulated muck and rubbish.

This was the first work site and the local community soon became involved. A great deal of favourable publicity was generated and the restoration had begun. It wasn't until the late 1980s, when it was decided that the canal could be fully restored, that actual reconstruction work would begin. Photo courtesy *Swindon Evening Advertiser.*

Kingshill Road Bridge, confusingly also sometimes known as Rushey Platt Bridge, carried the Turnpike road to Wootton Bassett. A 1912 view.

Kingshill Road Bridge, seen here in 1912, was built in 1803 and demolished in the early 1920s leaving only a slight hump in the road to mark its passing, the fate of so many arched bridges.

Wilts and Berks Canal Company,
GENERAL CARRIERS

Of Merchandise and Goods of all Kinds.

WHARVES AT

BRISTOL,	FOXHAM,	LONGCOT,
BATH,	DAUNTSEY,	CHALLOW,
BRADFORD,	WOOTTON BASSETT	WANTAGE,
MELKSHAM,	HAY LANE,	ABINGDON,
LACOCK,	SWINDON,	CRICKLADE,
CHIPPENHAM,	BOURTON,	STROUD AND
CALNE,	UFFINGTON,	GLOUCESTER.

FREIGHTS CARRIED IN COMPANY'S BOATS,

Which run regularly between Swindon and Bristol; and elsewhere as required.

THROUGH RATES QUOTED FOR FULL LOADS.

IN COMMUNICATION WITH ALL PARTS.—RATES ON APPLICATION.

BRISTOL DEPOT:—

Messrs. Gerrish & Co.'s Stone Wharf, Redcliffe Backs.

Best Forest, Somerset, and Smiths' Coal, Foundry Coke and Small Coal.

GARDEN GRAVEL.

THE ABOVE ALWAYS IN STOCK.

Goods of all descriptions Carried at Moderate Rates.

For dates of Company's Boats between the above places, carrying less than full loads, and for freights, general information, and full particulars, apply to

H. G. ALLEN, Manager,
CANAL OFFICE, SWINDON.

Mr H.G. Allen was appointed canal manager in 1882 by a group based in Bristol who had leased the navigation. In spite of the railway competition the company still believed that canal transport was a viable alternative.

68

Midland, Western, and Metropolitan
CANAL CARRYING COMPANY, LIMITED,

(Wilts and Berks Canal),

##

Of Merchandise and Goods of all Kinds.

WHARVES AT

BRISTOL,	DAUNTSEY,	LONGCOT,
BATH,	WOOTTON BASSETT,	CHALLOW,
BRADFORD,	HAY LANE,	WANTAGE,
MELKSHAM,	WROUGHTON,	ABINGDON,
LACOCK,	SWINDON,	CRICKLADE,
CHIPPENHAM,	STRATTON,	STROUD AND
CALNE,	BOURTON,	GLOUCESTER.
FOXHAM,	UFFINGTON,	

ALSO LANDINGS AT OTHER PLACES.

FREIGHTS CARRIED IN COMPANY'S BOATS,

Which run regularly between Swindon and Bristol; and elsewhere as required.

THROUGH RATES QUOTED FOR FULL LOADS.

IN COMMUNICATION WITH ALL PARTS.—RATES ON APPLICATION.

BRISTOL DEPOT AND WAREHOUSES,
COUNTERSLIP.

Best Forest, Somerset, and Smith's Coal, Foundry
Coke and Small Coal,

GARDEN GRAVEL
AND
ROAD MATERIALS ALWAYS IN STOCK.

Goods of all descriptions Carried at Moderate Rates.

For dates of Company's Boats between the above places, carrying less than full loads,
and for freights, general information, and full particulars, apply to

H. G. ALLEN, Manager,
Canal Office, Swindon.

A new name but the same management. By 1888 the Bristol group had lost £6,000 and after paying a forfeit of £1,000 gave up their lease. In 1891 another new group was formed, but this, The United Commercial Syndicate, had no more success.

In their attempt to rid themselves legally of the canal in Swindon the local councillors had many photographs taken showing the poor state of the navigation. This is Cambria Bridge looking east from Marlborough Street footbridge, c.1912.

John Webb's warehouse, wharf and timber yard, shown here c.1880, were just south of Cambria Bridge on the east side of the canal.

Milton Street Road Bridge in 1977 – again confusingly sometimes known as Commercial Road Bridge – with the imposing Central Club building towering over it which has now been demolished and replaced with an office block.

Looking east from Milton Road Bridge in 1896 is a sight still familiar to today's boaters – a canal stoppage. The reason had nothing to do with the canal but was to enable footings to be excavated for new buildings.

The canal line passes the buildings that were originally part of the Swindon Wharf area, c. 1950. The Murray John Building is now on this site.

Another part of Swindon Wharf is buried under the tented market area. As already noted Swindon is now one of the few large towns that does not have a waterway passing either through or close to it.

The unusual Golden Lion Bridge was raised vertically by the use of two windlasses. One can speculate as to whether there was a resident bridge-keeper or whether the boatman had to manage on his own. The gearing mechanism was mounted at the top of the columns. Looking east, c.1900.

In front of the lift bridge – this time with the winding gear exposed – is a foot bridge said to have been installed by the GWR railway works to prevent the workers being late due to the heavy boat traffic! Looking west c.1900.

First of a two part set of postcards. From John Street Basin, which was infilled during 1966, looking west from the junction with the North Wilts Canal towards Golden Lion Bridge in 1905.

The second card shows the vision of a local councillor, Ruben George, who was well ahead of his time. This artist's impression is reminiscent of Little Venice near Paddington in London.

Six

John Street Basin
to Latton

The North Wilts Canal was completed at a lower cost than engineer Whitworth estimated, a very unusual occurrence.

Priestley again comments:

> 'It commences in the Wilts and Berks Canal, near Swindon, 345 feet above the level of the sea, and proceeding in a pretty direct line towards the north-west, terminates in the Thames and Severn Canal at Weymoor Bridge, having passed the town of Cricklade in its way. The length is eight miles and three furlongs, and falls, from the Wilts and Berks Canal to the Thames and Severn, 58 feet 8 inches.'

This is the most important branch of the W&B, which opens up further cruising rings within the Wessex Waterways Network, especially now that the negotiations over the Latton Bypass on the Thames & Severn have reached a successful conclusion. It will eventually be possible for craft leaving the North Wilts Canal to travel down the Thames & Severn Canal to the town of Lechlade. Alternatively, boats will be able to cross over to the River Severn via the Thames & Severn and Stroudwater canals.

The North Wilts Canal heading off north out of the bottom of picture in 1912. Looking east down the main line is Wellington Street Bridge – also known as Queenstown Bridge.

Looking back to the west towards Golden Lion Bridge from the junction in 1914. There is now no sign of the footbridge. This area was infilled during 1960 and is now part of a shopping precinct.

Looking up the North Wilts Canal in 1912 from the junction towards John Street Bridge which was demolished in 1960. The wide canal with a towpath on one side and a footpath on the other is reminiscent of the new Birmingham main line.

The citizens of Swindon may have turned away from the old canal but they were enthusiastic about the new electric tram system. Mayor J. Hinton performs the opening ceremony on 22 September 1904.

Fleet Street Bridge – built in 1878 and called originally New Bridge – was the only turntable bridge on the navigation. According to Dr Tull the bridge was operated by a capstan situated at the north-east corner. The bridge had to be strengthened to a take the weight of the trams.

The reason for the construction of Fleet Street Bridge was to avoid the detours of the old fixed bridges in Sheppard Street and John Street, with the local authority contributing to the cost. An 1890s view.

It is a pity that the economic and social conditions at the turn of the twentieth century did not allow for large-scale community projects such as developing the old canal as a civic amenity. Today Swindon could have been benefiting from several miles of what is sometimes referred to as a linear park bringing the countryside to the heart of the town.

Bullens Bridge, which has several alternative names, is said to have been the first iron trellis bridge erected in Wiltshire. According to Dr Tull, the bridge is thought to have been built in the USA and exhibited in the Great Exhibition of 1851 before being brought to Swindon. A 1920s view.

Situated as it is, close to the canal, it is likely that this blacksmith would, in the past, have had plenty of dealings with the horses that were used to pull the working narrowboats.

John Webb moved his business to this building, still close to the canal, from his original site by Cambria Bridge, probably when any possibility of waterborne deliveries had totally vanished.

Swindon Top Lock with the massive GWR railway works behind it in 1920. At this time there was still water in the canal above the lock and the cottage was still occupied, but by 1922 the canal had been infilled (possibly) by GWR.

A day boat being pulled by two donkeys out of Swindon Top Lock in the early 1890s. This is probably the only picture of a working boat on the North Wilts Canal.

Rodbourne Road Bridge (also known as Telford Road Bridge) spans the tail gates of Swindon Lock number four. The area was infilled between 1920 and 1922, about ten years after this photograph was taken.

Looking north from Rodbourne Road Bridge, 1912. The children were not after tiddlers as you might expect but were netting butterflies in the dried up canal bed.

The bottom gates of Swindon Lock number four showing the signs of decay in 1912. Although the brickwork still looks in good condition the gates have certainly seen better days.

A final look over the bridge, guarded by its solitary gas lamp. The utilitarian bridge was constructed of iron instead of the more usual brick arch, but a saving grace was the trellis work side rails.

Look what I've found! Moredon bottom lock (or Moulden Lock) has been excavated to reveal parts of the bottom gates still in position and some of the chamber brickwork in reasonable condition.

The lock gates removed, waiting for a decision on their fate, while restoration of the lock gets under way. Since the excavation of the lock the canal back to Purton Road has been dredged.

Family members of Messrs Crapper & Sons, a major civil engineering firm, presenting a cheque to W&BCAG for £24,000 in December 1998, this being their latest donation under the Landfill Tax Credit Scheme. From left to right: Howard Crapper, Henry Smith (W&BCAG director), Harry Bromley (W&BCAG negotiator), Roger, Richard and Lawrence Crapper. Photograph courtesy of *Swindon Evening Advertiser*.

Work is well under way on the lock and the canal below has already been dredged as far as Moredon Aqueduct. The towpath along here has been reinstated and in places raised to prevent water spilling over the embankment.

Moredon junior school children being shown the Moredon Aqueduct over the River Ray, 1983. The aqueduct was in poor shape and badly overgrown. Photograph courtesy of *Swindon Evening Advertiser*.

W&BCAG Restoration Officer Ron Robertson, a full time employee, is responsible for an enormous amount of progress in recent years. There are few jobs that Ron won't tackle; whether it be bricklaying or heavy machine operation, he does it all.

The aqueduct has been restored. All the brickwork has either been repaired or replaced, including the arches, and a new layer of clay puddle has been laid on the canal bed.

Chelworth Wharf and road bridge were just south of Cricklade. A new bridge will be required here and consideration given to a back-pumping system to maintain water levels. The south portal of Cricklade tunnel is just beyond the wharf in this 1900s view.

The Southern end of Cricklade Tunnel in 1972. This tunnel was a three level arrangement. with the railway over the canal and the road over the railway. About 1965 the road bridge was removed and the railway was taken up.

A look into the tunnel shows that, when the road was re-aligned, steel pilling was driven down on either side of it and then the gap between was filled solid under the new road. Needless to say the canal will require a small diversion here.

Cricklade church in the background with the River Thames running alongside the canal. After West Mill lift bridge the canal crossed over the river on an aqueduct. This print is from a watercolour of unknown date.

After abandonment, a footbridge replaced the aqueduct over the River Thames to improve the water flow and prevent flooding. Some of the foundations of the original aqueduct are still visible. A totally new aqueduct will be required which could become an important feature of the canal.

Latton Basin looking south c.1895, possibly from the bridge over the junction with the Thames & Severn. In front of the lock house, as at Semington, was the stop lock. The boy is Joe, the son of Alfred House, the lock keeper. All business was conducted from the 'office' at the front of the house.

Latton is a name probably most familiar to members of the Cotswold Canals Trust. Their successful battle to secure a navigable passage through the Latton Bypass was a waterways success story. This route is crucial to the success of the Wessex Waterways Network.

Approaching the regulating lock from the south, *c.*1890. The recent feasibility study indicates that the lock is in 'fair' condition and that it should be rebuilt. It doesn't mention the basin, which in recent years has been used for many purposes including an animal pen.

Since this photograph was taken in 1970 the house has been completely renovated. After leaving Latton Basin the canal swings to the right passing over the River Churn Aqueduct to seek out the Thames & Severn Canal.

The terminus of the North Wilts Canal at its junction with the Thames & Severn Canal. From here it will eventually be possible to either travel over to the River Severn and on to the Midlands or turn down towards the Thames.

The Thames & Severn joins the River Thames a short distance upstream of Lechlade, from where one could carry on down to Abingdon to meet up again with the W&B.

Seven

John Street Basin to Uffington

In 1964 Martin Smith produced his *Swindon and the Construction of the Wilts and Berks Canal*. In this, so far, unpublished work he states:

> 'As far as Swindon was concerned, the building of the canal, which passed a mile north of the town, made trade unusually brisk as a large number of 'navvies' were brought into the area. The population of Swindon and its neighbourhood was doubled for a time in consequence of the large amount of imported labour, and bull-baiting was reintroduced for the amusement of the canal constructors. The cutting of the canal produced something more than a passing sensation; it was the greatest public work ever undertaken in north Wiltshire and the high level of the place called for great expenditure of capital and labour on locks to the east and west.'

Since then Swindon has just kept on growing, unfortunately almost obliterating most of the line of the canal at its centre but there is now the will and means to restore it. The alternative routes needed to circumnavigate central Swindon have been identified and substantial work has already been carried out.

Back on the main line of the canal going east is Whale Bridge which had a Victorian gents convenience on the left hand side. The original stone arch bridge was demolished in 1893 and this iron bridge assembled in its place survived until 1963.

Whale Bridge got its name from the adjacent Whale public house which in turn had been named after the old Cetus (Whale) Buildings next door. Fleming Way now runs along the line of the canal.

Looking west towards Whale Bridge and Skurrays Mill and Brickyard in 1912. This part of Swindon has now been completely redeveloped and B&Q and Halfords now occupy the site.

York Road Bridge – alternatively known as Graham Street Bridge – also disappeared during the construction of Fleming Way although the north side abutments can still be found.

Drove Road Bridge carried the turnpike road to Cricklade. It was culverted around 1921. This is now the sight of the 'Magic Roundabout' where the A361, A4311, A429 and A345 all converge.

The desire of the Swindon residents to have something done about the state of the stagnant canal is understandable when you see the sorry state of it and of Dunsford's Wharf. The photographer in 1914 would have been standing on Drove Road bridge.

A hayrick fire at Dunsford's wharf apparently caused by spontaneous combustion, *c.*1905. By the time that this photograph was taken the fire was almost out but still smouldering at the centre. There is now a fire station close to this site!

William Dunsford succeeded Joseph Priestley as canal manager and guided the canal through it's most successful period. In *Rural Rides* William Cobbett noted the fine appearance of the canal manager's villa which was just south of the canal, and supposed (erroneously) that the canal profits must be prodigious.

The young lady is posing on the outfall from Coate Water, c.1900. The reservoir was opened in 1822 shortly after the completion of the North Wilts Canal, which would have put a strain on the existing water supplies.

Many residents of Swindon would be amazed to be told that Coate Water was an artificial lake. For years it has been used as a water-based recreational amenity without any thought being given to its origins.

Our 1890s holidaymakers recommended that you should get to know the local canal workers, mentioning Mr Ferris, the Marston Flight lock-keeper, in particular.

Mr. Ferris,
Lock-keeper,
Marston Flight.

Jack Dalby, looking west at Acorn Bridge, which carried the Western Region main line, on the A420 four miles east of Swindon. The canal passed through the left-hand arch.

This is Bourton Wharf and Costers Lift Bridge, c.1900, which could eventually be the site of one of the many new businesses that will inevitably spring up along the canal as soon as boat traffic returns.

Shrivenham Arch Bridge, which carries the B4000 over the canal, was the second place to benefit from W&BCAG working parties. The accumulated rubbish was cleared and the area generally improved.

Shrivenham Arch Bridge, seen here in 1981, was also known as Station Road Bridge. Removal of the debris revealed the towpath under the bridge and the canal has now been dredged on both sides.

The West Vale Branch of W&BCAG have constructed a canal-side park at Shrivenham. To add to the amenity value of the site they have also built a new slipway by the car park ready for when the section is re-watered.

Looking south from Longcot Wharf back towards the junction in 1970. There are currently no plans to restore the Longcot arm but it could be considered at some future date.

Longcot Wharf cottages looking towards Longcot Road which, for obvious reasons, is closed to traffic. Harsh winters were always a problem for the canal; it could be shut for days, even weeks, if it became iced over. A 1962-1963 winter shot from the J. Brown Collection.

The mechanical drawbridge above Longcot Top Lock being wound with a windlass in 1895, probably by a crew member from *Dragon Fly*. The bridge and lock were just east of the junction with the Longcot arm. In 1946 both were infilled.

'We are entering the Vale of the White Horse, a thoroughly agricultural district smiling with fertility and giving such rich promise for the coming Autumn days'. This was Henry Taunt's description when he ventured off of the Thames to explore the canal. An early 1960s view.

Posing on the lift bridge at Uffington Wharf is postman Richard Rogers who was the letter carrier for the villages of Baulking, Uffington and Woolstone in 1900. From the J. Brown Collection.

Farmer John Jenkins, here with his family at Uffington Wharf in 1902, is said to have been the last man to operate a narrowboat on the W&B when he used one to transport his hay crop. Previously he had carried coal, salt, etc., between Swindon and Wantage. J. Brown Collection

Eight
West Challow to Grove

In 1970, Major R.V.G. Brown stumbled upon the canal close to his home in Wantage and in consequence produced a thesis entitled *Wantage and the Wilts and Berks Canal*. Here are some quotes from it:

> '.....even in the two years I have known Wantage, parts of the canal, and a few more of the people who remember it, have vanished.'

> 'In spite of the part played by the canal in the development of Wantage, relatively little is known about it locally.'

> 'The line of the canal is at present (August 1970) still clear in the Wantage area, although it is by no means unbroken.'

Major Brown, at that time, had no doubt that the canal was not restorable, but subsequent events, not least the opening up of sections of canal in the area, will (and I know he will be pleased about it) prove him wrong.

Since 1970 much has altered in this area. The Wantage Arm has totally disappeared and road schemes will mean that the canal will need some minor re-routing and repositioning of locks. Improvement work at several sites has meant that the canal, once again, has a distinct presence in the community and is already being enjoyed by the townsfolk.

There will be some need for the road to be re-aligned as there are sharp right and left hand bends on the existing West Challow Bridge. The canal line either side of the bridge is basically intact. A view from c.1890.

The remains of a lift bridge at West Challow with a water pipe across the canal bed. This is typical of the many 'minor' obstructions that will have to be dealt with. The negotiations with the relevant authorities usually takes far longer than the actual work.

Hunters Bridge with a young lady and her dog in the rowing boat, *c.*1890. One assumes that her companion has just 'nipped' ashore to take this picture.

Hunters Bridge from the opposite side at the same time. The abutments of the bridge still exist and consideration is being giving to rebuilding the arch bridge on the original site.

Barwell Bridge, just before the junction with the Wantage arm, is now forever buried under Mably Way. It is probable that a new lock will be constructed between here and Hunters Bridge to replace Grove Top Lock. An 1895 view.

Belmont Bridge on the Wantage arm was of a stone construction not the usual brick. This was the 'commodious and substantial Carriage Bridge' that Samuel Worthington, the owner of Belmont House, insisted on. A 1956 view from the British Waterways Archives, Arthur Watts Collection.

From 1901 to 1922 a Mr Pates lived in the Wharfinger's house at Wantage Wharf and hired out skiffs from the summer house on the south side of the basin. This view is from the top of the church tower, *c*.1900.

During 1970 Major Brown interviewed many people who still remembered the wharf and the canal, including those who reminisced about skating on it 'all the way from Abingdon to Swindon!' A 1900s view.

The buildings at Wantage Wharf still exist, although over the years they have had many different uses. Unlike at Calne there is really no hope of the canal ever coming back into the town, but fortunately the main line passes close by.

At the turn of the twentieth century, Wantage was a small market town whose claims to fame included being the birthplace of King Alfred and having built, in 1876, the first steam tramway in Britain.

The Jolly Waterman pub used to be in Mill Street and was popular for its hot food: 'the faggots of the Wantage pub were famous the length of the canal.' The street leads down to Wantage Wharf, *c*.1930.

Opposite: One of the most important buildings at the wharf would have been the stables as, without healthy well fed horses and mules, trade would have been severely impaired. The stable at Wantage has survived the decades in remarkably good condition. Here the stables are seen *c*.1970.

Grove Top Lock and cottage seen from the junction. Henry de Salis in his inspection launch, *Dragon Fly*, was probably the only person ever to travel the whole length of the canal in a powered boat. Fortunately his 1895 photographs survive.

This is probably the pound between Grove Top Lock and Limekiln Lock as seen in 1890. It is now known as the Elm Farm Section. This is one of the areas that has been restored and is now a very popular recreational walk for the local people.

When a section of canal is restored its appearance belies the amount of time and effort that has gone into it. At Grove Top Lock it took several years of regular work parties to achieve the desired result. The assistance of WRG is always appreciated, as at this summer workcamp in 1990.

The results are worthwhile. Not only was the pound cleared and dredged and the towpath rebuilt and laid with ballast but the tail end of the lock and wing walls were also reconstructed. With the area landscaped and having a foot path on the opposite side it is a very popular circular walk.

Raymond Bird was one of the founder
members of W&BCAG and has been a
enthusiastic worker at Wantage for
many years. Now in his early eighties
Raymond still makes a round trip of
140 miles twice a month for the regular
workparties. Of course, age brings
wisdom…and a fold-up chair.

No sooner was the Elm Farm section
officially opened in 1994 than the first
private boat appeared. This caused a
minor problem as no arrangements had
yet been agreed on boat licensing!

The bottom of the restored Elm Farm section is dammed off at the top of the derelict Lime Kiln Lock. Controlling the water level in the cut is an essential task and here Geof Austin has just opened the regulating valve in 1996.

Unpaid volunteers they may be but amateurs they are not. Shortage of funds is a perennial problem so in order to reach the tops of these dead trees a cage was constructed to fit onto the Hi-Mac which enabled the chainsaw operator, Roy Murrell, to work safely.

Grove Wharf buildings are now known as Ormond Terrace. This must have been an interesting place as the canal ran past the front and the Wantage tramway at the rear.

Looking west at Grove Common Lock tail bridge which was nearing completion. The lock will need considerable work as the brickwork is in very bad shape, but, as with much of the infrastructure, it only needs the men, money and materials.

Nine

Ardington to Abingdon

As recently as 1982 Ronald Russell's book *Lost Canals and Waterways of Britain* only encouraged us to explore the remains. This is indicative of just how quickly circumstances can change given the enthusiasm of the public and the will of authority. One day boats will again be able to leave the hectic Thames at Abingdon and cruise the peaceful canals of Wessex.

Mr Russell followed the line of the canal and wrote:

> 'If you approach Abingdon by the A34 you will find the canal bed at Caldecott; look for signs of an embankment on the west side of the road. Opposite the embankment, Caldecott Road takes the line of the canal towards the Thames. On the riverside at the southern edge of Abingdon is a cast-iron bridge over the River Ock, erected by the canal company and so inscribed. To the south of the bridge is the site of the canal entrance and the basin is in the yard of a laundry. Here, on Friday 10 September 1810, "a body of the Proprietors passed the last lock into the Thames amidst the loud huzzas of multitudes assembled to witness the spectacle".'

In the not too distant future we will be able to re-enact this event although, as with Semington, a new site for the junction will be needed.

Dragon Fly in Ardington Top Lock. This was Henry de Salis' third *Dragon Fly*. Built of steel, and steam-powered, it was just under sixty feet long and must have seemed the ultimate in luxury to the working boatmen in 1895.

The canal bed between the Ardington Locks, *c.*1970, showing, yet again, the resilience of a rural waterway. The recent study shows the section infilled for 750 metres between Cow Common Brook to Hanney Road with the rest 'a little overgrown'.

When Major Brown visited Ardington Top Lock in 1970 he found the remains of the Lock Cottage which has since been demolished. He also reported that the lock was 'in better condition than others in the area' and nearly thirty years later it is still being described as being in 'excellent condition.' An 1895 view from the Hugh McKnight Collection.

Lord Wantage was involved in a final attempt to revive the canal as a viable commercial concern, but by 1901 (the year in which he died) this too had failed. This 1912 postcard shows the memorial which was erected in his memory at Ardington church.

The railway bridge between the Ardington locks has been narrowed and culverted. Fortunately, there is a possible alternative line for the canal about 180 metres to the west.

Sweeping away the past to make way for the future. Cow Common Bridge was demolished in 1965, the year this view was taken, as part of a road improvement scheme to allow heavy loads to reach Harwell AERE and Didcot Power Station.

Steventon Lock and tailbridge will need to be rebuilt and could possibly be the site of a back-pumping station, one of several that are being considered in order to conserve water supplies.

One of the lift bridges between Steventon and Drayton Locks which have been infilled and the structures removed. When rebuilt, these bridges, as can be seen at Foxham, soon mellow to become part of the landscape. An 1895 view from the Hugh McKnight Collection.

One can only envy Henry de Salis having the time, money and opportunity to have been able to cruise the majority of the inland waterways at leisure. *Dragon Fly* moored by the lift bridge between Drayton and Tythe Barn Locks in 1895. Hugh McKnight Collection.

Demolished and culverted in 1912 this stone bridge, with Caldecott Road in the foreground, carried the Drayton Road over the canal. The bracing under the bridge indicates its weakened condition. This view was taken just before the work was undertaken.

Caldecott Road running parallel to the canal towards the lift bridge, which was surrounded by factories and warehouses. Beyond here was Abingdon Basin.

Abingdon Basin, c.1900, with Caldecott Road lift bridge in the distance. Today the canal line down the wide Caldecott Road is still quite apparent even with all the housing that now surrounds it.

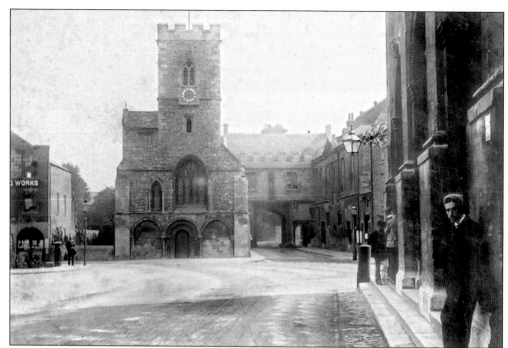

The fifteenth-century Abbey Gateway and twelfth-century St. Nicolas Church in Abingdon, *c*.1900. Present day visitors will encounter a much more hectic town now, but one still well worth a visit.

Some things don't alter. The river at Abingdon has always been a favourite location for photographers. This view shows St Helens Wharf, which stretched from the bottom of East St Helen's Street on the Wilsham Road to the mouth of the canal, with a collection of narrowboats moored alongside. A *c*.1890 view from the collection of the Centre of Oxfordshire Studies.

Looking upstream from the canal entrance, *c.*1860, at the boats that probably came from the St. Helen's Ironworks which, among other things, built and repaired steam boats of various types. Photograph courtesy of Centre of Oxfordshire Studies.

The Townsend family's pleasure launch at the entrance to the canal. They were probably here just to pose for this picture as I'm sure they wouldn't have taken their smart steam boat onto a 'dirty old canal!' Among those on board are Mr T.A. Townsend and his nephew W.A. Townsend. A 1910 photograph courtesy of the Centre of Oxfordshire Studies.

The walled-off entrance to the canal, with the Ock Bridge upstream. Although it is theoretically possible to use the River Ock to reconnect the canal to the River Thames this is an extremely unlikely alternative.

The cast-iron bridge at the mouth of the River Ock is often mistaken for the canal entrance because of the inscription. The bridge was, of course, installed for the convenience of the canal company.

126

In the not too distant future boats will once again be able to enter the W&B canal at Abingdon to cruise the more than sixty miles of what will be one of the most beautiful canals in the country. An 1860 view.

Postscript

The Wilts & Berks was never a well documented canal, it being one of the less important commercial waterways and succumbing to early abandonment. Much of the older photographic record is from the years of decline and decay. I have had to rely mainly on the archives of W&BCAG, the Jack Dalby Collection and members' own private collections. The historical content of the introduction was taken from material supplied by Peter Scatchard, a former W&BCAG chairman. I have tried to be as accurate as possible but the dating of some pictures amounts to no more than an educated guess.

It has been my intention to try to show that the W&B has survived the eighty-five years since abandonment and is rising, phoenix-like, to become the central part of the important Wessex Waterways Network. In the last few years, an amazing amount of progress has been made but there is still far to go and the driving force will, for the foreseeable future, remain the Wilts & Berks Canal Trust. As has been proved on similar ventures, it is pressure and commitment at grass roots level that eventually breeds success. New recruits are always welcome. Special skills or expertise are not necessary; just an extra pair of hands can at times make all the difference.

Acknowledgements

Response to my appeal for material led to me receiving in many instances several copies of the same picture from different sources. I have therefore, except in a small number of cases, not credited individual pictures. I would like to thank all the following (not in any order of precedence) for their assistance and encouragement: Graham Escott, Peter Williams, Tim Preece, Keith Walker, Rachael Baynard, Luke Walker, Ron Robertson, Alan & Di Tanzell, Ray Denyer, Jan Flanagan, Geof Austin, Jim Brown, Mr. F.E.J. Burgiss, Roger Halse, Bill Wood, Neil Dowson, Bob Codd, Keith Fisher, Barbara Small, Paul Carengia, Reg Wilkinson, Derek Parker, Chippenham Town Council, Chippenham Civic Society, Swindon Reference Library, Swindon Museum, Centre for Oxfordshire Studies, Pendon Museum, Judy Thomas & the Abingdon Area Archaeological Society, Mrs B. McCaul, Swindon Evening Advertiser, Alan Norris, Clem Barnett, John Henn, Neil Rumbol, Richard Porter, Liz Drury & the Friends of Abingdon, Ken Buckland, Harry Bromley, Bill Fryer, John Espley, Paul A. Williams, Eddy Cuss, Peter Scatchard, Chris Gibson, George Gibson, Mr & Mrs Nicholas Gardner, Major R.V.G. Brown, Melksham & District Historical Society, Hugh McKnight, Martin Fryer, Tony Sharp, Terry Onslow, British Waterways and all the members of W&BCAG who have been so helpful.

Further Information

Wilts & Berks Canal Trust

General enquiries   01628 544666
Email   Info@www.wilts-berks-canal.org.uk
Web site   http://www.wilts-berks-canal.org.uk

Membership Secretary:

Chris Toms,
16 Firham Park Ave., Harold Wood,
Romford, Essex, RM3 0SJ
Tel: 01708 342036

Books & Maps

Brown, R.V.G.   *Wantage and the Wilts & Berks Canal*
Dalby, L.J.   *The Wilts & Berks Canal*
Hadfield, C.   *The Canals of South & South East England*
Tull, Eric V.   *Canal Days in Swindon*

Maps – OS 163, 164, 173 & 174